Priestess

The Life and Magic of Dion Fortune

By the same author
AN INTRODUCTION TO THE MYSTICAL QABALAH
DANCERS TO THE GODS
GATE OF MOON

Priestess

The Life and Magic of Dion Fortune

Alan Richardson

THE AQUARIAN PRESS
Wellingborough, Northamptonshire

First Published 1987

British Library Cataloguing in Publication Data

Richardson, Alan
Priestess: the life and magic of Dion Fortune.
1. Fortune, Dion 2. Occult sciences — Biography
I. Title
133'.092'4 BF1408.2.F6

ISBN 0-85030-461-X

Printed and bound in Great Britain

Contents

Acknowledgements

I am indebted to a great number of people who have made this biography possible, many of them spending long hours of research into the sort of vital trivia without which I could not have managed. In random order I give them as follows:

Tom Firth OBE and his mother Helen, whose information on the Firth family background of their distant cousin saved me months of hard work; Leslie Price for his invaluable research in obscure sources that I would never have discovered on my own; Mrs M. Young of the Law Society for details as to Arthur Firth's dubious career; Rosemary Mower White of Great Missenden for details about the second Mrs Penry Evans. The staff of Watersmead, and the staff of the Fir Lodge, Bath; V. W. Williams of Pontardawe for details and memories of his cousin; Anne McCormack and Angela Doughty of the Surrey Record Office; Victor Gray and Miss Butler of the Essex Record Office, Chelmsford; M. G. Sims, Librarian of the Staff College, Camberley; A. G. Harfield of the Royal Signals Museum; Terence C. Charman of the Imperial War Museum; A. H. Wesencraft of the University of London Library; Richard Robinson of the Christian Science Committee on Publication; R. J. Eggins of the Limpley Stoke Hotel, Wiltshire; Pippa Robson of The Belfry, West Halkin Street; P. W. Ellis, Exeter County Library; Miss S. M. Stephens, Registrar's Office, University of Sheffield; Alexis Brook of the Tavistock Clinic; P. M. Coleman of the Sheffield City Libraries; C. D. Darroch of the Royal Hampshire Regiment; G. Langley, County Reference Library, Bristol; R. M. Perkins, Archivist, King Alfred's College, Winchester; S. R. Moles of the Library, Bishop's Stortford; Mrs C. Sacha, Waverley District Council; Mary Jack, of the Paradox Research Institute; Janet Jackson of Amersham County Library; Shelagh Head and Diane Coyne of County Hall, Hertford; J. M. L. of Woodspring Central Library; John Minor of the Theosophical Society; the staff and archivists of the South African Embassy; Jane Dansie of the Essex County Council Libraries; Ian Stevenson of the Ministry of Agriculture, Fisheries and Food; Mrs Norma Harvey of the College of Psychic Studies; J. E. Treble of the MOD, Hayes, Middlesex; J. M. Olive of the City of Sheffield Local Studies; Dr Weisart of the University of Heidelberg; Mr G. N. Pratt of The Grange, Taverner's Green; Duncan Mirylees of Guildford Local Studies Library; the editors of 'Light'; and the Society of the Inner Light.

Out of all these complete strangers could I draw attention to the help afforded me in particular by the staff of Llandudno library, namely Mrs E. A. Mitcheson, Miss J. M. Thomas, Elan Rivers, and Mr Huw Pritchard; without them, and the kind help of Ivor Wynne Jones, the Wales-wise journalist, I would have given up a long time ago.

In other fields I could not have managed without the expert knowledge of John M. Hamill, Librarian and Curator of the Grand Lodge of England, and the Reverend T. W. Shepherd, from another side of the square; plus the kind help of Dr Alan Cooper of the Masonic Centre, Cape Town.

Harry Edwards of the Old Cliftonian Society and R. G. Smallshaw of Hugh Sexey's Middle School have helped in more academic ways; while my good friends David Annwn and John Winter have always been on hand with advice and expertise in many areas.

Thanks also to Patricia Villiers Stuart and Charles Shepherd for helping me to look in odd corners and evoke atmospheres; plus Tim and Jenny Owen, Johnny and Janet Maxwell, Barry and Valerie Fuge for present and past help, and happy times.

In more esoteric fields there are Basil and Roma Wilby, Jed and Murry Hope, Jack and Lara Kavanagh, Bill and Bobby Gray, Robert and Anne Greig, Mike and Dolores Ashcroft Nowicki for their practical help and wisdoms; while I must not forget that this book rides upon the scholarship of Ellic Howe, Francis King, Gregory Tillett, Geoffrey Ashe, R. A. Gilbert, Ithel Colquhoun, D. N. Redstone, and Paul Devereux.

There is also June Stubbings of Bishop's Stortford for helping to find Moriarty, David Light of Bournemouth and Philip and Jan Carver for helping me put it into context, and Juliet Burton whose faith has always kept me going.

Carl Weschcke has been on hand with disinterested advice and comment, as have Pat, Tony, Paula McCarroll and George Richardson, plus the Johnsons of Winsley: Brian, Brenda, Stuart and Teresa.

Finally, there is Nigel and Billie John, who did so much graft for the sake of a mutual friend; Clive Harper and Chesca Potter who cheerfully did all the dirty work and gave me riches they will never imagine; E. Marion Griffith, a Wise Mother who has taught me much in this new youth of hers; G. H. Harris of Limpley Stoke, Caroline Mallinson, Mr. E. Barnes, Arthur Swallow, Sue Tolley, and Mr. and Mrs. Francis; plus

Sir Hugo and Lady Susan Marshall, for their lovely sanctuary and enchanted valley.

And beyond even these there is Michelle, for whom all things are done; and our daughter Zoe, who will one day do them for herself.

Then I saw why there must be priestesses as well as priests; for there is a dynamism in a woman that fecundates the emotional nature of a man as surely as he fecundates her physical body; this was a thing forgotten by modern civilization which stereotypes and conventionalizes all things, and forgets the Moon, Our Lady of Flux and Reflux.

Dion Fortune
The Sea Priestess

1.
DAUGHTER OF HEAVEN AND EARTH

> And there is a way perhaps, in which the world in the long run is more affected by legends than by the manipulation of power: legends alter the way people think. This is on a higher level (if they are recorded) than that of power.
>
> Leonard Mosley

Dion Fortune was the pen-name of a woman who died of leukaemia on a bleak day in January 1946. Her real name was Violet Mary Firth. She was fifty-five years old when she died and had been living as a divorced woman for the previous five years. 'Dion Fortune' was the public expression of a personality which had devoted the entirety of at least one life to a passionate study of the Gods. This mask became so fixed that at the end of her life no one, least of all herself, could possibly have removed it. Violet Firth died some time in the 1920s. Dion Fortune went from strength to strength.

In simple terms she was a powerful psychic. Contact with dead souls, with entities from other systems of evolution, and with near-forgotten deities, was as natural to her as breathing. This converse, and an attempt to discern the inner workings of life, meant everything to her. She was born a child of Empire and was to be one of its last priestesses; and in her mediations between the land and the people she was to go as deeply into the Otherworld as any person had ever travelled. Some say that in so doing she lost a portion of her humanity.

She is best remembered as having been a magician. In one sense she was womanhood's answer to Aleister Crowley: although he was an essentially evil man with a few streaks of goodness, she was an essentially good woman who had strands of darkness within. By her own definition magic was 'the art of causing changes to occur in consciousness'. This is the best definition ever given. By learning to change one's consciousness under full control of one's will, she averred that we could become more surely aligned to our proper destiny, more closely drawn to the Gods. Further, by using certain techniques to bring out faculties that we all possess, she felt that she could transcend Time and Space and bring influences to bear upon the collective life of her sex, her nation, and her race. It was largely her role in life to bring through to the rest of us all those evolutionary energies that the bright spirits had to offer. If Woman today, for example, has any of the freedoms or insights that were denied her in the pre-war world, then the shade of Dion might insist that this was due in no small part to the rites she worked in her various temples off the Bayswater Road, off Belgrave Square, at the foot of Glastonbury Tor, and within her own soul.

This was the path of High Magic. She believed in it with all her heart.

She may not have been aware of it, but the name of Dion Fortune can be broken down into two parts. Dion as a personal name means 'Daughter of Heaven and Earth', while Fortune, or Fortuna, means 'Woman of Destiny'.

It sums her up exactly. She was a shaman, she was a priestess, she was a simple piece of human equipment — like an electrical conductor. And as far as the Gods were concerned she was as easily discarded and replaced when she had burnt herself out.

Born under the sign of the Archer on the Hill of the Bow within the influence of the Great and Little Dragons, she sent her arrows of consciousness toward the star of knowledge that she saw as sinking into the West, aiming them beyond the utmost bound of ordinary human thought. She believed, as did all of her pupils, that she had been born to the task, destined to walk between the worlds. With care and with the proper illumination, we could each of us follow on behind.

When Dion died she was held by some to be a very rich woman. This was partly because she ruled a group of people who were, by and large, reasonably wealthy — some of them eminent in their class and profession. But it was also because of her maiden name, Firth. It was always added, sometimes by herself, that she was one of *the* Firths, of Sheffield steel fame. In fact when she died her wealth totalled exactly £9,781 18s. This was a large sum for the times but by no means a huge sum. With the exception of a small payment to her cousin, it was bequeathed entirely to her own Society of the Inner Light, as the group which she had formed was called. The money would be scrupulously administered for the furtherance of the Work. This was how she had always spent her money; she had no time for fripperies, little interest in the sensual possibilities of the material world, and no hobbies or interests beyond the sphere of Magic.

Her wealth, such as it was, had its origins in the good earth of Yorkshire. And although she was proud of her roots she always stopped just short of being the sort of professional Yorkshirewoman who would parade her country background like a splinter from the True Cross.

There is only one observation on record about her presence there. This probably took place during one of her vacations from her boarding school. It was at the time of the Cutlers Feast, in Sheffield, when the Master Cutler is installed for a year. The young and strapping George Keyworth, himself a trainee cutler, found himself being pressed by his parents to dance with the attractive Miss Firth. His parents had hearts of gold but an eye for the main chance — and Miss Firth was perceived as a very good dancer. However, nothing came of it.[1]

Despite the vagueness of her actual contact with that county, a Yorkshire lass she always claimed to be. This was partly pride and partly camouflage. Knowing that someday someone might attempt a biography and yet abhorring the idea, Dion was deliberately elusive in describing her life. Even so, this had precisely the opposite effect to what she might have wished: it led people to her. They were drawn by, among other things, the mystery of the woman.

The themes of her life can be summed up in Moons and Dragons, Water and Virgins, and the secrecy which is at the heart of power. And Dion, be it noted, had power. She was like The Priestess in the tarot card of that name, fey and private, ever-young and knowing, bright with moons and seated between the pillars of those opposites which drove her on. In her lap was the mystic book of the Gods' lore, which said no more than that the land and the people are One. Behind her was the curtain which led to her Mysteries: ocean can be glimpsed — the cold waters of the Atlantic. Were we to pull the curtain aside completely we would find a panorama which included the Great and Little Orme in North Wales, the long finger of Brean Down, the rounded mass of Glastonbury Tor, and all those places in which she had lived and worked Magic. To her, living and working Magic were inseparable acts. To her, the land of her birth meant all things. It was alive and feminine. It was fecund and maternal in a way that she could never be.

The whens and whereabouts of her life on this earth are like the rock and soil of some prehistoric long barrow: they form a tunnel down into the darkness, into the Otherworld and towards the stars.

And sometimes, if conditions are right, her spirit will come to the mouth of that tomb to meet us.

The origin of her wealth and her Yorkshireness, such as these might be, lay within Sheffield. It is a city which lies on three hills at the meeting of two rivers, the Don and the Sheaf, at the heart of Britain — a nation which Dion saw as a great and vital goddess, brooding and powerful, looking ever Westward.

Beneath the surface of Sheffield lay the rich Silkstone seam of coal. This seam was the basis of the city's wealth just as much as carbon is the basic stuff of the universe. Charcoal was made from this, and it was used to smelt the apparently endless quantities of iron ore that the Yorkshiremen also found, making steel in their own homes from Chaucer's time onwards. These early industrialists were known by a title which will bring a smile to the lips of any magician: they were known as the 'Little Masters'.

Of the many firms which specialized in making steel during the nineteenth century, one was Sanderson Brothers and Company, whose chief smelter was Thomas Firth. In 1833 Thomas Firth was commanding the then huge wage of seventy shillings a week. This was Dion's great-great-grandfather. He had two sons, Mark and Thomas junior, who, on leaving school in that year, joined the same firm. Before very long they were both earning a straight pound sterling a week. To the manager's astonishment they felt it was not quite enough, and he promptly turned down their demands for an increase. This demand, prompted out of avarice, dreams, or plain Yorkshire canniness, marked one of those otherwise trivial moments in history which are, in retrospect, charged with import.

The rejection of their demands prompted Thomas and Mark to buy their own six-hole furnace in Charlotte Street. Where and how they got the capital is not recorded. It was probably from their father's savings. At first they manufactured steel exclusively for home comsumption, but gradually extended their operations to Birmingham, which was by now superseding Bristol as the second city within England. The brothers were still in their mid-twenties. When their father died in 1848 it was agreed between them all that Mark would be the head of the firm. Within a year they had acquired an unspecified but allegedly immense American connection, followed by the building of the Norfolk works in their home town which covered thirteen acres. They bought up other works at Whittington in Derbyshire, covering twenty-two acres, as well as several forges at Clay Wheels near Wodsley.

They owned land; they made it pay. Their wealth came from the very elements of the earth. Dion, whose wealth was to be of a very different kind, was to do exactly the same.

Her great-grandfather's company did have one speciality. Mark Firth knew that if by 1850 the British Empire was not quite at its height, and Britain not yet the most powerful nation of all, then it was only a matter of time before it became so. To this end he was more than willing to assist in its expansion. So his speciality was casting steel blocks for ordnance, and various kinds of shot, plus a large variety of heavy forgings for engineering purposes. Most of all the firm made guns. One of their gun-blocks was sixteen inches in diameter for a massive 81-ton gun, which was then the heaviest single casting ever made.

By the middle of the nineteenth century all the steel used in the manufacture of guns for the British government was Firth's steel. They gave the Empire its firepower. The guns which sank the Chinese fleet in 1857 were Firth guns; the weapons which suppressed the Indian Mutiny were Firth weapons; and when the British bombarded Kagoshima in reprisal for the murder of a single Englishman, the cannon used were Firth cannon.

These were the years of gunboat diplomacy, and through their known science the Firth family brought together the elements of earth and water, fire and air, and brought half the world under their sovereign's control.

The principal feature of their business was the refinement and manufacture of steel. In this they were unrivalled. When they were not making guns for their own country they were importing immense quantities of foreign iron from Swedish mines, where they had concessions. They also supplied the Italians and the French (at that time allies) with gun tubes of their own.

The Firth family were prominent and productive members of a race of people who were, in their own eyes at least, the true Lords of the Dazzling Face, splendid in their azure seats. The ancient symbol of Britain, the white horse, which Dion felt linked them to Atlantis by evolutionary routes via the eo-hippo, had been superseded by the lion, an altogether different beast, and symbol of a new type of consciousness which ripped and clawed its way across the world.

By 1840 three younger brothers had joined the family firm: John, Edward, and Henry. It is John who concerns us most, for he was to be Dion's grandfather. In a sense it was he who created Dion Fortune and gave her power. He did this because he gave her more than the mere name of Firth, he gave her the family motto too: *Deo, non Fortuna.*

If the adoption of a family motto was a sign that the Firths had left the world of the working classes and entered the realm of the *nouveau riche*, touching upon the upper stratosphere of British society, it would be the same motto that would enable Dion to leave the mundane world entirely, and help her plumb the depths of the astral plane, and the collective subsconscious of her race:

> In my own experience of the operation, the utterance to myself of

> my magical name led to the picturing of myself in an idealized form, not differing in type, but upon an altogether grander scale, superhuman in fact, but recognizable as myself, as a statue more than life-size may yet be a good likeness. Once perceived, I could re-picture this idealized version of my body and personality at will, but I could not identify myself with it *unless I uttered my magical name.* Upon my affirming it as my own, identification was immediate. Consciousness transferred itself to the form thus visualized, and I stepped forth into the world of dreams *naked*. Upon that nudity, as of an antique statue, I could, by a simple act of imagination, put on whatever robes or drapery I desired to symbolize the part I wished to play.[2]

'Deo, non Fortuna' was this magical name, given to her by the family's emergence from the herd. To the rest of the Firths it was little more than a novelty, the icing on the cake — or not even that, but rather a little pattern on the icing itself. None of them could have imagined the power that one of the later additions to the dynasty would find within this harmless piece of snobbishness.

John Firth was married twice: first to Elizabeth Bowden, who died in 1852 after only four years of marriage, and by whom he had one daughter Jessie, and a son named Thomas. After four years of being a widower he married Charlotte Harding, by whom he had four sons and two daughters.

Charles Harding Firth was born in 1857 from this second union, married one Frances Ashington, and became one of the most prominent historians of his time after graduating from Balliol College, Oxford. Knighted in 1922, he was a Fellow of the British Academy, a Trustee of the National Portrait Gallery, and Regius Professor of Modern History at Oxford. He specialized in the period of the English Civil War, with emphasis on Oliver Cromwell, and was a noted contributor to the monumental *Dictionary of National Biography*.

Lewis John Firth, about whom almost nothing is known, was born the following year.

However, in Edward Harding Firth we have another who made an impact upon our times in the field of theology. Ordained in 1882 he became the curate of St Agnes, Bristol, and later the Rector of Micheldean, Gloucestershire. From 1916 until 1933 he was Rural Dean of Romsey and Honorary Canon of Winchester Cathedral the town where King Alfred, in an act of talismanic magic, buried a golden dragon for the safety of the realm.

But it is the fourth son who concerns us most. Born on 13 February 1862 in the year that the speed of light was first measured, when Elizabeth

Barrett Browning wrote her *Last Poems*, and when Clark identified Sirius B in the heavens, this was to be the father of Dion Fortune. Born in the sign of Aquarius, the man carrying water, he was ruled by a symbol that a magician named Moriarty felt was a prophecy of the return of the Goddess. And indeed it was. Firth junior carried more than just his own deep hopes: he carried the seed of she whom the world would think of as the Sea Priestess. It was inevitable, too, that he was called Arthur: the father of the woman who would one day invoke the spirit of the Pendragon *had* to be called Arthur.

The brothers all attended Clifton College, Bristol, which had been newly formed with the sort of high moral and academic standards that tended to attract those new dynasties who had no benefit of family entrée to the more established public schools of the day.

In 1886 he formed a partnership with Frank Bowman to start his own law firm of Bowman and Firth Ltd, Sheffield. They seem to have been an amicable pair because Frank Bowman was best man at Arthur's wedding. Even so Firth does not seem to have practised as a solicitor for very long despite the fact that at his death in 1943 this would still be given as his profession. In fact his registration expired in 1893 and he never renewed it. There is, indeed, no record of him ever having practised after this year.

Presumably his real line of work was not sufficiently prestigious for him to give it. So, like the Arthur of myth and legend he comes down through the bare records as a remote figure, stern even, who made no provision in his will for his only child Violet, as he deemed, rather sniffily, that she had been 'more than adequately funded' by the terms of her marriage settlement. But, unlike the Arthur of legend, he seems always to have been subservient in some way to others: his father and uncles, his more illustrious and successful brothers; most of all to his father-in-law. It is ironic that he was hidden from the more accessible records, such as the old Post Office Directories, by virtue of being overshadowed by a man whose very name suggests blandness, or else Everyman.

This man was John Smith, Gentleman.

John Smith and Arthur Firth would have commended themselves to each other by the fact that they were both of the blood, belonging to the sacred clan of Yorkshiremen. John was born in 1834 in Sowerby, which was then a small town lost in the moors, approached by valleys that were once thick with oak, ash and thorn. In ancient times the inhabitants lived above the tree-line in summer and only came down from the moors in winter, to move along the valleys towards the coast. Burial sites and circles abound, and the Brigantes were the tribe to be fought when the Romans came there as they did everywhere else, bringing their peculiar *pax* along with their short swords.

John Smith is of course the commonest of names within the English-speaking world. The only nobility it can command is through its mythic associations, harking back as it does to the trade of smithcraft, once the most sacred and magical of arts. Wayland the Smith, one of the oldest of Gods, was once the most popular, whose smithy is still visited, still venerated, and still potent, next to the dragon-like figure of the White Horse at Uffington.

It is not known when Arthur first met his future father-in-law, nor what segment of the Wheel of Fortune — choice or chance, fate or fancy — should bring them together. However it was probably in the year 1885.

As to where they met, this is much easier to guess. Which brings us down to a precise and identifiable spot within the lunar core of the great goddess figure of Britannia, in the Moonraker County of Wiltshire. Viewed through the magical eye — it had to be there.

So, when Arthur Firth came down from the solar centre of Sheffield with all its fire and steel, to stay at a spa hotel in a small village in a lost valley in the West Country, without knowing it he had brought Lord Sun and Lady Moon together in a rite that revolves without end.

The Church of St Mary the Virgin lies on a side road which leads down from the busy A36, sloping and winding toward the plush and trim village of Freshford. Hidden by hedgerow and dry-stone wall it can easily be missed by the motorist. In all the centuries it has not changed much. Long before Christ, long before the Romans, longer still before the Druids, this had been a holy place. Even now the actual site of the original pagan temple still survives within the church grounds, although it is marked by no more than a curvature of the wall. Legend has it that the original builders tried to put the church lower down the valley, but that the Devil himself made them put it where it now stands. From that unexceptional curve in the wall the land beyond drops steeply though not dramatically. The eye is made to fly like a witch over the curvature of fields towards Westwood.

Once, I believe, a young and fertile goddess was worshipped here, nubile but sightless, ever-giving but ever-chaste. By the time the Christians came the goddess was changed to St Mary the Virgin. Even the early Fathers understood something of the true nature of virginity, which meant not so much an intact hymen as a consideration of being one-in-herself, as only a goddess can be.[3] This way, female deities of the fields and the corn were to be transmuted into the Virgin Mary, who according to the system of the magicians, was also Isis, and Keridwen, and Fian, Herne's own lady, queen of the valley and streams. Although the colours might change a little, all else remains always the same. Within the churchyard itself are the tombs of thirteen Anglo-Norman nobles. Sometimes, sitting very still, so quiet that the other senses can come out as delicate as mice, they can still be sensed: brooding but not hostile, autocratic but not cruel. They were men who became rich on wool as their newish and nominal lord, Jesus, became mighty through the formula of the Lamb.

I had passed this church a thousand times and always promised myself a visit one day, thinking it was the sort of place that might hold secrets. Involved as I was with my full-time job, as well as writing *Gate of Moon* and then researching the Firth family up Welsh hill and down Yorkshire dale, I never dreamed that it was here, on my own doorstep, that Dion Fortune's parents were married.

Arthur Firth was probably in the West Country visiting his brother Edward in Bristol. It is more than likely that at some point in his holiday he decided to take the waters. Taking the waters was something of a fad in that era, although there were really only three centres in Britain where one could do this: Harrogate, Leamington Spa, and Bath. They became the refuge of the beau monde — those who could afford the treatment. Spas were born from Mystery. They were always holy places, though it was the Romans who brought opulence to the process of bathing and worship. The town of Aquae Sulis, so-named by these conquerors, exemplified this. Set within a U of hills that are open to the north — like the initiation mark of some Raven-Priest of Mithras — the atmosphere of the town today is still impregnated with the feel of Minerva, and behind her the death-goddess Sulla, with the sun-god Bran.

If Arthur was attracted here by the prospects of therapy, John Smith came down in 1879 purely and simply to make money. He took over the Hydropathic Establishment in nearby Limpley Stoke and ran it with his friend and partner George Crawford, from 1876 to 1888. Neither of them was deterred by the lack of any natural spring outlet in the Hydro itself and neither did they see fit to advertise the lack. Large stone tanks in the basement were filled with mineral waters transported from Bath and thence applied to the residents through a variety of options. They could have Turkish or Russian baths, needle or spray baths, lamp or sulphur baths, douche or electric, followed if required by massage and rubbing administered by male or female masseurs, depending on choice or propriety.

Dion would have liked that: water, the universal symbol of the unconscious, was being used to cleanse and heal; water from the warm and fecund depths of the earth. In the Magical system she would come to develop, using an equal variety of rituals, she would attempt to do much the same sort of thing.

The Establishment was only three minutes' walk from the station and the Post and Telegraph Office, on the Bath and Salisbury branch of the Great Western Railway. It had fourteen acres of grounds, with facilities for tennis, boating 'and other out-of-door amusements', as well as a commodious Reading and Writing Room in which conversation was forbidden.

It had a certain reputation, although it never quite attracted the cream of British society. The Hydropathic Establishment tended to appeal instead to vicars and spinsters, little-known artists and retired teachers. The now-forgotten novelist Mrs G. de S. Wentworth-James made this the setting for her romance *A Mental Marriage*, from which we can pluck out the line: 'Of course, I came here because you once told me that the Dimpley Oak Hydro was the best place to live in after one's own home.' There was also a drill instructor to provide daily drill and exercise in calisthenics, with piano accompaniment, 'free of charge'; and there was family worship morning and evening.

Persons suffering or recovering from infectious diseases, or unsound mind, or otherwise unsuitable, were not admitted. Neither were dogs allowed in the house.

To outward appearances the house is largely unchanged today, although now it is simply known as the Limpley Stoke Hotel. It is a popular place for wedding receptions and parties, with the stroboscopic delights of the disco thrown in where necessary. Really, in wondering at the forces which brought Arthur Firth here to meet the girl he would marry, Sarah Jane Smith, we ought to look for the hands of the Gods.

Sometimes in a magician's life he gets moments when the entire cosmos seems to be manipulated for his sole benefit — or punishment. It is an experience than can be easily dismissed with some trite psychological term, but it is a powerful and intensely real perception nonetheless. The magician finds himself at the end of a series of events which are often national in scale, in which climate, politics and mass human aberrations appear to be involved. He becomes quietly and privately staggered by how certain and crucial events in his life come to pass.

Arthur might well have felt something of this. Most people do in the early ecstasy of falling in love. They believe themselves star-crossed, destined, in some sense 'chosen' — and in his case at least this was entirely correct. Arthur, who was doomed to an undistinguished life by any professional standard, and Sarah, who would never make more impact upon the public records than as the mother of one child, were brought together for the purpose of making a priestess through whom the Gods and Goddessses would talk.

Sarah was John Smith's youngest daughter. He also had Emily and Amy who were eleven and three years older, respectively; and the adopted Lizzie, who was two years younger than Sarah.

We know that Sarah and Arthur were married on 19 August 1886. This was the year that Stevenson wrote his *Dr Jekyll and Mr Hyde*, that Gladstone resigned; the year that the Statue of Liberty was dedicated in New York, and all the claimants to the throne were expelled from France. Marie Corelli, who had little talent but enormous popularity, wrote *A Romance of Two Worlds*; while on 29 December the anniversary of Becket's murder, Thomas More along with fifty-three other English Catholics who had been executed for their loyalty to the Church of Rome during the reigns of Henry VIII and Elizabeth I, was beatified by Pope Leo XIII. Although she was not yet born, this last event, as we shall see, was one of the most important in Dion Fortune's life.

As a sidelight upon Sarah and Arthur it is interesting to speculate that they may well have had one acquaintance in common before they ever met. This was Francis Younghusband, who often stayed with his aunt in Sharpstone House, a little way down the valley slopes. Born in the Punjab and a student at Clifton College, like all the Firth boys, Younghusband would gain the reputation of an explorer-mystic, widely known and greatly respected as a writer on India and Indian religion. He explored Manchuria; he was the first Englishman to reach India from China overland; he was special correspondent for *The Times* on the Chitral expedition; and British Commissioner to Tibet in 1903-4. It was his celebrated mission to this country which led to the unveiling of the forbidden city of Lhasa.

So the man who did so much to bring the East to the West once lived a short distance down the valley from the mother of a woman who would one day try to send it all back again, insisting that in spiritual terms the East has little to teach us.

The Limpley Stoke valley gave something to Sarah and Arthur. It infected them with some of the magic of a lost age. It is one of the places that is most surely if quietly alive, with the parish church at the top of the hill like a beacon for those who came afterward.

We can imagine that day in the autumn when they married. A small pathway leads from the church down toward the Hydro, cutting the valley side at an angle. We can see the guests setting off back after the ceremony eager for the reception, like the image in Samuel Palmer's visionary oil and tempera 'Coming from Evening Church', where the air throbs with a sense of Otherness, the figures pulsate with hints of a world beyond.

John Smith, gentleman, would have done his daughter proud that day, though it was to be another four years before he would get the granddaughter that he would adore.

In the space between the worlds, in the bright no-time between lives, the soul is given the choice of where and when and with whom to incarnate. It is not whim but Law. Sometimes it is possible to remember this, although the act of description diminishes the experience as the mind manages to conceive the near-inconceivable. The parents-to-be are seen; they are sensed as part of the watching soul — separate but still a part of the watcher. They are seen as oddly young, as the child will never know them. There is a sense of rightness, a feeling of pattern.

Using her own magical vision, Dion was able to discern what happened next:

> At the moment of sexual union a psychic vortex is formed resembling a waterspout, a funnel-shaped swirling that towers up into other dimensions. As body after body engages, the vortex goes up the planes. In all cases the physical, etheric, and astral bodies are involved; the vortex therefore always reaches as far as the astral plane; a soul upon the astral plane may be drawn into this vortex if it is ripe for incarnation, and thus enter the sphere of the parents. If the vortex extends higher

> than the astral plane, souls of a different type may enter this sphere, but such extension is rare, and therefore it is said that man is born of desire, for few are born of anything else.[4]

We may assume that the psychic waterspout created by Arthur and Sarah's lovemaking reached far beyond the lower astral levels and attracted just such a 'different type' as Dion proved herself to be. Beneath it all she was quite aware of her uniqueness; often, she found such knowledge appalling.

And so this pre-life spark of hers, this 'seed-atom' as she would call it, chose precisely the sort of place, body, and circumstances as would imbue her whole career upon this earth with a background of hint and symbol. As she herself saw it, magicians such as she did not much show people the Path, they *were* the Path. The champion of the West, the priestess of the Serpent Power and the cult of the Dragon Kings, the often dark and fundamentally sterile Woman, could not have chosen better.

2.
THE SECRECY AT THE HEART OF POWER

> Saturn is indeed one of the Old Gods and is concerned with the mineral aspect of earth. He is throned upon the most ancient rocks . . .
>
> Dion Fortune

Violet Mary Firth was born in the Sign of the Archer on 6 December 1890, at Bryn-y-Bia in Llandudno, in the country of the Red Dragon, or Wales.

Dragons, which are symbols of ancient sexual powers taking wing, traditionally guard secret treasures; they are linked with the Moon and dead souls, and the subtle and profound Mysteries of Women.

Bryn-y-Bia means 'Hill of the Bow', which was the site of a decisive battle between warring races, from the corpses of which a 'yellow monster' arose to devastate Europe in the sixth century. Dion, therefore, had been born in what was once a plague-infested burial ground.

That she was born in the sign of Sagittarius, the Archer, is important too, for here we are in the realm of the philosopher-kings, and the centaurs. From this strange union of woman and beast came Dion's deep knowledge of humanity's bestial origins, and a deep sadness at her own differentness. It made her the alien, the outsider. It made her appear as someone who saw too much.

And there was the year 1890 itself, when Booth wrote *In Darkest England*, when Degas painted his *Dancers in Blue*, and Paul Claudel produced his play *Tête d'Or*. It was the year in which Cleopatra's tomb was discovered, moving-picture films were first shown in New York, and Lockyer came out with his theory of stellar evolution. It was also in this year that Sir James Frazer wrote his massive and influential study of comparative folk-lore and myth called *The Golden Bough*.

Dion would come to like that book: she would live out large parts of it.

Llandudno itself is situated on a long flat spit of land between two limestone headlands. These headlands are called the Great and Little

Ormes. 'Orme' according to the most felicitous interpretation derives from 'wyrm', or 'worm'. It is synonymous with that beast which has so long dominated the darker aspects of the British psyche — the dragon.

The name of the town comes from '*llan*', meaning a sacred enclosure, and 'Tudno', the name of an old Celtic saint who was associated, indirectly, with a legendary drowned city in Cardigan Bay.

When John Smith took his caravanserai of professional bonhomie and therapeutics there, the town had its scattering of churches: there were English and Welsh alternatives for the Presbyterians, Wesleyans, Baptists and Independents, plus two Missions and one synagogue. The 'old religion' of Catholicism was catered for by the Church of Our Lady Star of the Sea.

Tudno's sacred enclosure, then, was bounded by the two Ormes. The former was once an island, joined to the mainland only by the neck of land on which the town was built. It consists of alternate beds of chert and limestone, arranged in convenient terraces on which traces of an Iron-Age fort remain, plus fragments of a cromlech, and what is left of a once-impressive avenue of upright stones in the shape of a letter L, leading to a circle. Once, the Romans mined rich veins of copper there which they held sacred to the goddess Venus. It is a headland pitted with caves, the most curious being the one called Llech, or 'The Hiding Cave', at the point of the promontory, rumoured to have been a grotto, or 'pleasure house' in an earlier century. Another cave, destroyed by the construction of the Marine Drive, once housed a happy couple and their fifteen children. The wife, Miriam y Ogo, or Miriam of the Cave, died in 1910 at the age of ninety-one.

Caves, as we shall see, became important to Dion. She would have known and liked Miriam y Ogo. Everyone did.[1]

Little Orme lies at the eastern point of the great crescent moon of the bay. It is not so high as the other but its cliffs are more sheer. It too has many caverns, the best known being Porth Diniweid, the Innocents' Gate, and Ogof Cythrenliaid, the Devil's Cave, this being large enough to row into at high tide. From the summit of Little Orme you can see Penmaenmawr, and the druid-isle of Anglesey on which the best and last remnants of British wisdom made their stand.

It was at the foot of this lesser dragon that Violet was born, in the old house they lived in until the purpose-built Limpley Lodge was finished as the permanent housing for the owners and managers of the Craigside Hydropathic Establishment.

Smith seems to have paid for this building himself. In many ways it was the Limpley Stoke Hydro all over again, but on a considerably bigger scale. Residents could stare out over the Ormes from the various and varied dining rooms and drawing rooms. By reason of the rising ground on which it was built, the tide, so to speak, was always in. Its rise and fall was considerable.

This new Hydro had all the treatments of the former but an indoor heated swimming pool was a notable extra. Unlike the relatively modest venture in Wiltshire, the Craigside Hydro attracted the real cream of society up to and including royalty. There was even a resident physician, John Miles Chambers, who was Arthur's brother-in-law. It was Dr Chambers' daughter, Enid, who was the only real friend that Dion Fortune would make and retain outside the sphere of magic.

Arthur Firth undoubtedly used his legal skills to put this business on a sound footing, although by 1902 he was giving his address as The Grand Hotel, next to the pier. It is not clear whether he was living here in personal splendour or if he was connected with its management. It was pure snobbery on his part that he always, until his death in Torquay in 1943, gave his profession as solicitor. He was neither more nor less than a hotelier, aspiring to be the sort of 'gentleman' that John Smith always felt was his proper station in life. Having lost his father at the age of seven, and spent only a single term at Clifton College in 1875, he must have found the large Smith family a haven of warmth and companionship. If nothing else they were both Yorkshiremen in alien counties; they spoke the same language. One small branch of the steel-making Firths at least, was devoted to Smiths.

Nothing is known of the circumstances surrounding Violet's birth, but the mythophiliac nature of sorcerers and their apprentices makes sure that there is enough to make us marvel. It was always rumoured, for example, that Violet was an orphan, and only brought up by the Firths because they were childless. As we have seen, this is not true, but behind the popular urge to foster that myth was the idea of changeling birth, and other-than-human conception. The young and naive needed this myth; they needed to believe that she was in some way 'different'. As indeed do magicians themselves, many of whom have their private stories to tell about the circumstances of their own birth. In fact some of these stories are largely true, and they tend to bear out the idea that the real magicians of this world are born and not made. Dion hinted at a marvel around her own birth in her last and most revealing novel, *Moon Magic*:

> To add to the complications I was supposed to have died as a baby. I was declared dead and lay dead for many hours in my mother's lap, for she could not be persuaded to lay me down; and at dawn I revived, but the eyes that looked at my mother, she told me many

> years afterwards when I asked her the cause of my strangeness, were not the eyes of a child, and she knew with the unerring instinct of a mother that I was not the same one.

It is unlikely that this was case: but in her more glamorous moments she would secretly want it so. Magicians can be like that.

Violet, in the language of flowers, means 'modesty'.

Mary derives from the Hebrew Marah, which means 'bitter sea', which links with the Great Sea of Life.

And Firth means a sea inlet.

A modest inlet of the sea of life. That is what her outer name means. She would have liked that.

We do not know much about Violet's life in Wales. There have been rumours that she caused alarm among the locals with her outbursts of psychism, but this is not likely. As we have noted, most people have assumed (and Dion encouraged the assumption) that she had been born and brought up in Yorkshire, for she never described herself as anything other than a Yorkshirewoman or an Englishwoman, which begs the thought that she may well have attended a boarding school in that county; or else that her parents were so besotted with their own background, as Yorkshire people can be, that they never let her identify with her adopted home. Then again, perhaps she was so unhappy there that she never wanted to identify.

There is an essay written in 1905 in which she recalls a typical Welsh cottage:

> The interior of a Welsh farm-house when the lamps are lit, might furnish a study for Rembrandt, with its brasses, old oak, and the pot swinging over a glowing peat fire.
>
> All round the room, near the ceiling, runs a wide shelf laden with polished copper pots and pans disposed to best advantage; these are the household gods, and they are never demeaned by use, a common black kettle being kept for the purpose of boiling water. As my grandmother used to keep two pokers — the parson, or brass one, who lay at his ease on the fire-dog, with his feet stretched towards the blaze; and the curate, or little black poker, who stood stiffly upright at the side of the hearth and was used for poking the fire — so did these good people with their copper kettles.
>
> There is always a tall, black dresser — who does not know a Welsh dresser, with its rows of willow-pattern cups hanging by their handles from the edge of the shelves, while the top shelf is generally consecrated to the hideous ugly china ornaments which, though of repulsive aspect, have value for a collector?

> The great open fireplace looks quite mediaeval, with the stones on either side, and the cauldron of caul swinging from a long chain; and half-way up the chimney the sides of bacon are hanging in the peat smoke. When the larder runs low, a boy is sent up the chimney to return, black as a sweep, with a ham equally grimy, but of excellent flavour.
>
> There are still hand-looms in use in these cottages, on which are spun the famous Welsh shawls; the women knit stockings by the dozen, and the men carve those long pear-wood spoons so rarely seen outside Wales. The tall hats and scarlet cloaks of the Welsh peasantry are now never worn, but they are still carefully preserved in the family chest, and rank with the kettles and the carved spoons.
>
> The old-fashioned farmers do not put much faith in banks, so they pull a couple of stones out of the wall, tie up their money in a little bag, put it in the cavity, and then replace one of the stones. This bag passes on from father to son and at the death of a farmer it is taken out and counted, and as a rich man will have some six or seven hundred pounds in gold, silver, and even copper, it takes his heir some time to compute the amount of his legacy.
>
> The Welsh, as a nation, are very generally misunderstood. The Celt and Saxon standpoint is so utterly different that it is almost impossible for the one to judge the other. This essay, therefore, is not a criticism, for I am no critic, but just an account of Welsh farm-life as I have seen it.[2]

That is an accomplished essay for a girl who had not yet reached her fifteenth birthday; a keen eye for detail and a definite style. And her concluding comment: 'The Celt and Saxon standpoint is so utterly different . . .'. Is she here speaking as a Saxon who has done her best to understand the natives? I think so. She did not know then, but she uttered a fine prophecy for the turbulence she would know in her marriage to a dark and handsome Celt whom she, and everyone around, referred to simply as 'Merlin'.

This essay, really, presents the sum total of biographical knowledge concerning her time in Wales. In her adult writings she makes a few comments about the occult potency of such areas as the Plynlimon mass and Snowdon, home of the Gods, but there is nothing personal. And there is her novel *The Winged Bull* which was written in 1935 in which the protagonists escape to Llandudno itself. But nowhere does she give any indication that she was born there.

We do, however, have a few words about her inner life during her childhood. Wherever she was living at the age of four, she began to have visions. These were visions of what she came to regard as her true home on this planet. They were visions of Atlantis.

In not a few people there linger memories of past lives. Shadowy and fragmentary, like the memories of a home left in early childhood, the picture images survive. Far less rare than we realize are these memories of the past. Many children have them, and the romancings of childhood are not infrequently recollections.

Life soon buries these dim memory pictures under layer upon layer of fresh impressions and absorbing interests. There are some children, however, who find a strange fascination in these pictures of the past that rise unbidden into consciousness, and who dwell upon them, until they develop into whole landscapes and life histories. The child himself may regard them as nothing but story-tellings that amuse his idleness; the adolescent may forget them altogether, but sometimes there comes a day when an interest in transcendental subjects may lead him to dip into the literature of occultism, and in the investigations of some psychic into the records of the lost continents, or the researches of some scientist into their surviving relics, he may suddenly find he had come face to face with his own long-forgotten imaginings.

What are they worth, those musings of childhood when the brightly-coloured pictures rise one after the other in the magic lantern of the mind? If we could collect them all together, might we not be able to reconstruct some picture of the lost civilization that history has forgotten?

Here, for what they are worth, are some memories of the phantasies of childhood — pictures that formed themselves unbidden in the mind in that interval between the putting out of the nursery light and the oncoming of sleep.

First, a constantly recurring image of a sandy foreshore with a level plain behind it and mountains rising abruptly in the distance. A sluggish river made its way across the plain; a few queer-looking trees like feather dusters straggled at intervals along its banks, but it was not safe to go near these trees because there were dangerous beasts in the river that might gobble you up. For the same reason it was not safe to go too near to the waters of the shallow sea that rippled over the sands; things like giant jellyfish were believed to swim there, and fat, black, shiny, porpoise-like backs could sometimes be seen further out.

There was glowing warmth, a lush grassy vegetation, the sky was a very dark indigo blue; and the sun, strangest of all, was copper-coloured. The copper-coloured sun made a great impression.

What does subsequent knowledge say concerning these things? Remember, they were the imaginings of a very young child, somewhere about four years of age, who was unfamiliar with books and had never been far from home.

The sandy foreshore, shallow sea, and level plain reaching back to the abrupt mountain range are a well-known type of geographical formation. The plain is composed of alluvial silt, probably brought down by the slow-moving river from the mountains.

What were the 'feather duster' trees? Why did they persist in the imagination of a child who was accustomed to the ordinary English woodlands? May they not have been the tree-ferns of primaeval times, before the hardwooded timber-forest had evolved?

What of the copper-coloured sun, glowing hot but dull in its indigo sky? Psychics tell us that the atmosphere of lost Atlantis contained far more water-vapour than any climate known to us today. It is also noticeable that the childish imagination pictures a lush 'grassy' vegetation; there were no bushes present to the eyes of the four-year-old. Botanists tell us that it was a grassy vegetation that would go with the tree-ferns, for most of the plants that clothe the earth today had not then evolved.

As for the 'walloping, lolloping beasts' seen out in the water, we have only to look at the picture of a prehistoric scene reconstructed by the scientific imagination to know that the four-year-old was not very wide of the mark.

It was also known to the pondering child-mind that very few people lived near the sea shore; only very poor people who were fishers, and they lived in little low round huts made of basket-work; and they went out fishing in small round baskets, too, and very often they did not come back, because the beasts ate them. It was also dangerous to go near their huts, because the fisher-people themselves ate strange children when they could get them.

For the most part the sea shore was bathed in broiling stewing sunshine, but sometimes it was swept by terrific storms. These came up suddenly, so one was always on the 'qui vive' when one visited the coast, for what with the 'walloping beasts' and the fisher-folk of cannibalistic habits, and the sudden storms, the coastal country was a dangerous and undesirable place. Yet one kept going there. Home, however, was some miles inland, in a cave at the base of the mountains.

Why should the childish imagination conceive that, although 'home' was in the much safer and pleasanter country some miles inland, it was necessary, despite the dangers, reluctantly to visit the coast from time to time? The four-year-old did not know the reason for these perilous expeditions, it only knew the fascination of the dangerous forbidden waters and the dread of the treacherous foreshore. Had the bright scenes, tropical, yet barren, been the memory of some picture, seen and forgotten, whence came the impression of repeated, reluctant visits to this sinister coast?

The habits of primitive peoples at the present day may throw some light on the subject. Where trade is not developed, the inland tribes come down at regular intervals to the sea shore to obtain salt.

The cave-life was a particularly vivid and delightful memory. There were two distinct types of scenery attributed to this dream-country of the copper sun — the low-lying, oppressive flats of the estuary and the broken country at the foot of the mountains. These were densely wooded, so densely that there was a perpetual green twilight. There were three different qualities of light in these dream pictures, and the impressions of each were very vivid and distinct, for each kind of light seems to carry with it a distinct emotional quality; it was the light that was the most important thing about the vision scene, the thing that determined the mood.

There was the fascinating, coppery sunlight with its treacherous risks. The child loved the sunlight and dared the risks in order to enjoy it. There was the green underworld of the trees where one was at home, where one could hold one's own with all comers. And lastly, there was the firelight of the caves, flickering on the shaggy skin-clad companions and the high cleft roofs that led up into darkness.

These were some of the pictures that haunted a child's mind and were the source of endless fascination and not a little fear. Whence did they come? How do we account for their presence in the mind of a four-year-old? Are they the recollections of scenes in a picture-book that caught the fancy? The child did not attribute them to any book, they were just 'there', rising spontaneously. They were among the earliest memories. It was not till much later that the child found that imaginary adventures could be pictured among these scenes; in the earlier stages, there were no adventures, only the shifting, broken pictures flickering through the mind, like the glimpses of lighted interiors seen from a train after dark.

Were the racial memories of the childhood of mankind reproduced in the mind of a child?

Were they memories of previous experiences of that soul in its far-away childish past, which were able to come through into consciousness when the mind of the present was at a similar stage of development?

There are many possible hypotheses; nothing can be proven. The story is told for what it is worth.

This piece was included anonymously in the monthly magazine that was produced for the group that she was then running, known as the Fraternity of the Inner Light. Although she did not sign her name to it, the article, entitled 'Atlantean Memories' was undoubtedly by her.

It is interesting to note, therefore, the words 'a child who was accustomed to the ordinary English woodlands'. Was she being elusive here, settling herself firmly into the guru-act, covering up the mundane background for the sake of greater mystery? The Firth family were certainly in Llandudno until 1902, when she was then twelve years old. It seems that the dragon-powers that she would come to mediate through the ancient pantheons of the Arthurian cultus, and which came to a head (almost literally) through the Great and Little Orme, never seem to have manifested in Dion as any form of real affection for her birthplace.

Nothing much is known about her childhood beyond these images and this story offered 'for what it is worth'. Failing the appearance of schoolgirl diaries, nothing ever will be known. Like all great magicians she probably went through great and intense periods of loneliness that were only relieved by moments of personal epiphany; there may well have been active rejection by her peers. It is almost inescapable in someone like her. Magicians, regardless of the validity of their systems, are *different*. It is a subtle difference and not easily identified but it is there, and other children, having the peculiar perceptions of their kind, would always sense this. Loneliness is the first lesson that any magus has to learn.

It has always been rumoured that she was brought up, as an orphan, in a family of Christian Scientists. The first was certainly a myth as we have seen, and the second is unlikely.

Christian Science did not arrive in England until 1898, when the first church was founded in London. There is certainly no question of anything organized in Wales or the West Country existing prior to 1890, which rules out the idea that her parents were already committed members of the Church when Violet arrived in their lives. Nor is there any record of either Sarah or Arthur ever having been members in either Sheffield, Weston-super-Mare, Llandudno or London: or anywhere else. Nevertheless, she did have a tenuous and brief connection with the Christian Scientists when she was old enough to make up her own mind, but we will discuss this shortly.

In September 1901 the heart seems to have been ripped out of John Smith's world when his wife died. At her own request she was buried at the place where she had spent her happiest years, back in Limpley Stoke. Her grave is found in the Church of St Mary the Virgin where her daughter had been married fifteen years before. When I went to look for it I knew, upon entering the gate, that there was really only one place for it to lie: beyond the Anglo-Norman tombs, up against the curved wall where the goddess had once been worshipped.

The Smith family next appear in Weston-super-Mare. By this time, a year after his wife's death, John was seventy years old and no age to run anything very much. Perhaps he just wanted to retire, for there are no records of any Hydro in that town.[3] Their address was 'Lynwood', 18 South Road, which lay at the foot of the hill on which the remains of Picwinnard's Cairn stands. Fishermen used this cairn to invoke the sea-gods' favour. It is also linked with one of the great leathery, flying beasts of Wessex.

The dragons, the winged serpents, were still guarding their child.

We only know for certain about the family's appearance in the West Country because Violet wrote a book. She wrote her little poems in the same year that an as yet unknown man in Egypt was busy writing a piece of prose-poetry called *The Book of the Law* at the behest of a praeter-human intelligence called Aiwass. Two further extremes of humanity can scarcely be imagined than young Violet and the quickly notorious Aleister Crowley. *The Book of the Law* was worlds apart from the simple vision expressed in the aptly entitled *Violets*, but in twenty years' time she and her work would rival and counterbalance both.

The front of her book bore the words 'These Poems are offered to the Public in the hope that those to whom the author is now a stranger may some day become her friends.' They would indeed, though it would take three generations. The declaration is either that of a very lonely child or an extremely secure and affectionate one.

Violets was almost certainly financed by Smith, for whom she wrote 'The Gorgonzola', explaining that he was in the habit of buying cheeses that were so ripe as to be almost sentient, capable of wreaking havoc all round. A long poem, it begins:

> One day our dear grandpa went into town,
>   And chose a nice cheese with a rind that was brown;
> It was greenish inside, and he noticed with ire
>   That it bore unmistakable signs of the wire.
> Dear grandpa went off with an innocent mind,
>   Not knowing what havoc at home he would find,
> Nor the number of persons to ask with a sneeze
>   If 'he'd pay for the damages done by his cheese?'

It is the doggerel of a clever young girl, but no more than that. An intelligent one, but no genius.

On the other hand we can catch glimpses of the woman she would become in the rest of the poems with titles like 'The Hills', 'The Corn-Field', 'Music in Nature', and 'The Song of the Sea'. Already the earth and sea were beginning to talk to her. In later years they would talk through her.

Of them all the most interesting is perhaps 'The Song of the Sea', although less because of its content than because of its sense of rhythm.

'The Song of the Sea'

What are the billows murmuring?
  Singing so soft and low,
As, retreating, they bare the sea-sands fair
  With a ceaseless ebb and flow:

Do they sing of the South Sea Islands
  Where the feathery palm-trees grow?
Or the Northern Sound, where they're chained and bound
  With the bonds of the King of the Snow?

Do they sing of the terrible battles
  And victories long ago?
How the sea-mew screamed, and the cold stars gleamed,
  And the scud flew wild and low?

How they lash their sides with anger,
  And the wild winds fiercely blow;
Like a grey velvet pall, there hangs over all
  The Storm-fiend, on wings of snow.

And fiercely the north wind bellows,
  And loudly the billows roar;
With an impotent rage, that nought can assuage,
  They rush on the rock-bound shore.

Their songs brings back a scene to me
  That I saw in days of yore —
How the mad waves strove, in a rock-bound cove,
  To drive a ship ashore:

Bravely she struggled against them,
  But what may man avail
When the ocean doth rise, with angry eyes,
  Lashed by a northerly gale?

Madly the brave ship struggled,
  But they pressed her more and more,

Till she struck on a rock, with a shattering shock
  That was heard by those on the shore.

Her crew all stood on the fore-peak,
  Dimly seen through the gloom of the night;
Through the torn storm-veil the curlews wail,
  And, engulfed, she sinks from sight.

At other times, I've seen the sea
  Like a maiden lying asleep;
Her bosoms gently rise and fall, a silver moon shines over all
  As she rests in the arms of the deep.

February 1904

Nearly thirty-three years later she would write a novel called *The Sea Priestess* which stands today as the finest novel on real Magic ever written, a novel that is absolutely soaked with the rhythms of the sea to an almost hypnotic degree, and of which this childhood effort is almost a prophecy.

But in some ways the importance of *Violets* lies not in the glimpses it allows us of this unknown period of her life, but in the fact that it was reviewed in *The Girl's Realm*, accompanied by the only known photograph of Violet as a girl. The article appeared in the May issue for 1905, and reads:

> Violet is a lover of Nature, and it is when her childish muse sings of Nature that we listen with most pleasure. Life, with its puzzles and problems, is not to be fathomed by the plummet line of a child's intelligence, no matter how gifted that child may be. But a child is near to Nature's heart and to it . . . she whispers her secrets and sings her sweetest songs. So we turn the pages of *Violets*, as the little volume is aptly named, and wonder whether Time, the Tester of all things, has indeed in store for us another Elizabeth Barrett Browning, or another Emily Brontë. And meanwhile wise little Violet Firth works hard at her school at Weston-super-Mare all the term, and reserves verse-making for her holidays.

Wise little Violet. The reviewer could never have known that one day the sweet young poet would go beyond Time, and appear to people in their dreams, or in vision, directing the currents of their lives.

The face which looks out is an ambivalent one, although undoubtedly attractive. In discussing it with modern magicians I find them torn in their interpretations between that of an essential purity and spirituality, as opposed to a thinly veiled precocity and burgeoning sensuality — or 'jail-bait' as one of the more libidinous of the adepti said. Really, she is all things to all magi. That is the nature of a priestess.

Echoes of rumour and speculation have it that she once attended the grammar school in Weston-super-Mare. This is unlikely, to say the least, as it was not built at that time. But the reviewer's words in *The Girls' Realm* — 'Violet Firth works hard at her school at Weston-super-Mare all the term, and reserves verse-making for her holidays' — suggest that she may well have attended a boarding school there.

To this extent I would offer the possibility of her having attended one of the first co-educational boarding schools in the country. Ironically for an exponent of *tantra*, or sexual magic, this was and is known as Sexey's School, Blackford, which at that time simply gave its postal address as Blackford, Weston-super-Mare, which might explain the reviewer's comment.

The original version of *The Sea Priestess* came out in 1938, a novel set in the West Country in the fictional towns of Dickford and Starber. Her protagonist, Wilfred Maxwell, is an ineffectual little man heading toward a lonely old age in company with his mother and sister. One day after an uncharacteristic spot of anger he decides to leave the house, named as 'Cedar House', and live in the old barn-cum-stables at the bottom of the garden:

> Everything was abominably overgrown but I shoved my way through, following the track of a long-lost path, and came to a small door with a pointed arch like a church door, set flush with the wall of ancient brick . . . On one side were the horse-stalls, and on the other the harness-room, and in the the corner a corkscrew staircase led upwards into cobwebs and darkness. I climbed this cautiously, for it felt pretty rickety, and came out into the hayloft.

Dion invariably used real places for her novels, although she tangled up the details when she felt it necessary. So the description of the first days of Sexey's School are noteworthy in this respect.

In 1897 several men of substance in the Wedmore and Blackford area set up a committee under the chairmanship of a Mr J. C. Smith, a local solicitor. It is not known whether or not he was related to John Smith, but it is unlikely. However this new Smith did manage to find some suitable premises where a school could be started, and these were at a house in Stoughton called Cedar Tree House. Nearby was a two-storeyed barn which, with the help of a local craftsman called Stickland, was adapted for a schoolroom.

The first headmaster was one Edward Henry Smith, who was born in Godalming, Surrey in 1863. Along with his wife and his assistant, Mrs MacKenzie, he seems to have run a lively and happy school from 1897 until his retirement (to become Rector of Enmore) in 1923.

The original buildings of Stoughton were given up in 1899 when the school moved to its present location at Blackford.

Smith himself was something of a writer, and a keen naturalist. At the end of his years he published *Happy Memories of West Somerset*, in which he shows an extensive knowledge of the area, especially Brean Down, and comments on two occasions that many churches 'built upon hills overlooking the sea, and on rocky islands not far from the mainland are dedicated to St Michael'.

Was it he who first pointed this out to Violet? And in later years, as she cast around for names for *The Sea Priestess*, did she derive Dickford from nearby Cocklake – a name that would have caused much merriment to adolescent girls? And was the stream which so excited Wilfred's imagination the same once-holy stream which flowed from Blackford and which was said to cure scrofula as well as to turn silver to yellow?

The records for the school do not go back earlier than 1912 so we can never know for certain. On the other hand there is the possibility that one photograph which we have from that era may well be of Violet. Included in the small history of Hugh Sexey's School which was published in 1957 we can see the little group of girls in one of the school brakes, on an outing. The background is not clear: it could be a dusty road the wheels are on, but it is more likely to be Brean Sands, a hard, flat and endless stretch of beach which runs from the Down, off toward Burnham. The girl to the left forefront bears a marked resemblance to the known photograph of Violet Firth, although this could be mere wishful thinking. Others who have seen the picture are less than convinced.

But, if Violet did not attend Sexey's School, lost within the once-drowned lands of Somerset, where the sea was only kept at bay in mediaeval times by the labours of monks along the coast keeping up the sea walls, and where the soil is rich with the blood of warring races which strove to gain supremacy of the land – a land pregnant with the seed of Arthurian myth – if she did not go there, then it can only be said that she *should* have done.

It was the ideal place for her, in fact. Odd and haunted, little known, only the great gates at Bridgwater in her time held back the full flow of the sea, the Bristol Channel having one of the highest tides in the world. She would have come to adolescence among people who could remember when the waves had licked right up to the foot of distant Glastonbury Tor itself, and the otherwise landlocked hills like the 'isle' of Wedmore becoming, in truth, islands in a green sea.

Water and earth . . . these are the constant themes of her life. She was living out a ritual long before she ever knew the meaning of Magic. If the monks, and long before them the Romans, held back the waters by artifice, then she by her magic would teach the world how to do similarly, how to create channels whereby the right amounts of the moon-stuff could flow, in specific directions, under full control.

There is no doubt that around this time, 1906, whether she was a student at Sexey's School or not, she discovered the power of Brean Down.

The Down itself is an outcrop of carboniferous limestone which prods out into the sea some 1½ miles, confounding the feminine imagery for once and adding a touch of androgyny to the magical scheme. At the very end are the remains of an old fort which was built in 1866, designed to hold thirty men and twenty horses, and armed with enough seaward pointing guns of good Firth steel to blast any intruder who might dare to venture that far up the Bristol Channel. The north side of the mass contains what is left of two limestone quarries, and on the heights, which command views over the whole bay of Weston are the remains of an old stone circle and a later Roman temple to a now unknown god.

Moves were afoot in Violet's day to make this into a bird sanctuary, and some sort of a nature reserve generally. Peregrine falcons and ravens made their home there, while the botanist could delight in finding campanula, harebell, gentian, sea holly and rest-harrow. Years later the atmosphere of the Down would stay with her; in her imagination she restored the old fort and made it into her private sea-temple. At the very tip, where the jagged rocks disappear into the waves, her fictional persona would commune with the powers of the ocean, and draw upon the lost knowledge of the Atlantean temples from whence she had come and to which the finger of the Down still pointed. This knowledge, she felt sure, would help change the way Man and Woman looked at each other.

Was her paganism awakened there? Did she make contact with the raw, untutored power of neighbouring Brent Knoll? Or did she hear the sea-spirits around the Down which even now call to the inner ear and seek to draw the unwitting soul into their cold green world?

No one will ever know.

On 12 May 1906 Violet's dream came to something of an end. John Smith died of broncho-pneumonia at the age of seventy-two. Arthur promptly decided to uproot everything and move to London, to 53 New

Broad Street, possibly comforted by the knowledge that his father-in-law had left him and Sarah the sum of £1,477 16s 9d. At his own request Smith was buried next to his wife in the church at Limpley Stoke, while Arthur spent the next years doing no traceable work, but indulging himself in the manner to which younger Firths ought to have become accustomed.

The West Country could wait for Violet's eventual triumphal, if unheralded, return. For the next few years she had London to contend with . . .

London: the capital of Empire. If Wales had given Violet access to the dragon-powers that are part and parcel of the *tantra*, if Yorkshire had given her enough to put her in touch with a previous life as a warrior-woman, and if the Summerlands of the West had given her glimpses of drowned worlds and ancient ways, then London was the cauldron which brought it all together and made it boil. According to one contemporary authority the very name was derived from *Luan-dun*, or City of the Moon, in Celtic. Tradition held that there was once a temple of the Moon-Goddess Diana on the spot where St Paul's now stands. This interpretation may not be correct by the standards of modern etymological research, but in magical terms it is perfect.

At that time London was unrivalled in its powers of assimilation. Quite as much as to Paris, the civilized world went there to absorb the atmosphere and energy, and bring otherwise alien flavours to the broth. It was the place to go when you were wide-eyed and with social cachet; the place to marvel at for its myriad novelties and wonders; the place to set you yearning for an entreé to its round of receptions and Court life, its theatres, shows, and endless amusements for body, mind, and soul. Hours could be spent at a music-hall, or an evening in Parliament where world-famous men could be watched discussing important policies; or a quiet morning could be spent in company with one of the multitude of poets who lived there, some of whom would come to abide in English literature with Keats and Shakespeare. There was no end to its depths, a bottomless cauldron of nourishment . . .

This encounter with London was as important to Violet's inner life as anything she would encounter on the astral planes. Although before she could really come to terms with either, she had to come to terms with Christian Science first.

When the Smiths arrived there in 1906 many people in the city had still not forgotten the controversy that the religious group had aroused only eight years before when the novelist and journalist Harold Frederic had died as a direct result of his Christian Scientist teacher, Athalie Mills, forbidding him the orthodox treatment that would surely have saved him.

This was not something that would have worried the teenage Violet. The controversy, the challenge to the Establishment, the appeal to mysterious forces — these were all just what she wanted. She could sympathize with the idea that one must find a true relationship with God. And under her later persona as Dion Fortune she would change this to the plural, and advise people to adjust toward the Gods. As far as the founder Mary Baker Eddy was concerned, it was all a question of systematic Bible study, plus the opening of one's heart and mind to the love and law of Christ. It meant, in short, being born again.[4]

This would certainly happen with Violet, but not for some years. And in any case it was not Christ through whom she was reborn, but through the divine and androgynous being known as Melchisedec of Salem, who had no earthly headquarters, and who existed on the Inner Planes alone.

Christian Science was the first manifestation of this dichotomy which ran right through her life: between the Gods and the One God; between the Mystery in Bethlehem and those of Karnak, Atlantis, and Avalon.

She was not unique in this construction within her psyche: the English, despite their traditional outward air of calm and logic, of stolidity and sang-froid, are actually the most individual and eccentric of peoples who live closer to the unconscious than any other, their paganism capped-off with a thin Christian cover like the sacrificial well in Glastonbury. But with Violet it was almost as though the two parts were initially equal, bound together yet constantly striving to part, like one of those amorphous, bi-sexual creatures that the early Theosophists claimed to have been Man's direct ancestors.

Although her mother was apparently a keen Christian Scientist, there is little evidence that it was anything but an adolescent passion on Violet's part; and only one piece of written material specifically links with that time. This is a poem that appeared in the *Christian Science Journal*, Volume 26, April 1908.

Angels
Violet M. Firth

When thy Dead Sea apples are ashes,
And the light has died out in thy home,
While the sea of thy sorrow updashes,
Whitening thy robe with its foam,
Shut out from pity or pardon,
With thy hope in thy hand lying dead —
Remember the tomb in the garden,
And the words the angel said.

Now to the rock-hewn chamber
Thou comest with spice and balm,
As the sky with its wan pale amber
Heralds the morning's calm.
A stone seals the tomb's low portal,
Too great for thy strength to move;
And thy heart tells thee all things are mortal,
And frailest of all, thy love.

But lo, the stone no longer
Closes the door's low way!
One other than thee, and stronger,
Stayed not for the break of day.
What humble friend remembers,
Now that thine all is destroyed?
Who fans thy life's chill embers?
Behold, the tomb is void!

It is a good poem, skillfully crafted for her age and showing promise of some considerable talent ahead if it were developed. But there is nothing there to give any real hint of the unique achievements that were to come.

She last mentions Christian Science in a book that she wrote at the age of forty, this being one of the stock-taking years in a person's life. Knowing by this time that she would never have children, and that a certain potency had gone forever whether she regretted it or not, she began to look back on something quite different to the normal concerns of women: she began to look back upon her Magic instead. It is from this point on that we can begin to pick up her own testimony.

The book in question was given the ghastly title *Psychic Self Defence*, and subtitled *A Study in Occult Pathology and Criminality*. Many of her books were simply collections of essays on a rough theme, but this one was purpose-built. It was less a treatise on defence against malign entities than a magical autobiography. It is a unique book, though one that is not always to be believed. In places, it is also a very beautiful one.

It is here that she gives us her first anecdote about her early years, dating it to around 1910. It is worth quoting here in full.

> As a young girl of twenty I entered the employment of a woman who I now know must have had a considerable knowledge of occultism obtained during a long residence in India, and concerning which she used to drop hints that I could make nothing of at the time, but which, in the light of later knowledge, I have come to understand. It was her

custom to control her staff by means of her knowledge of mind-power, and she had a steady succession of most peculiar breakdowns among the people working under her.

I had not been with her very long when she wanted me to give evidence in a lawsuit. She was a woman of violent temper, and had dismissed an employee without notice and without wages, and he was sueing her for the money due to him. She wanted me to say that his behaviour had been such that she was justified in thus dismissing him. Her method of collecting my evidence was to look into my eyes with a concentrated gaze and say, 'Such and such things happened.' Fortunately for all concerned I had kept a diary and had a day-to-day record of the whole transaction. If it had not been for this I should not have known where I was. At the end of the interview I was dazed and exhausted, and lay down on my bed in my clothes and slept the sleep of utter exhaustion till the next morning. I suppose I slept for about fifteen hours.

Soon after this she wanted my testimony again. She wished to get rid of my immediate superior, and wanted to find sufficient grounds to justify her in doing so. She repeated her previous manoeuvres, but this time I had not got a diary record to fall back upon, and to my intense surprise I found myself agreeing with her in a series of entirely baseless charges against the character of a man I had no reason to believe to be otherwise than perfectly straight. The same exhaustion and the same dead sleep descended upon me immediately after this interview as after the preceding one, but an additional symptom now manifested itself. As I walked out of the room at the end of the interview I had a curious sensation as if my feet were not in the place I expected them to be. Anyone who has walked across a carpet that is bellying up with the under-floor draught will know what I mean. Occultists will recognize it as having to do with the extrusion of the etheric double.

The next incident to occur in this curious menage did not concern myself, but another girl, an orphan with considerable means. My employer kept this girl constantly with her, and finally persuaded her to put the whole of her capital into her schemes. However, trustees descended in wrath, forced my employer to disgorge, and took the girl away with them then and there, leaving all her belongings behind, to be packed up and sent on to her afterwards.

Another incident followed quick on the heels of this one. There was an elderly woman in the establishment who was slightly 'minus' mentally. A dear old thing, but childlike and eccentric. My employer now turned her attention to her, and we watched the same process of domination beginning. In this case there were no trustees to interfere, and the poor old lady was being persuaded to take her affairs out of the hands of her brother, who had hitherto managed them, and commit them to the tender mercies of my employer. My suspicions had by now been thoroughly aroused. It was more than I could bear to see old 'Auntie' rooked, so I took a hand in the game, woke 'Auntie' up to the situation, pushed her belongings into a box, and got her off to her relatives while my employer was away for a brief absence.

I hoped my complicity in the affair would not become known, but I was soon disillusioned. My employer's secretary came to my room one night, after 'lights out,' and warned me that the Warden, as we called our employer, had found out who it was that had engineered 'Auntie's' escape, and I had better look out for trouble. Knowing her to be of an exceedingly revengeful nature, I knew that my best refuge was flight, but flight was not altogether easy to achieve. The institution in which I was employed was an educational one, and a term's notice had to be given before leaving. I did not look forward to working out that term under the unchecked control of a spiteful woman. So I watched for an opportunity that should justify me in walking out. With my employer's uncontrolled temper it was not long to seek. I was up late the following night packing, in preparation for my intended flight, when there came to my room another member of the staff, a girl who seldom spoke, had no friends, and went about her work like an automaton. I had never had any dealings with her, and was more than surprised at her visit.

It was soon explained, however.

'You are going to leave?' she said.

I admitted that it was so.

'Then go without seeing the Warden. You will not get away if you don't. I have tried several times, and I cannot get away.'

However, I was young and confident in my untried strength, with no means of gauging the forces arrayed against me, and next morning, dressed for the journey and suitcase in hand, I went down and bearded my formidable employer in her den, determined to tell her what I thought of her and her methods, quite unsuspicious that anything save ordinary knavery and bullying was afoot.

I was not allowed to get started with my carefully prepared speech, however. As soon as she learnt that I was leaving, she said:

'Very well, if you want to go, go you shall. But before you go you have got to admit that you are incompetent and have no self-confidence.'

To which I replied, being still full of fight, that if I were incompetent, why did she not dismiss me herself, and anyway, I was the product of her own training-school. Which remark naturally did not improve matters.

Then commenced a most extraordinary litany. She resumed her old trick of fixing me with an intent gaze, and said:

'You are incompetent, and you know it. You have no self-confidence, and you have got to admit it.'

To which I replied, 'That is not true. I know my work, and you know I know it.'

Now there was no doubt that much could be said concerning my competency in my first post at the age of twenty, with a great deal of responsibility on my shoulders, and newly inducted into a disorganized department; but nothing whatever could be said against my self-confidence, except that I had too much of it. I was quite prepared to rush in where archangels would have hung back in the collar.

My employer did not argue or abuse me. She kept on with these two statements, repeated like the responses of a litany. I entered her room at ten o'clock, and I left it at two. She must have said these two phrases several hundreds of times. I entered it a strong and healthy girl. I left it a mental and physical wreck and was ill for three years.

Some instinct warned me that if I admitted I were incompetent and had no self-confidence my nerve would be broken, and I would never be good for anything afterwards, and I recognized that this peculiar manoeuvre on the part of my employer was an act of revenge. Why I did not pursue the obvious remedy of taking refuge in flight, I do not know, but by the time one realizes that something abnormal is toward on these occasions, one is more or less glamoured, and just as the bird before the snake cannot use its wings, so one cannot move or turn away.

Gradually everything began to feel unreal. All I knew was that I had to hold on at all costs to the integrity of my soul. Once I agreed to her suggestions, I was done for. We went on with our litany.

But I was getting near the end of my resources. I had a curious sensation as if my field of vision were narrowing. This, I believe, is a characteristic phenomenon of hysteria. Out of the corners of my eyes I could see two walls of darkness creeping up behind me on either side, as if one stood with one's back to the angle of a screen, and it were being slowly closed upon one. I knew that when those two walls of darkness met, I should be broken.

Then a curious thing happened. I distinctly heard an inner voice say:

'Pretend you are beaten before you really are. Then she will let up the attack and you will be able to get away.' What this voice was, I have never known.

I immediately followed its advice. With my tongue in my cheek

I asked my employer's pardon for everything I had ever done or ever should. I promised to remain on in my post and to go softly all the days of my life. I remember I went down on my knees to her, and she purred complacently over me, well satisfied with the morning's work, as she had every reason to be.

Then she let me go, and I went up to my room and lay down on the bed. But I could not rest until I had written her a letter. What that letter contained, I do not know. As soon as I had written it and put it where she would get it, I fell into a sort of stupor, and lay in this state with my mind completely in abeyance till the following evening. That is to say, from two o'clock one afternoon till about eight o'clock of the following day — thirty hours. It was a cold spring day with snow on the ground. A window close to the head of the bed was wide open and the room unheated. I had no covering over me, but I felt neither cold nor hunger, and all the processes of the body were in abeyance. I never stirred. Heartbeat and respiration were very slow, and continued so for several days.

I was found eventually by the housekeeper, who revived me by the simple application of a good shaking and a cold sponge. I was dazed, and disinclined to move or even to eat. I was left to lie in bed, my work taking care of itself, the housekeeper coming to look at me from time to time, but making no comment on my condition. My employer never showed herself.

After about three days my especial friend, who thought I had left the house, learnt of my continued presence, and came along to see me; an act requiring some courage, for our mutual employer was a formidable antagonist. She asked me what had happened at my interview with the Warden, but I could not tell her. My mind was a blank and all memory of that interview had gone as if a sponge had been passed over a slate. All I know was that out of the depths of my mind a most terrible state of fear was rising up and obsessing me. Not fear of any thing or person. Just plain fear without an object, but none the less terrible for that. I lay in bed with all the physical symptoms of intense fear. Dry mouth, sweating palms, thumping heart and shallow, hasty breathing. My heart was beating so hard that at each beat a loose brass knob on the bedstead rattled. Fortunately for me, my friend saw that something was seriously wrong and she sent for my family, who fetched me away. They were exceedingly suspicious. The Warden was exceedingly uncomfortable, but no one could prove anything, so nothing was said. My mind was a blank. I was thoroughly cowed and very exhausted, and my one desire was to get away.

It began then, when the malign aspects of magic made themselves felt whether she wanted to know them or not, and it was some years before she learnt the techniques which would enable her to protect herself. In *Psychic Self Defence* she portrayed herself as something akin to the brave Fool of the tarot, unaware of the precipice. But the truth was closer to the vision of herself that she had had four years earlier, in her first novel, *The Demon Lover*:

> Only the most rigorous self-denial had enabled her to get through her training; the third term had been one of semi-starvation, and this, added to the strain of the final examination, had reduced her to an abnormal state in which she floated rather than walked, and saw grey ghosts about her rather than men and women . . .

If every man's first novel portrays the author as Christ, then in *The Demon Lover*, she set herself up as the Virgin Mary, albeit unconsciously. She was not The Fool, then, so much as The World, wrapped up in herself, naked and innocent, yet to be born into the Otherworld, chaste as only women of her class in that era could be chaste. The Warden of that 'educational establishment' would take her psychic virginity and rip open the womb of her innocence in a single dark act.

It is not known exactly where this assault took place. It could have been in St George's Secretarial College in Red Lion Square, which place she knew well and alluded to in another early novel; it may well have been outside the City of the Moon's ambience, near Thor's Ley, or Thursley in Surrey, at the British Colonial Training Institute that she seemed to describe in her collection of short stories called *The Secrets of Dr Taverner*, and where at some time, in some way, at least some of the raw material of her magic was hammered into shape.[5]

Whatever, the end result was that Violet had a nervous breakdown. She went away to recuperate. Her health was very poor. Of course it was no inner deity that spoke to young Violet and told her to pretend to give up; it was her common sense, no more, assuming audible tones within her psyche out of sheer exasperation. Had she been less proud, less stubborn, she might have taken this obvious way out immediately. Instead she insisted on a battle of wills and got a nervous breakdown as a result. It is a testament both to folly and integrity. Had she been two-faced as the great run of humanity is two-faced, she could have walked out of that office with impunity. As it was she *made* the Warden's magic effective.

In the months following her escape she continued to find herself easily tired, drained of all her once-considerable vitality. She deliberately forced her memories of that terrible encounter out of her mind, feeling that if she dwelt upon it the shock and strain might prove so severe that her mind would give way altogether. She kept her psyche together with the help of an old school arithmetic book, spending hour after hour doing simple sums to keep her mind from racing itself to pieces, every now and then sidling up to the memory and then shying away from it like a frightened horse.

> About a year after the incident, my health still being very poor, I went away to the country to recuperate, and there came across a friend who had been on the spot at the time of my breakdown. It had apparently caused a good deal of talk, and I found here one who was not inclined to explain away my experience, but asked pertinent questions. Another new friend became interested in my case and hauled me off to the family doctor, who bluntly gave it as his opinion that I had been hypnotized. It was before the days of psycho-therapy, and his ministrations to a mind diseased were limited to patting me on the back and giving me a tonic and bromide. The tonic was useful, but the bromide was not, as it lowered my powers of resistance, and I speedily discarded it, preferring to put up with my discomfort rather than to render myself defenceless. For all the time I was obsessed by the fear that this strange force, which had been applied to me so effectually, would be applied again. But although I feared this mysterious power, which I now realized was abroad in the world, I cannot tell what a relief it was to me to find that the whole transaction was not an hallucination, but an actual fact that one could rise up and cope with.

In effect she had had none of the classic journeys through madness, going through the three stages identified by Joseph Campbell as, first, *Separation*, whereby the whole personality falls apart. In many Eastern systems of occult training the guru deliberately humiliates his disciple, constantly and in public, with the intention of smashing the hapless wretch's ego in order to begin again anew. In the West however, life itself is the guru. Then there is *Initiation*, whereby a piece of personal courage or achievement enables the individual to reconstruct his personality along better and more flexible lines. Dion was to achieve this only when she took a magical initiation into the occult Order with which she eventually trained, the basis of the whole problem being that her etheric aura had been damaged, to use the parlance of occultism, and she leaked 'prana', or vital energy. And finally comes the stage of *Return*, when this newly-made heroine goes back to the very Source itself. Dion spent the whole of her life doing this.[6]

In considering this nervous breakdown, it is interesting to note the comments of Jack Gratus in his otherwise tedious book *The False Messiahs*, when he discusses the links between rebirth and baptism. Quoting the psychiatrist August Hoch, who mentioned 'the psychology of wiping the slate clean for a fresh start', he notes: 'The idea, expressed theologically, is to become like Melchisedec, the priest who typifies the Christ-figure: "Without father, without mother, without descent, having neither beginning of days, nor end of life"'. More significantly he goes on to say:

> The stages of development into the new identity may not be as clearly marked out as I have indicated, but they usually follow this pattern: crisis, interlude of apathy and dejection, followed by visions and dreams of death, possibly by drowning, the hearing of a command to take up a new identity, and finally a 'call' to reveal this new identity and the mission that accompanies it to the whole world.

As we shall see, the figure of Melchisedec had great significance in Dion's life for he was the head of the Order to which she belonged. She did in fact have just this sense of mission that Gratus identifies as one of the prerequisites of the Messiah, although her youthful passions stopped short of any such delusions for herself. She was a woman for one thing. The nearest she could get to it was in the Sleeping Priestess themes she used in her later novels.

It should be added, too, that she was by no means alone in making such a link with Melchisedec: her whole group did so; magicians today, having little interest in Dion Fortune or her Society, are still doing so.

But we are jumping ahead.

In the years immediately preceding the Great War the young woman was still, with the help of her arithmetic book, a tonic, and her friend's advice, struggling to come to terms with the complete destruction of her ego. As a means to reconstruction she did what so many people do who have suffered in this way; she took up the study of psychology. Psychology, she felt, would put all things on a rational basis.

Magically, it was the worst thing she ever did.

If taking the waters was something of a fad for her parents' generations, the study of psychoanalysis was much the same for hers. The rolling billows of the unconscious mind seemed like the Atlantean depths she had glimpsed as a child. Below the surface, if one could dive or peer deep enough, were all the secrets of life.

Freud, Jung and Adler were the names on educated lips: a trinity of wise men of differing views but essential unity of purpose. Freud with his emphasis on the 'love experience', Jung, with his ideas on the archetypes and the inward alchemies, and Adler with his assertions that all humans strive toward power. Love, Wisdom, and Power . . . they were almost like the three rays in Dion's cosmology.

Psychology had one marvellous and over-riding virtue in the eyes of people like Violet: anyone could practise it. No formal qualifications were needed. It was the Alternative Therapy of the time. There was even full and fierce debate as to whether lay analysts would or should be accorded the full recognition of their more orthodoxly qualified fellows. In the end they were not, and Violet never forgave the British Medical Association for it.

Nevertheless she became a lay analyst. In her own words she became the highest-paid lay analyst in London, just before the Great War. This alone is testimony to the faddishness of the art, for Miss Firth, at the height of her brief and lucrative career tinkering with people's minds, was then twenty-three years old. There is no such thing in this world as a mature and insightful twenty-three year-old. It was the novelty which attracted her customers, nothing more.

She seems to have attended classes at the University of London as organized by a Professor Flugel, an open-minded man of broad interests who was also a member of the Society for Psychical Research.

Records of the time have all been destroyed during the two wars, but we do know that Violet referred to herself as having worked in a Medico-Psychological Clinic in Brunswick Square. This was not the Tavistock Clinic as has been reported; nor was it identical with the Medico-Psychological Society which was formed at that time and which still exists, but has no record for her, and which was situated in Chandos Square in any case.

It would seem that the actual clinic she referred to was run within the jurisdiction of the London (Royal Free Hospital) School of Medicine for Women, a title which is fully explanatory and almost incantatory. It had 165 beds and numerous out-patient clinics. One, for 'Mental Pathology' was run by W. H. Stoddart, while another person connected with it was Henry Albert Reeves FRCSE, of whom more later.

The hospital was linked to the University of London, which promised that in due course the successful graduate of the theoretical courses (as given within the University) and also of the practical aspects (as achieved within the Hospital) would be formally recognized as professionally competent in the art of psychoanalysis. To Violet's annoyance, they never were.

When it came to her clients, she encountered people whose complaints are now part and parcel of everyday life: there were abnormal deviants of both the male and female sex — that is to say homosexuals; there were a number of unmarried mothers who had failed to hang on to their most precious asset; and most of all there were the compulsive masturbators. Her clinic seemed to heave with compulsive masturbators.

She gave public lectures. Some of these were collected and published in 1922 as *The Machinery of the Mind*, with an introduction by the brilliant botanist A. G. Tansley. It makes dismal reading today, but that is hardly her fault. It is not so much that her psychology was trivial or shallow: the problem is that psychology itself is trivial and shallow.

Freud, Jung and Adler and all the rest of the neo-Gnostics have done more damage to magic than any of the supreme rationalists in the scientific establishment. But it is changing, as Violet would have wanted it to change. In years to come magicians will look upon psychology as a fad akin to the hula-hoop: useful for the exercise of certain otherwise forgotten muscles, but scarcely the best or most dignified way of proceeding through life.

Her best virtue in this pseudo-profession of hers was her honesty and directness. Society was built upon the 'done' and the 'not done', the 'U' or the 'non-U'. There were subtleties of converse and behaviour that were expressed through unwritten rules. To be an Englishman was to belong to an exclusive club; membership of that club was dependent upon proper expression of all those factors which make for Good Breeding. Violet's Yorkshireness was well-suited for cutting through the cant like a witch's dagger, letting the life come out into a greater world.

She was honest, and often ruthless with her honesty.

Bernard Bromage, writing about her some ten years after her death, had an acute ear for those nuances which derived from this time. Writing about the time when he knew her in the mid 1930s he comments:

> Dion Fortune never ceased to impress on me that she . . . had attained the greater part of her knowledge of magical techniques solely by a study of psychological principles. I, as it happened, was well acquainted with the training of the Jesuits regarding fundamental psychological precepts; and she was enormously interested to hear my account of this highly-skilled and severely disciplined school of investigation.
>
> She had attended many courses at that highly 'liberal' institution, the University of London, in such related subjects as psychology, psychoanalysis, mental therapy and the like, and she tended to use

> the terminology employed in these circles in what seemed to me a rather over-facile and slightly too credulous manner. She was full of 'ab-reactions', 'compulsive neuroses', 'psychosomatic conditions' and the like. I saw her essentially as an epigone of the Central European School which owed its main allegiance to Freud and which dominated the minds, not to mention the morals (or lack of them) of so many of the young and eager intellectual spirits of the 'twenties. She had fallen for a time under the influence of the doctrines of the psychologist Aveling; but it was the trumvirate Freud, Jung, Adler who had awakened her extraordinarily intelligent interest in psychological principles and orientated her towards a position in which she saw quite exceptionally clearly the close connection between modern empiricism and tried and tested tenets of the great Tantric and Qabbalistic ritualists.
>
> I recall many discussions with her on these and kindred topics: on the nature of the love technique and how it is the woman . . . who awakens the energy in the male and so makes him positive; of the part played by the ancestral subconscious in the formation of character and personality; of the tremendous and sometimes terrifying power of suggestion and its use in propaganda; of the nature of the child and the perception of animals.[7]

He knew Dion at her psychoanalytical best, when she was a woman of some substance in her late forties. Had he known her in her days at Brunswick Square, Bromage would have been irritated by it all.

On the other hand he was not really equipped to understand the extent to which she was beginning to analyse her experiences in the light of Magic. Freud himself would have envied the more esoteric of her clients. Not every psychoanalyst had the good luck to be able to number real vampires among his case-load.

> When psychoanalysis was first introduced into England I took up the subject, and became a student, and eventually a lecturer at a clinic that was founded in London. We students were soon struck by the fact that some cases were exceedingly exhausting to deal with. It was not that they were troublesome, but simply that they 'took it out' of us, and left us feeling like limp rags at the end of a treatment. Someone happened to mention this fact to one of the nurses engaged in the electrical department, and she told us that the same patients 'took it out' of the electrical machines and that they could absorb the most surprising voltages without turning a hair.[8]

This is nonsense, of course. She is looking back upon her experience with a lurid eye and trying a little too hard to gain the support of the scientific world (via the electrical department) in her discourse upon a highly dubious topic. The fatigue that she and her fellow-students felt is common to all who work in the field of mental illness, and scarcely needs the concept of vampirism to explain it — the more spectacular aspects we will describe later. Even so, she was less concerned with the romantic approach of Bram Stoker than with understanding those curious relationships where a mordid attachment existed between two people — 'most commonly mother and daughter' — whereby one seems to drain the life force from the other. And before she goes on to narrate a genuinely magical tale of vampirism which was dealt with by her mysterious and all-potent occult teacher, we find the following and possibly revealing paragraph:

> I am of the opinion that what Freud calls the Oedipus complex is not altogether a one-sided affair, and that the 'soul' of the parent is drawing upon the psychic vitality of the child. It is curious how aged Oedipus cases always look, and what little old men and women they are as children. They never have a normal childhood but are always mentally mature for their years. I persuaded various patients to show me photographs of themselves as children, and was much struck by the elderly, worried expression of the childish faces, as if they had known all of life's problems and burdens.

She might have been talking about herself: she never had a normal childhood and was mentally mature for her years, knowing all of life's problems and burdens . . . But when she lay, thankfully, on her death-bed in 1946 it was as though she had stepped through the mirror at last: she who had never had a proper life, and who had been bent in spirit in her last years by the weight of the burdens she had carried to and from the Otherworld on behalf of her motherland, was suddenly freed from it all. Those close to her then thought that she had never looked so serene, so beautiful — and so very *young*.

As a psychologist she *had* to be a Freudian — and not just because his was the most famous name, and the first known to the educated public. There was the sexual basis to his philosophies which had enormous appeal to young people, enabling them as it did to 'sail near the wind' in intellectual terms, while apparently offering clear and obvious solutions to life's problems via impulses that were common to, and becoming increasingly more demanding within, the dishonest society of the time. She would have championed Marie Stopes too, as well as D. H. Lawrence — although her own later attempts at 'Lawrentian' novels stopped far short, of that man's explicitness. Later on she would outgrow

Freud as everyone should and take far greater interest in Jung, who was becoming more obviously a magician himself, though a very shackled one.

The terminology which Bromage found so facile in its use still remained. It was only the surge of her psychism which saved her.

Wisely or not, psychology for Violet was the Outer Court, as she would come to express it. It was her means of making magic acceptable to the world at large — a world which rode with increasing speed upon the concepts of scientific rationalism as it geared itself towards the first scientific war. It enabled her, she felt, to justify the philosophy and practice of magic, and draw the right sort of (intelligent) people toward the enchanted circle in which she now found herself, outside of which she never stepped:

> As soon as I touched the deeper aspects of practical psychology and watched the dissection of the mind under psychoanalysis, I realized that there was very much more in the mind than was accounted for by the accepted psychological theories. I saw that we stood in the centre of a small circle of light thrown by accurate scientific knowledge, but around us was a vast circumambient sphere of darkness, and in that darkness dim shapes were moving. It was in order to understand the hidden aspects of the mind that I originally took up the study of occultism.
>
> I have had more than my full share of adventures on the Path; have known men and women who could indubitably be ranked as adepts; seen phenomena such as no seance room has ever known, and borne my share in it; taken part in psychic feuds, and stood my watch on the roster of the occult police force, which, under the Masters of the Great White Lodge, keeps guard over the nations, each according to its race; kept the occult vigil when one dare not sleep while the sun is below the horizon; and hung on desperately, matching my staying-power against the attack until the moontides changed and the force of the onslaught blew itself out.
>
> And through all my experiences I was learning to interpret occultism in the light of psychology, and psychology in the light of occultism, the one counterchecking and explaining the other.[9]

When she wrote her dismal little books on psychology with names like *The Psychology of the Servant Problem*, *Machinery of the Mind*, and *The Problem of Purity*, she was Violet M. Firth. But when she wrote her luminous books on Magic she was Dion Fortune. It is the Magic which has survived, as Magic always will. As an analyst she was never more than a clever amateur, despite her high earnings. As a magician, despite the low returns in material riches, she was superb.

The months before the Great War were in many ways the most important in her life. She was approaching twenty-four years of age, a tall and handsome woman, flaxen-haired and no one's fool, well-meaning toward her fellow-humans but unfulfilled in her attempts to help them. She was in her prime, really, and might well have turned her thoughts toward the idea of marriage if the conflict in Europe had not removed the entire generation of marriageable men that she could have wed. This, in common with so very many women who were born at the same time, was why she did not get married until late in life — not because of any sexual conflicts as to her own orientation, as has been implied. Given that it was just not done then to marry even fractionally below one's social stratum, it will be seen that her entire social class of eligible bachelors was wiped out at the Somme, Passchendaele and Ypres. During the years of the war her femininity was to go to seed like the poppies which have become such a symbol for the slaughter in Flanders.

Twenty-four was the ideal age for a woman to marry at that time. She would have had the sort of 'fling' that was allowed to women then, and achieved some experience of her own. Ideally she would have met and married some tall strong and brooding man (and in fact she would one day do exactly that) but she had ahead of her one disastrous romance with someone that she would come to believe was non-human, and before *that* she would meet another kind of entity altogether. This was the year that the mundane and wordly self of Violet M. Firth began to fade. This was the year that the denizens of the Otherworld, tired of waiting, began to make themselves known to her. It was the year that, long before she made inner contact with the austere and self-created being known as Melchisedec, she met an entity altogether more personal and approachable. 1914 marked the troubling of her life. This was the year she first met her Master . . .

3.
THE TEARING OF THE VEIL

> We have in our midst a widespread organization that has an open platform. The Eastern Mahatmas are working through it, but where are the Western Adepts?
>
> Dion Fortune

Now Henry Steel Olcott was not the Master in question: far from it. He was not in fact anyone's Master, but rather an American lawyer whose job it had been to root out corruption as a Special Commissioner for the War Office. For his talents and success in this field his government had awarded him the rank of Colonel. He was one of those men, without especial qualities, who nevertheless come to achieve world renown in certain areas of interest. In short, every occultist in the past century has heard of him.

He was an intelligent man, within definite limits, but no more than that. He was also scrupulously honest. Unlike the Masters whom he would serve, he had a knack for setting people's teeth on edge — at least in Europe. But that was ever the American karma. Born in the first quarter of the nineteenth century he was, in middle age, a broad and strongly-built man, his pleasant and genial face surrounded by a large silver beard which tended to make him look older than he actually was. Lively and vital, his only real physical defect was a disobedient eye that would turn in all directions at the least likely moment. To the snobby Europeans among his various audiences it must have seemed a great mystery as to why the Exalted Ones should have so singled him out for their attentions.

In effect his life began in middle age. In the year 1874. On 14 October to be precise. This was the exact date that he met the woman who would profoundly change his life and, ultimately, affect the occult movement throughout the world.

He met her at a seance, at the Eddy homestead near Chittenden in the State of Vermont. Here, the Eddy brothers were having great success, by all accounts, in materializing the spirits of the dead. Olcott was there on behalf of the *New York Daily Graphic* to report on this.

Eighteen seventy-four was a good year for Spiritualism in America. It was a fad of the sort of proportions and intensity that can only originate in that country. This was long, long before the years of jogging, T. M., est, self-help psychologies such as T. A. and P. E. T. — not to mention the heady times of chewing gum and skate boards. At its height, which would not last long, over a million adherents were claimed for the spiritualist movement, and few people had not tried their hands at table-rapping, ouija boards, and the more advanced forms of mediumship.

Olcott, although a keen convert, did not entirely lose himself within the morass of the movement. He was too honest a man to be taken in by all but the very cleverest — or the most genuine — of mediums.

And on 14 October 1874 it was not a dead soul made manifest which took his attention but a woman who was present at the same seance.

'Good gracious, look at that specimen will you?' he said to a friend.

The specimen in question was a certain Madame Blavatsky. Helena Petrovna Blavatsky. Known to all and sundry, friend and numerous foes, as HPB.

Madame was a tall woman, unusually stout. Her face was massive, with high cheekbones and a flat nose, surmounted by a mop of frizzy hair. She described her own features as Kalmuco-Buddhisto-Tartaric. Her huge eyes, which everyone commented upon, were of the most startling blue. A chain-smoker, and keen devotee of hashish, she was capable of language that would make a Marseilles dock-hand blush when she got angry. She was afraid of no one in this world, and not very many from the next.

Olcott was just a prop to this woman, though an important one. It was she who introduced him to the Masters, she who brought them to the West, while Dion, who followed her, would do her best to send them home.

By her own account Blavatsky first met a Master when she was only twenty years old. This was in 1851, in Hyde Park, next to the Serpentine. The moon was shining brightly at the time. The name of the Master in question was Morya, or the Master M, as she often called him. He was a representative of what she called the Great White Brotherhood, or the White Lodge. He and others Masters such as Koot Hoomi lal Singh, (often contracted to Kuthumi) and Djwal Kul, were said to reside in the Himalayas but could and did manifest themselves anywhere at any time if they so wished. And when there was Work to be done, they frequently so wished. With almost limitless powers, they were the true rulers of the world.

All this was pieced together by Olcott as his relationship with Madame progressed. If he was not exactly Boswell to her Johnson, he did enable us to learn the story of the Theosophical Society from one of the innermost angles. Because of this gnosis to which he had been exposed, he gave up his wife and sons without a second thought. For the rest of his days he was Blavatsky's man and no one else's; although it has to be said that they never got to the point where they thought of sharing a bed. In their own words they were 'chums', no more. As the Colonel confessed to A.P. Sinnett: 'Do you think that I would stand going about with that mad Frenchwoman if I did not know what lies behind her?'

He was wrong on two points here: she was not from France but the town of Yekaterinoslav in the Ukraine, where she was born on 30 July 1831; and she was not mad, but had been cursed with glimpses of the Goddess. To the mob, the two states are often difficult to separate.

At this time, in 1874, Olcott did not yet know the full extent of just what lay behind his new mentor. He simply thought of her as an exceedingly powerful medium, for which she already had something of a reputation. Together they formed the Miracle Club, intent on more phenomena, which were duly if dubiously provided. But by 1875 the tempo had quickened somewhat. Olcott came to learn about Blavatsky's psychic contact with one John King (a typically bland spirit-name) who was well-known in circles on both sides of the Atlantic. She had, he learned, known this entity since 1863. 'The spirit of John King', she wrote, 'is very fond of me, and I am fonder of him than anything on earth. He is my only friend, and if I am indebted to anyone for radical change in my ideas of life it is to him alone. He has transformed me and I shall be indebted to him . . . ' To her, King was no mere non-entity (no pun intended) which always seemed to abound on the Otherside with names such as Chan, or White Cloud, coming from a historically unverifiable period. His was a real and warm personality — quite as much so as that of her newfound *chela*, Olcott. She believed King, in his earthly existence, to have been the swash-buckler Henry Morgan.

How could the poor Colonel compete — if indeed he ever tried?

Yet fond as she was of King, she revealed to Olcott that the spirit was a mere messenger: a messenger from some very exalted souls indeed. In due course (and this was still some time before the Himalayan Masters appeared) he was put in touch with them himself. This came not from the primitive methods of table-rapping and ouija boards, but in the form of handsome letters, marvellously precipitated from thin air, and properly addressed too. His communicants were members of the mysterious Brotherhood of Luxor, a company of adepts, three of whom were named as Serapis Bey, Polydorus Isurenus, and Robert More. These illuminati belonged to the Ellora, the Solomon, and the Zoroaster sections of the Brotherhood, respectively.

And, when Olcott wanted to contact these adepts, all he had to do was to write a letter himself, give it to Madame Blavatsky, and await his reply after she had duly precipitated the letter to them by a reverse process.

Had Olcott not been such a transparently honest wretch, and had Blavatsky not been such an enormously magnetic creature, no one in this world would have believed it was not all a hoax.

In fact many did disbelieve, but for the moment the couple were such small game that it was not worth expending shot on two minor eccentrics. Yet Blavatsky then did two things that immediately and for all time put her a great way above all the little mediums and rogues that abounded. She wrote a book, and she founded the Theosophical Society; and the former was the foundation for all the glories of the latter.

The word *theosophy* is a compound of two Greek words meaning 'divine wisdom'. They decided upon this title on 13 September 1875, after rejecting titles such as the Hermetic, the Egyptological, or the Rosicrucian Society. The word Theosophy somehow felt right to them all. The early members were few: a Mr J. H. Felt who was a dabbler in the occult with a penchant for evoking and controlling Elementals; the Freemason and bibliophile Charles Sotheran; a New Yorker and his poet wife; a Signor Bruzzesi who had been a former secretary to Mazzini and who had studied Magic in Europe; and William Quan Judge, who had been a clerk in Olcott's law business. And Blavatsky herself of course. They were nothing without her and what she promised. They wanted *real* wonders, aided and abetted by the Masters she kept telling them about.[1]

In fact this term 'Masters' had a maddening and mighty appeal to the minds of the middle and upper Victorian classes on both sides of the Atlantic. It conjured concepts of power and grandeur and absolute authority. In that century, more than in any other, these were seen as entirely desirable qualities. More important still, every man or woman could, according to this new female prophet, come to bask in the favour of a Master if he or she proved of suitably noble soul. Proving of noble soul involved believing in Theosophy, doing the Masters' bidding (as expressed through Madame Blavatsky) and sublimating the sex-force.

The Victorians were doing an awful lot of sublimating the sex-force at that time. On collective levels, in Britain, the armed forces were doing it very well indeed, through time-honoured methods of invasion, domination and massacre.

Interestingly, the concept of these supernatural beings did not, despite popular belief, originate with this complex and labyrinthine Russian woman. As Ithell Colquhoun notes in *The Sword of Wisdom*:

> The tradition in Europe of Superiers Inconnus goes back further than Madame Blavatsky . . . to the founders of Masonic fraternities like Martinez de Pasqualli (d. 1774) Louis-Claude de Saint-Martin (1743-1803). Even before these, the Strikte Observanz of von Hund (1722-76) had its Unknown Supermen. Though such doctrines were popularized by Madame Blavatsky's Theosophy they did not originate with it.

The book that HPB wrote, *Isis Unveiled*, we will deal with very shortly. However much her critics laughed off her ideas of the Masters, they could not so easily dismiss such a monumental work — except by ignoring it completely.

But it is here that we have a sticking point in tracing the magical influences which led up to the creation of Dion Fortune. Because Dion herself, although she believed implicitly in the concept of, and *Inner* Plane reality of the Masters, did not for one moment believe that they had any physical existence. Indeed, she even made her own brief psychic contact with 'They of the Himalayas', but still after that could not accept that they had physical bodies anywhere on this earth. She who would walk along that same Serpentine bank as Blavatsky had done in 1851, she who at that time habitually wore a long black cape and broad-brimmed hat, meditating as she walked upon the Mysteries of Egypt — she would never accept that any exalted being had once appeared to HPB, or anyone else, in the flesh. Writing about the judgements made upon Blavatsky by some acidic and not very judicious researchers, she made the snap judgement:

> My verdict is 'guilty', with a strong recommendation to mercy. Being myself the head of an occult organization with Masters behind it, I know the difficulties she had to contend with and the temptations to which she was liable. I think she faked the Letters, but I do not think she faked the Masters . . . I am also of the opinion, in the light of my own experience in the same field, that the tales of personal meetings with the Masters on the physical plane, and all the evidence for their local habitations and names, is also bunkum, and I do not believe that whoever originated these stories, or whoever substantiated them, has ever been sincere.[2]

This is a far cry from the little girl in Weston-super-Mare who wrote rather sweet poems about cornfields. The voice which speaks here with typical forthrightness could also have been Blavatsky's. It is the voice of just such another as Blavatsky: the voice of a Priestess of Isis.

It is not meant in any vaguely poetic sense, but literally. Dion would resurrect the Mysteries of Isis in a converted chapel off Belgrave Square and live within the aura of that goddess daily; while half a century before would see Blavatsky comment in a letter to her sister Vera:

> You may disbelieve me, but I tell you that in saying this I speak but the truth; I am solely occupied not with writing *Isis* but with Isis herself. I live in a kind of permanent enchantment, a life of visions and sights! I sit and watch the fair goddess constantly. And as she displays before me the secret meaning of her lost *secrets* and the veil becoming every hour thinner and more transparent, gradually falling off before my eyes, I hold my breath and can hardly trust my senses![3]

Blavatsky is referring to her epic book, *Isis Unveiled*. Originally, when John King was still the major influence and before he had been supplanted by her Eastern guides, it was to have been called *the Skeleton Key to Mysterious Gates* — a largely forgettable title. Later, under a more exalted inspiration than that of poor John King, she changed it to *The Veil of Isis*. This was a reference to Plutarch who described the veiled Isis in front of her temple at Sais, with the famous inscription: 'I am everything that has been, and is, and will be, and my veil no mortal has uncovered.' This was a far better title, but it was pointed out to her that had it already been used in England for a book on Druidism by W. Winwood Reade. And so she settled on *Isis Unveiled*.

It is a formidable work, even discounting the blatant and unacknowledged debt she owed to the book *Anacalypsis*, by Godfrey Higgins, which was subtitled 'An Attempt to Draw Aside the Veil of the Saitic Isis; or an Inquiry into the Origin of Languages, Nations, and Religions.' Higgins was a high-grade Freemason, a student of occultism, and may well have been a member of *An Uileach Druidh Braithreaches*, a Druid order believed to be a precursor of the Hermetic Order of the Golden Dawn. No matter that she stole from him for her vision, or that Dion's own seminal book *The Cosmic Doctrine*, which was claimed to have been dictated by *Western* Masters, was in many ways a re-working of lectures given by her mentor. Neither of these things matter. It was the end result that was important. And in Blavatsky's case the end result was a book which stunned the occult world, even if it left the more orthodox literary circles totally unmoved.

John Symonds, in his neglected little biography of Madame Blavatsky, attempts to sum up the content and themes and impact that *Isis Unveiled* had when it appeared in 1877:

> What is *Isis Unveiled* about? . . . If Atlantis had really existed, and if one person, a single Initiate, had been selected by the Gods to give to the world the arcane knowledge which was swept away when Atlantis was submerged, then HPB was that Initiate, and Isis Unveiled a repository of that knowledge. Indeed, Madame Blavatsky believed that she alone . . . had been selected by the Master to reveal forgotten wisdom. Thus we learn for the first time of the Secret Science which was expounded by the rishis of old who included among their august number Buddha, Confucius, Lao Tze, Zoroaster, Pythagoras, Plato and Apollonius of Tyana. And Christ, too, in spite of the anti-Christian sentiments in *Isis Unveiled*. We are also told of the existence of Hidden Masters who are said to be living in the flesh, but who are hardly bound by the physical laws which govern the rest of Mankind. These Masters or Brothers inhabit remote places like Tibet, or Yucatán in swamp-covered Central America . . .[4]

One can imagine that when Dion came to read the book she would have paused at one point early on in her studies to get a red pen. She, who had had her own memories of Atlantis as a little girl living in Llandudno, knew that Isis allowed of different visions and interpretations, channelled through many priestesses.

Poor Olcott knew nothing of the controversies which surrounded Blavatsky's scholarship. He was not learned enough to question the accuracy of her theologies, too englamoured to doubt her powers, and only really concerned with the fact that he had, himself, seen one of the Masters in the flesh.

> I saw him towering above me in his great stature, an Oriental clad in white garments . . . long raven hair hung from his turban to his shoulders; his black beard, parted vertical on the chin in Rajput fashion, was twisted up at the ends and carried over the ears; his eyes were alive with soul-fire . . . He was so grand a man . . . so luminously spiritual, so evidently above humanity that I felt abashed in his presence . . .

This was the Master Kuthumi, real and in the flesh; appearing from nowhere and disappearing likewise. Dion would never have liked Olcott. He would have set her teeth on edge.

Despite this antipathy, by 1914, some twenty-three years after Blavatsky's death, and only seven after Olcott's, Violet was about to meet her own Masters as a direct result of linking with that 'magical current' begun by the founders of Theosophy.

At this time the Theosophical Society had begun to attract a very larg

The Firth family crest

Letter-heading for the Craigside Hydropathic Establishment

The Limpley Stoke Hydropathic Establishment

Violet as pictured in *Girls' Realm*

A school outing. Is the girl to the forefront Violet Firth?

Helena Petrovna Blavatsky

following, numbering some 25,000 members world-wide. It attracted those free-thinkers who were weary with the Church and its dreary stranglehold; it was also very popular with women of a certain class who entered the Society as a counter, perhaps, to the Freemasonic clannishness of their men. They too would have their secrets. They too would have portents given to their lives. It was, to many, a safe way to become anti-Establishment; a respectable way of becoming outrageous.

Violet was quite aware of the Theosophical Society as it stood at that time. This was when she still a student of psychology, and as self-certain of psychology's innate wisdom and rightness as Olcott had been about Kuthumi's flesh and blood. Quite likely she would have, at this point in her thinking, dismissed the Colonel's teacher as no more than a piece of psychological compensation, or subsconcius upwelling. Had she gone deeply into Jung she would have ascribed the whole saga to the provenance of archetypes and had done with it all.

Although she was not to become a true member of the Theosophical Society for another ten years, she went along to a meeting held not far from her work-place in Brunswick Square. The group she describes was probably one of those suggested by Charles W. Leadbeater, who was then the brightest star within the Theosophical firmament, but whom Dion would soon come to lambast as a homosexual black magician.

She tells the story herself in the monthly *Journal of the Society of the Inner Light*, at a time when the figure of the Christ still had some resonance within her psyche, a few years before the pagan contacts swept in.

> The capital I is an overworked letter at the best of times, and autobiographic details cannot be justified unless they have intrinsic value, or the person they concern is of eminence. I am far from eminent, nor am I so egoistical as to think that my experiences are of interest to any one but myself *save in so far as they are of evidential value.* We are only too familiar with the person who has a friend to whom wonderful things happen, and who ten proceeds to relate an anecdote told about the late Dr Dee. This is not evidence, and it is a great pity that it is ever offered as such, thereby bringing esoteric science into ridicule. I can at least speak of that which I have seen. I know the Masters are real because I have not only seen Them with the Inner Eye, but have time and again felt Their power in the world of form, and promises made to me have been kept. If the things I have to relate are not what I believe them to be, what are they? At any rate they have produced not only a complete change of life, but also of circumstances, which I regard as evidence of objectivity. But whether subjective or objective, they have brought to me the big things of life beside which I count all else but loss.

At the time when I first came into contact with occultism I was a student of psycho-analysis, which I had hoped to make my living as well as my life-work. I had achieved some standing among my fellow workers, but was gradually being brought face to face with the fact that I had very little success in alleviating human misery, and this was a thing for which I was sincerely concerned. I felt very great compassion for the suffering with which I had to deal; it made me genuinely unhappy when I saw cases drag on and patients spend their little all in the hope of a cure of which I knew there was no prospect.

About that time a club was founded for young Theosophists, a club designed to act as a channel for the work of the Masters. It was joined by many who desired to serve the Masters, and by some who merely wanted a decent meal in a district where most of the other restaurants were of a type which is a good pull-up for cabmen. I joined this club, not because I was in sympathy with its aims, for I knew nothing whatever about them, but because it was near the clinic where I worked, and was a pleasant place to get a meal.

Here I met for the first time with the teaching of Theosophy, and I am afraid the introduction was not a very happy one. I heard a great deal of irresponsible talk, which I thought was foolish, and with the arrogance of youth, I dismissed without further enquiry the whole philosophy and science from which it appeared to be derived, and indulged in a little gentle leg-pulling. Young Theosophists produced their best psychic experiences for my edification, and I replied that we had patients suffering in a similar way at the clinic, but they were getting better under treatment. This naturally led to strained relations. People will turn the other cheek to persecution, but not to ridicule.

One day, in an idle moment, I thought that I would patronize the meditation class. I am afraid my mood was one of mischief rather than enquiry, and during the earlier part of the proceeding I meditated chiefly on the hardness of the chairs. The matter in hand was the transference of thought-forms, and with my usual amused contempt I looked on at the performance. Then to my surprise there arose before my mind's eye what psychologists call 'hypnogogic', a small, brightly coloured picture, such as is seen when looking through the wrong end of an opera glass. I saw a vision of an herbaceous border, full of tall blue plants. The leader of the group then announced that she had made a thought-form of delphiniums, which I thought was a curious coincidence. Next there appeared in my consciousness a picture of that unlovely vegetable known as a 'red-hot poker', and again the group leader announced that this had been the subject of her meditations. Two more experiments were made, and in each case the image in my consciousness preceded the announcement. I said nothing, because I knew that I was in an unfriendly atmosphere, but I thought a great deal. I had dismissed contemptuously the ill-considered stories that had often been told me, but I saw that this time I was dealing with something genuine, and was honest enough to admit it.

I realized that if thought transference were a fact, it had a very important bearing upon psychotherapy, and I proceeded to experiment upon the lines laid down at that meditation class. I saw that in thought-reading we have a method which would enable us to discover dissociated complexes without the use of the cumbersome and painful method of psychoanalysis; I experimented with it very carefully, and found it to be reliable, and then having scrapped the greater part of the analytical side of psychotherapy, proceeded straight to the re-education, and found that the re-education itself, if based on right diagnosis, could produce a synthesis of the dissociated materials.

But in the meditation class I had not only had a personal experience of thought transference, but some power had touched me that produced a profound spiritual upheaval; I looked my psychoanalytical work straight in the face, and knew that I could no longer go on with it, threw up my post and joined the ranks of the Land Army.

Looking back, I believe that, the Masters being invoked at the founding of that club, they were truly using it as a channel, and that, because I genuinely desired knowledge in order that I might alleviate the suffering, I was brought to that contact. I think, too, that were a little more love mingled with the Wisdom and Power, many would now be Theosophists who are simply independent students of occultism. I have often wondered why it was that those conducting the affairs of the club did not realize that a change was taking place.

A time of testing followed my resolution to pursue such dim lights as I had. The conditions were terribly severe when the first women were sent out on the land, but I did not feel free, during that time of great national need, to return to the pursuit of my own affairs. This again, I think, was one of the tests of the Path. I endured for a year, and then the way opened up for me to undertake more congenial work of national importance, and I found myself in charge of a laboratory where research work was being done in connection with food-stuffs. A large proportion of my task consisted in spending long hours watching and waiting in a great empty building while bacterial cultures brewed in an incubator. A more ideal situation for that which was to follow could hardly have been found.

I suppose the enforced quiet must have had the effect of turning attention inward, for astral sight suddenly opened and gave me one of the frights of my life. I know of nothing more alarming than astral vision without the necessary knowledge to control it.

I saw at once I was experiencing that which I had thought such nonsense when I had heard it discussed in those Theosophical circles to which I had accidently penetrated. I saw also that I had got the clue to a certain type of insanity, for if any one who had floundered out on to the astral plane as I was doing, were to lose their nerve and panic, they would be in a very bad way indeed.

I knew that Theosophy possessed knowledge concerning that which I was undergoing, and I therefore went to the library which was then in Tavistock Square, and browsed among the books.

My first choice fell upon *The Ancient Wisdom*, and I began to read, coming presently to that wonderful passage wherein are referred to 'The brotherhood of the Great White Lodge, the Hierarchy of Adepts who watch over and guide the evolution of humanity'. I read the pregnant words: 'Still They teach eager pupils, showing the Path and guiding the disciple's steps; still They may be reached by all who seek Them, bearing in their hands the sacrificial fire of love, of devotion, of unselfish longing to know in order to serve; still They carry out the ancient discipline, still unveil the ancient Mysteries.'

Upon me the effect of this passage was mantric, it ran in my head like a tune, and my whole nature gathered itself up into a one-pointed desire to find the Masters. I say that my nature gathered itself up, for the conscious will was submerged in the tremendous uprush of the depths, the blind will of the primitive self that is usually expressed in savagery was in me turned to the desire for Light. Fierce as thwarted love and stronger than the fear of death was that desire, and there was no price I was not willing to pay. The Masters had only to make known Their conditions for me to comply with them.

All day long I moved in a dream, my body performing its duties automatically; my first waking thought was of the Masters, and my last thought as I fell asleep, and my dreams were coloured by my desire. I seemed to range over rocky deserts in a grey twilight, not upon toiling feet, but with powerful wing-beat and the speed of the wind; I had a sense of irresistible power, and always that tremendous desire drove me on, as if it were something outside myself. It was like the throb of the screw on board ship; awake or asleep, it was always there; one felt it under foot on deck, one heard it if one woke in the night; it never ceased to drive the ship towards the port for which her course was set, though it lay invisible as yet below the horizon.

I come from that part of Yorkshire which was under the Dane Law, and I suppose I reverted to type and 'threw back' to some Viking ancestor. Mildest of people in the ordinary way, we are liable to go baresark upon occasion, and I went baresark in my quest of the Masters.

For ten days I continued in this state, and then I found that which I sought. Upon the tenth night I went to sleep in the ordinary way, and began to dream. I dreamt that I was going down a long passage with many doors opening on to it, and the end of the passage led into the reading room of the old library in Tavistock Square. The passage had been dark, but the reading room was full of sunshine. I stood for a moment in the ray of golden light that came through the window, and then the whole side of the room opened out and I seemed to be caught up through space and found myself upon a plateau among great snow mountains, which I knew to be the Himalayas, and I was kneeling at the feet of two of the Masters. I could not see Their faces, for they were lost in a blur of light; nor could I see the hands, for they were concealed in the loose sleeves of the robes They wore, but I knew that one was the Master Jesus; the other I did not know, save that I felt Him to be a tremendous intellectual force. I have since learnt to know Him as the Most Wise, one of the Lords of Mind, on the Hermetic Ray; to the Master Jesus was given the title of Most Holy, Lord of Compassion.

The Master Jesus was clad in a purple robe, and the Most Wise in a robe of dark indigo blue. I was in Their presence for some time, but of what was said I can remember nothing save that I was bidden to have more reverence for that which was holy. I no longer had any sense of power such as had been with me upon my journey, but was awed, almost cowed, by the tremendous presences before Whom I found myself. The Most Holy took no part in the interview, but stood a pace or two behind His companion, and seemed slightly remote, aloof, and very weary, as if some great strain rested upon Him; the weariness gave me the impression of physical exhaustion through which the spirit shone undimmed. The Most Wise, however, seemed to have tremendous driving force, dominant, intellectual; and while I feared Him, I adored, and asked nothing better than to enter upon His service. I have learnt since that He is one of the Greatest Masters upon the Blue Ray, a Lord of Hermetic wisdom and ceremonial magic.

The Master Jesus gave me the impression of having an infinite patience with the weak, and pity for the lowly. Though He would lead by rough ways, He would lead gently and slowly, suiting His pace to the most foolish and footsore of His sheep. I have sometimes been asked why it is that I can work with people who have neither intellect nor education, and I think it must be because I myself was trained by a Master who did not look for qualities of intellect in His pupils.

I must have been about half an hour in the presence of the Masters, and then I felt conditions change, and I seemed to re-enter the room in the library through the gap in the wall, which closed behind me. Vision changed to dream, and I awoke. But the memory of that transcendent experience remained with me, and has remained ever since. Was it a dream, or an actual experience? That is a matter of opinion; I only know that not only my inner consciousness, but the outer circumstances of my life were totally different thenceforth.

When in the morning I looked back upon that breathless adventure, seeking to recover every detail of its memory, I found in my consciousness the certain knowledge that I had been accepted as a pupil by a Master. But here is a curious point, for although the whole bent of my temperament was towards the Master of Wisdom, I had been handed over to the Most Holy, the Master of Compassion, and I was not at all happy about it. I wanted the pace and driving power of the Most Wise; I felt myself to be strong and wished to be worked to my full capacity; I was impatient with the patience of the Master of Compassion; I thought it was a colourless service compared with that of the Master of Wisdom, and there were many struggles before I would submit to that gentle yet compelling force. I can see now why I was placed under His guidance and not given to the more intellectual type of Master who was congenial to my temperament; it was in order that I might not develop the powers of the mind with the faults of character uneradicated. Before I had gone very far with my training, however, I was very thankful that my Master was a Master of Compassion, who would not quench smoking flax. I do not know how the pupils of the Masters of Wisdom fare, I am sure I could never have stood the training.

During the next three days the memory of my past incarnations returned to me, right back to my first initiation in Atlantis; it was a practically unbroken record of temple work, save my last incarnation, which was most lurid, and into which I seemed to pack all the experiences I had forgone during the rest of my evolution. Now it is quite a simple matter for any one to equip themselves with a series of egotistical phantasies by way of past lives, but in my case I got back not only the memory of initiations and temple lives, *but also the memory of the teaching I had received during those lives.* The Ancient Wisdom is a very intricate and elaborate philosophy and science, and I defy anyone to think it out for themselves in the course of a few days without any previous study on the subject. Therefore I regard the fact that I have never had to work for my knowledge of occultism, but have recovered it, not even piecemeal, but in the mass from memory, as strong evidence in favour of reincarnation.

Arriving at this experience without any previous study of the subject, I have been greatly interested to note the extent to which my experiences have been confirmed by subsequent reading. I was particularly interested in Dr Bucke's book on cosmic consciousness, which was quite unknown to me at the time, and also in Dr Besant's writings on the Way to the Masters of Wisdom. It was very heartening to me to find that I, travelling alone and in ignorance, had struck and followed the well-beaten track, and this gave confirmation to my belief that my experiences, though subjective, had relation to objective fact, and were not of a purely arbitrary nature.

To distinguish between subjective and objective phenomena is a delicate task, especially when it be recalled that all experience, philosophically speaking, is subjective; we ought more strictly speaking, to distinguish between that experience which begins and ends within the self, and that which receives its stimulus from the not-self; and we have also to remember that any given experience not only may, but is bound, to have both elements in its composition, for the objective must always be interpreted in terms of the subjective in order to be comprehensible. I have therefore refrained from attempting any explanation of my dream, vision, hallucination, or experience, whichever it may be, because I, being the subject, am the last person to be able to form a just estimate; I have merely recorded it as it appeared to me, though I ask my readers to believe that I am not so naive as to think that what I perceived was an actual representation of what occurred, for how can a consciousness, habituated to form, produce a simulacrum of That which has no form? It has to rely on the images already stored in its memory to produce a symbolic equivalent; it can approach no closer than this.

Had my experiences ended with this vision, I should have accounted them purely subjective, though I should not have valued them the less for that reason; but from that time onwards the circumstances of my life were entirely changed; I seemed to have passed within the veil and never to return again to mundane life. Had I heard the story of my adventures from the lips of another, I should not have believed it. But it is true, even though incredible.

No, as a psychologist she would not have believed it. Had someone come to her as a patient and told her this story she would have, privately, deemed it incredible and professionally would have reduced it to no more than a sexually-orientated quirk from the unconscious.

But having experienced it personally she had found out, as so many have done before, that contact with the Otherworld — despite all the problems and errors and delusions — is indeed possible. She had found out that there is more to such visions than mere mental imagery. Beyond anything else, and far more important than the pictures, is the overwhelming sense of *presence*. A sense that is as real as if a flesh-and-blood person were standing near enough for you sense his body-heat, and smell his body-odour.

Her contact with these two entities is hardly to be compared with Saul's vision on the road to Damascus, but the impact upon Dion was much the same. This simple and indeed rather dreary vision proved to be one of the most crucial moments in her life. This, in the true meaning of the word, was an Initiation, a moment of beginnings, when Violet began to fade away into the furthest arc of the rainbow and Dion, the Daughter of Heaven and Earth, began most firmly to appear. Even though her formal training was not due for a few more years, and even if she had not yet made her mind up as to the precise nature of these Masters who had come to her in the silence of her young womanhood, she became a priestess from that point on.

The Master Jesus, under whose jurisdiction she had been placed, was not regarded by the Theosophical Society as any higher than the other, Himalayan, Masters. Many Theosophists were indeed rather condescending in their attitude. In fact they made a clear distinction between him and the 'Christ Force', which the Master Jesus had once allowed to enter into his body. He was by no means the Son of God, they averred, but a vehicle for something greater — even if his was a most august and venerable soul.

The poor fellow is almost given a simpering quality in Violet's vision. Laudable and necessary though his qualities of compassion might be, they were no doubt seen by her as of secondary interest to the rampant energies of pure magic that were exuded by the other anonymous Master.

This was, by name, a certain Master R. The leading Theosophists, using language that was ostentatiously trying to conceal, called him 'The Master the Count'. The Count in this instance was Le Comte de St Germain, a legendary figure who strode through the centuries, ageless and marvellous, exerting influence upon the courts of kings. The Master R was one and the same, a later manifestation. His earthly name was Rakoczi, and he was the leader of a noble and very real Hungarian family. It is not clear which of the bloodline was regarded as the Master in question but it was probably Francis II (1676-1735) who came to the throne of Transylvania in 1707 but spent some years wandering in Poland, France, and Turkey, before retiring to Rodosto in Asia Minor where he died. His previous lives were well-documented: Francis Bacon, Lord Verulam, Robertus the Monk, Hunyadi Janos, Christian Rosencreutz, Roger Bacon, Le Comte de St Germain, Droclus and St Alban.

Despite her declaration at the time, the Master Jesus was soon relegated to almost a secondary position within the Society she came to form; before too long she gave full bent to the type of energies that the Master Rakoczi preferred. Even so, although others among her pupils cultivated this contact, and although the Master R had prominence within the lodge after her death, she rarely used the contact in her last years.

Jesus and Rakoczi were Dion's first Masters but they were not the most important. She was quite candid as to the identities of the former but very secretive about the identities of the three entities that she would meet upon Glastonbury Tor, whom we will discuss in detail later.

For the time being, in the months before the Great War, it was sufficient that she had had something startling thrust upon her inner gaze. Perhaps in other years she would have gone on bended knee to Mrs Besant and

Bishop Leadbeater who ran the Theosophical Society at that time and been accepted into the élite core of the group, becoming just another of the seers of the Esoteric Section, bringing forth messages to the world from Masters — but always under the scrutiny and approval of Leadbeater himself, whom she would soon come to scorn as a sodomist with a penchant for little boys.

As it was, the assassination of the Archduke Ferdinand in Sarajevo was one of the best things that could have happened to Violet. War was duly declared. Violet put her race before her revelation, her nation before her numinosum. If she was a proud Yorkshirewoman, she was also a proud Englishwoman. Ideally she would have liked to fight alongside the men; yet because she had no aptitude for nursing and little attraction for anything on clerical lines, she did what she thought was the next best thing: she joined the Land Army instead. When her war ended, and she took up her inner life once more, she would be too wise and strong a woman ever to bend her knee to any earthly authority again.

Remembering the moment over a decade later she was to feel, and rightly, that this mass movement of the women on to the land was an important moment in Woman's history. There was something deep and fitting about the female sex going to the Great Mother like the serpent lines of women in one of the ancient rites at Avebury. Women were slowly, without anyone noticing, taking up the places that men had for so long denied them.

Each county formed its own Women's Agriculture Committee and saw the appointment of Organizing Secretaries. Then came the Travelling Inspectors to supervise the work in areas, followed by the Group Leaders in the villages. From the solitary woman officer first appointed to the Ministry in 1916 developed a large staff of women both at the Ministry and in the country, to deal with the organization and equipment needed to send the many volunteers out on to the land.

All of this was carried out at breakneck speed with no precedent and no time for preparation. Lloyd George, himself an inspiring hustler, put the project under the control of the Food Production Department and then sat back to count the volunteers.

Ultimately some 45,000 young women applied to enrol. Of this number about 50 per cent were rejected by the selection panels set up throughout the country. The feeling behind these panels was that nothing would be more damaging to the whole scheme than the girl who would not or could not cope. About 23,000 were finally enrolled, of whom Violet Firth was one.

And she, like so many of the English middle classes who expect to find that the countryside is nothing more than a large garden, and that life on the land is an endless idyll, discovered two truths: that the Great

Mother can also be a dark, cold and howling bitch; and that the one thing She demands of Her children is hard, sweaty and unremitting toil.

Violet at this time was still very much a child of her class, stuck in some 'Circle of Art' to use a magical term. Her world was still alive with the pretty attitudes of William Morris, rather than the truer colours of Hieronymous Bosch. In her late forties she would understand this, and describe the twin aspects of the Great Mother as those of the Black and the White Isis. During her year as a Land Girl it was the former she met, the howling that she knew.

No records have survived which might direct us with certainty to the farm at which she worked, but it was probably on the border between Hertfordshire and Essex, down a little road which once led across moorland but which now stops short at the runways of Stansted Airport.

This speculation is based upon the details she gave in a novel which she wrote in 1936 called *The Goat-Foot God*. Clive Harper, an inveterate, careful and sometimes inspired researcher in these realms deduced that the farm which formed the *mise en scène* of the novel was a certain 'Monks Farm' situated, according to Dion, on one of the 'lines of force' connecting Tintagel, Avebury, and St Albans. It was possibly here that she worked as a Land Girl under the supervision of a Mr Fothergill who owned the farm at that time. One presumes that she enrolled at the selection panel in Bishop's Stortford.

There is a story surviving from her time there. After she had worked long and hard at her tasks, her employers still had not paid her. So, summoning up her ancestors' baresarker spirit she forced a confrontation with them in which she stood next to the cess-pit and threatened to throw the entire bunch of the farm's keys into the faeces if her money was not immediately forthcoming. It was, and she left.

She had stated in her article that she had only worked on the land for a year. But in *The Psychology of the Servant Problem*, written in 1925, we find the lines:

> I cannot claim actually to have worked as a domestic in other people's houses, but during the war I had three years on the land, in which time I was made to realize the servants' point of view, for the simple reason that working as a lady gardener, I was virtually in the position of a servant under private employers and knew the servants' position from personal experience. Moreover (and it may be that I was lacking in proper pride) when I found that my interests were identical with those of the servants, I made common cause with the kitchen, and because I was also a servant and had to come in at the back door, I got to know the minds and feelings of the girls I met during the

> three years in a way I could never have done had I descended upon them from an upstairs Olympus, however democratic my intentions might have been.

Three years as opposed to one year. And this does not sound like the sort of working farm that Monks Farm was. Nevertheless, wherever it occurred, the story of Violet, the keys, and the faeces is a good one, and probably true.

And although we might dismiss the idea put forward in *The Goat-Foot God* that the farm was on some psychically tangible ley-line, it is surely food for thought that some years after Dion's death Stansted Hall, just a few fields away from Monks Farm, became Britain's first residential training college for Spiritualist mediums. The founders were entirely ignorant of, and indifferent to, the significance of the farm down the lane.

After this, by her own words, we find her undertaking work of 'national importance' in charge of an equally time-lost laboratory 'where research-work was being done in connection with food-stuffs'; no doubt under the aegis of the Food Production Department of the Ministry, where some responsibility must have been felt for those women who could not cope with conditions on the land. It is likely, too, that Violet had some genuine grievance against her quondam employers on the farm, and that the Ministry did its best to give redress by means of this cosy transfer. So she spent long hours in an empty building, watching and waiting, 'while bacterial cultures brewed in an incubator'.

She made a discovery too, and one which would have made her a fortune had she applied herself to the matter.

> The manufacture of a vegetable milk from the soya bean is a matter in which I was interested during the war, and I think I may claim to be the first person, in this country at any rate, who succeeded in making a cheese from vegetable casein. Shortly after the war the company that was making the soya milk closed down, the milk was unobtainable, and I lost touch with the matter.

This was Violet in her back-to-nature self, and this was Violet's war: she sat in a large and silent and empty room, and watched the growth of cultures. The land may have been too much for her as yet, but this microcosm under glass was fine. Despite the opening of the astral sight which silence and stillness can often provoke, this was the last chance of normality that she would ever have.

4.

'AN ADEPT, IF EVER THERE WAS ONE.'

> But let it be clearly noted that the personal contact with an initiated adept, though the turning-point of each career, is no more than a clue to be unravelled.
>
> Dion Fortune

Magically Violet had a lot to learn, even if her past lives had come welling up at once, like those quasi-living figures which rise to the Higher Self in the tarot card Judgement. Mystical revelations are not always consistent with earthly wisdom, and the Masters — no matter how intense the inner contact — are not always the best teachers. What she needed was someone here and now and in the flesh to point her in the right direction. Of course, as always happens in these instances, she found just the teacher she needed.

If we can determine to a year when she met her Masters on the Inner Planes, it is not quite clear how or where she met the man who provided the physical focus of her studies, and who taught her magic.

Large parts of *Psychic Self Defence* are taken up with anecdotes about him. All of them are flattering and even awe-inspiring, deeply coloured by her own fondness of marvels. Dion, who had no small insight by this time into the peccadilloes of the magi, was not one for elevating characters too far beyond the limits of reality; but she made an exception with this man. When she wrote about him he had been dead for seven years. This was long enough for her to get a clear look, but not long enough to twist the truth too much. She described him as having been 'an adept if ever there was one.' Having known a few adepts in her time, this was real praise.

Here was a man who could see auras, who could explore the remote past with his visionary talents, who could project his astral body with ridiculous ease, and cause (like Blavatsky) objects to precipitate themselves into the room from unknown or else foreign locations. Here was a man who had witnessed the machinery of the universe grinding away and who was able to describe in some detail the manner of its working. He was a man who had once been a high priest in Ancient Egypt and also in the Temple of the Moon on lost Atlantis.

Dion actually started writing about him when he was still alive; a fact which must have caused him no small embarrassment. These were short stories that were printed in the *Royal Magazine* between May and October 1922. They bore titles like: 'Blood Lust', 'The Soul that would not be Born', 'The Death Hound', and 'The Riddle of the Sign'. Because the subject was still alive and still very much engaged in teaching, the locations were deliberately altered, putting the events into the moorland near Hindhead, in Surrey. Later these stories were collected into the single volume called *The Secrets of Dr Taverner*. It bore the dedication:

> 'Dr Taverner' will no doubt be recognized by some of my readers; his mysterious nursing home was an actual fact, and infinitely stranger than any fiction could possibly be. It is a curious thing that the picture of him drawn from fancy by the artist who illustrated these stories for the *Royal Magazine* is a recognizable likeness, although that artist

> had neither seen a photograph nor had a description of him.
>
> To 'Dr Taverner' I owe the greatest debt of my life; without 'Dr Taverner' there would have been no 'Dion Fortune', and to him I offer the tribute of these pages.

His real name was Moriarty. The name Taverner seems to have been taken from Taverner's Green, near Hatfield Broad Oak, a pleasant ramble from Monks Farm and an even easier one from Bishop's Stortford. Everyone called him *Doctor* Moriarty, and because of his identification with Dr Taverner it was assumed by outsiders that he was a physician. Even the person who witnessed his death certificate made the same assumption giving his profession as a medical practitioner. He was not, and neither did the nursing home where Dr Taverner effected his miraculous cures have any existence as Dion stated; she was merely drawing upon her experiences at the Clinic in Brunswick Square. When she stated that the nursing home was 'an actual fact' she was using a common writers' device to give fictional stories impact, as well as camouflaging Moriarty's real locale, which, as will be guessed by now, was in Bishop's Stortford.

Moriarty was, rather, a PhD, having gained his doctorate at Heidelberg during a break from his many and varied travels. Or so he claimed. In fact the university at Heidelberg has no records for anyone of that name.

The good doctor was almost certainly fibbing. 'To fib' is a nice and grossly under-rated English verb which is much less offensive and aggressive than the verb 'to lie'. Fibs are tolerable, they are forgivable. Fibs are essentially harmless. They can often be charming.

Magicians, be it said, fib a lot. We all do. But with the magi it is partly to do with the formula through which they work. This is the formula expounded by Ignatius Loyola, founder of the Jesuits, who enjoined his followers to act 'as if'. A magician who used this method to great effect in the 1930s defined it as follows: one must act *as if* the Gods are real, act *as if* the poignant inner experiences have some valid and independent reality. 'If you can do this', he added, 'you need not worry about the whys and wherefores of the human reasoning mind; gone are the semi-sacred tabus of the superstitious past. You are free, for now has begun the Age of Aquarius, the Airy sign of the free man who strides across the wide firmament of the boundless realms of the Great Mother, carrying his own burden upon his shoulders.'

Clearly, there is a thin line indeed between using the Ignatian formula for magical purposes, and the simple act of fibbing for very human ones. Leadbeater, Mathers, Westcott, Crowley — all men who had glimpsed the faces of the Gods and lived to tell us — all these fibbed about aspects of their personal lives.

Likewise Moriarty. It is a common conceit of the magus to claim academic distinctions. He sees himself — and accurately — as far more intelligent than peers who have gained degrees by more orthodox means. He is aware that, because of his own karmic propulsion through life, the scholarly prizes were denied him. Sometimes, because of this, he feels that he with his infinitely wider and more original knowledge, entirely self-taught, *should* be so distinguished. The line between *should* and *as if* becomes blurred; doctorates appear like invoked spirits.

Moriarty was not an MD. He was not even a PhD. He just fibbed a little.

He was born on 27 July 1873, at 5 Upper Gloucester Street, Dublin. His father, William Moriarty, was a Captain in the Royal Navy stationed at Malahide just up the coast. His mother's maiden name was Mary Anne Reid. Beyond all things Theodore Moriarty was an Irishman. It is an influence that was quite as important to him as Violet's Britishness was to her, which points a curious difference between the races generally: the English, belonging to the country which by force of arms, diplomacy, and royal marriage contracts, managed to dominate the Scots, Welsh and Irish, invariably think of themselves as British. The Scots, Welsh, and Irish, no matter how amiably they feel toward the conglomerate, would always put their own nationality first, and mention their Britishness only begrudgingly, if at all.

Moriarty was born long before the Troubles, long, long before there was a border between the North and South of Ireland. He was a member of the Anglo-Irish middle classes, but it was the Irishness which would always prevail, in the last analysis. He was like John Smith in some ways, never going back to his native county but always inordinately proud of it.

Desmond Kavanagh, who had the dark mysticism of the Celt in his veins, ventured that his Irish kin-folk were spiteful, malicious, child-like and resentful in their dark aspect, but also redeemed this completely with their sense of wonder, humour, and imagination. All qualities which the English of that period, being too cautious emotionally, would regard as almost dangerous. This fits Moriarty, and the way he was regarded.

We have brief details about Moriarty's life that were gleaned from him by his pupils. When he was a young man he ran away from home and joined the Merchant Navy. Here, he was fortunate enough to meet a ship's officer who gave him books on philosophy to read. Later he studied at Dublin (and again Trinity College at least has never heard of him) before going on to take that degree in philosophy at Heidelberg. While still a young man he suffered from advanced tuberculosis and was told by his doctor to get to a dry climate. This he did, emigrating to South Africa, which completely cured him. In South Africa he worked at road surveying and later in the Customs Service, and made extensive anthropological studies of the Bushmen and other tribes. During this time he was very active in Freemasonry.

These are the bare details that he was happy to let his students in England know. It is, however, possible to flesh them out a bit.

Moriarty went to South Africa in 1897, at the age of twenty-five. He was an Examining Officer with the Customs and Excise Department; in other words, he was a Civil Servant. In 1904 he was taken to court for debt, owing the sum of £50 to a Mr George Eyre. This was incurred by the need to send his wife to England for urgent medical treatment, which proved 'entirely successful.'

Such is the South African system of records that it has not yet proved possible to find out any details about his wife and the two children he was said to have. His pupils, during the magical heyday in London, were so fascinated by the man himself that they showed no interest in such peripheral details. (Besides which, in that era, it was rude to ask.)

What we do know is that on 28 July 1903, he was initiated into Freemasonry in the St Blaize Lodge No. 1938 (of the United Grand Lodge of England) at Mossel Bay. It is at this point that we come close to the first swirlings of those currents which directed him.

Masonic Halls in the colonies were often the main gathering places for English emigrés. For the men, to be a Mason was to be ensured a place of relative import that was not necessarily dependent upon grossly unfair principles of heredity. One is reminded of the apocryphal definition of the Aga Khan in one of those tomes which analyse the British aristocracy: 'The Aga Khan is believed by millions of Moslems to be the very incarnation of God. Equivalent to an English Earl.' In Masonry however, titles, old school ties and the like, were always less important than the degree of Initiation.

The origin of Freemasonry has been traced, by their own standards of research, back to the time of the erection of the Tower of Babel — or more likely Solomon's Temple — the roof of which was supported by the three pillars of Strength, Beauty and Knowledge. Those pillars would become very important to Dion. Whatever the origin of the Craft, as they called it, there is clear enough evidence that modern Freemasonry in England dates from the foundation of the Grand Lodge in 1717; that of Ireland in about 1725; and Scotland in 1736. Although mediaeval operative Freemasons were actually engaged in erecting and repairing church buildings, they did not always have due reverence for Church doctrine and were eventually proscribed.

As time progressed a knowledge of ordinary masonry was no longer a requirement for membership. The rites, the activities, became symbolic. They began to re-create Solomon's Temple in different ways, on other levels deep within the spirit.

Although Moriarty had begun within the Grand Lodge of England he transferred in 1906 to the Edward H. Corgland Lodge No. 247, under the jurisdiction of the Grand Lodge of Ireland. This was in Johannesburg. Within a short time he became Master of the Patricia Lodge No. 406 at Port Elizabeth. Four years later, in 1911, he joined the Unanimity Lodge No. 3126 (of the United Grand Lodge of England again) at Walmer, near Port Elizabeth.

During this period he wrote, in collaboration with Thomas N. Cranstoun-Day, *The Freemasons Vade Mecum* (1909) and *Notes on Masonic Etiquette and Jurisprudence*, the latter being a tedious and nit-picking analysis of do's and don'ts which would interest only the most inflexible of the members. Nevertheless, the fact that it was written with Cranstoun-Day is noteworthy, for he was the formidable Head of the English Constitution in the Cape for a great many years, and head of all the side degrees to boot. He held office until he was ninety, being something of a living legend by this time. In documents Moriarty would sign himself as 'W. Bro. T. W. C. Moriarty, P. M. 406, I.C.; 18°; IV□', which means — from the eighteenth degree — that he had taken the Rosicrucian initiations that are open within Freemasonry.

Hints of all this filtered through to his pupils, impressing one in particular. In the *Dr Taverner* stories the physician-mage is given an assistant called Rhodes, whose voice is really that of Dion herself, but whose name is either taken from that of Moriarty's friend and co-worker in the Customs Department, one H. M. Rhodes, or else from Cecil Rhodes, Bishop's Stortford's most famous son. In the short stories the fictional Rhodes is fascinated by the powerful brotherhood to which his employer belongs. He talks about secret signs and mysterious words; he describes the lodges being able to contact each other across the world by means of trance-mediums, speaking to each other as if over the telephone.

It is obvious that Dion had only a vague, over-romanticized and occasionally ludicrous idea of what Freemasonry involved. Her comments and descriptions are those of an outsider wanting keenly to get in — even though she would be forever denied by virtue of her sex. In the story, 'The Return of the Ritual', Taverner saves someone by arranging for him to leave the country by ship. When Rhodes comes back from seeing him off, he comments:

> Yet another example was afforded me of the widespread ramifications of the Society. At Taverner's request I looked up the sea captain on his return from the voyage and asked him for news of Robson.
>
> This he was unable to give me, however; he had put the lad ashore at some mud-hole on the West Coast [of Africa]. Standing on the

> quay stewing in the sunshine he had made the Sign. A half-caste Portuguese had touched him on the shoulder, and the two had vanished in the crowd. I expressed some anxiety as to the fate of the inexperienced lad in a strange land.
>
> 'You needn't worry,' said the sailor. 'That Sign would take him right across Africa and back again.'
>
> When I was talking the matter over with Taverner I said to him: 'What made you and the captain claim relationship with Robson? It seemed to me a perfectly gratuitous lie.'
>
> 'It was no lie, but the truth,' said Taverner. 'Who is my Mother and who are my Brethren but the Lodge and the initiates thereof?'

The young Dion would have thrilled to all this. She would have wanted nothing better than to have the mysterious comradeship that would have been hinted at in all Moriarty's dealings. Denied entry into Freemasonry, and choosing not to join the rival Co-Masonry — which admitted women but was heavily influenced by Messrs Leadbeater and Besant, whom she detested — she came in time to form her own Lodge, working on lines that were closely parallel. She became in time her own Mother, and was to have many children.

Plainly, Moriarty was a man of enormous magnetism; this is a hallmark of the adept. Sometimes it attracts and sometimes it repels, depending upon one's own polarity at the time. On occasions, when the adept is in his power, or 'on his contacts' as they say, the magnetism is almost tangible. It tends to set up a resonance within those sympathetic souls near him. Rhodes/Fortune made the comment: 'It is a peculiarity of the mystic that his presence stimulates the psychic faculties of those he is with, and Taverner was a mystic of no ordinary type.'

Moriarty, and later Dion too, was well aware of the effect that such magnetism could have. They managed to make some safeguards both for themselves and for the sake of others. In Moriarty's case this sometimes took the form of a deliberate aloofness, a certain remoteness. Had he not done this then the magnetism would not have lasted for long, but would have been drained away. He built a wall around himself: he had to. Only a very few got close to him, or were allowed entrance through the secret gate. His favourite pupil in fact was not Dion but Gwen Stafford-Allen; yet it was the former, tall enough to peek over the wall, who would preserve him in the world of legend.

As well as her 'factional' descriptions of his activities in the *Dr Taverner* stories, she describes his physical appearance in her first novel *The Demon Lover,* written four years after his death:

> . . . the strange, impassive countenance . . . the deep lines of the parchment skin, the hollow cheeks, the high cheek-bones, the great jaw and the lofty forehead. The eyes, deep-set and glittering, were those of the hawk. He gave the impression of tremendous power, utterly impersonal, completely under control.

and also:

> . . . a face that was neither young nor old, but strangely deathless in its calm, as if all the races of the earth had risen and fallen before its unageing wisdom and power.

Dion was never very popular with the other members of the little community that came to be centred around Moriarty (they felt that she arrogated too much to herself, was too pushing) but they were all agreed that her perceptions of Moriarty's status were quite accurate.

He seems to have come to England permanently some time during the Great War. According to Dion in *Psychic Self Defence*, he was involved with her in the Medico-Psychological Clinic. We do know that he was patronized by three sisters, who were the daughters of Francis Allen, JP, of Cockley Cley Hall, Swaffham, Norfolk.

One of the women was Elsie Reeves, who was the widow of Henry Albert Reeves, once the Consulting Surgeon to the Hospital for Women, and to the East London Children's Hospital. Another was Ursula Allen-Williams, whose husband had a notable career in the Army and made it into *Who's Who*. And the third was Gwen Stafford-Allen, who was regarded by everyone as the one most likely to carry Moriarty's torch after his passing — but who would do no such thing. Possibly she understood that it was the man who was important, and not his philosophies.

The mind's eye is taken here to those pre-Raphaelite paintings, luminous with myth, that show King Arthur, the dying and sacrified God, being borne away to Avalon by the three queens. When Moriarty came back to England he was by no means a wealthy man. Yet these women supported him, allowed him to use their homes for his residential lecture courses, and bore with him until the end — which was not very long in coming. It links us with the Triple Goddess concept, which is the true manifestation of the White Goddess. Moriarty, who felt that the glyph of Aquarius, the man carrying water, was a prophecy of the return of the Goddess after all these cruel and patriarchal years, enjoyed and understood the patronage of these women. It was their wealth which was used to give him a platform for his work in England. No one knows how they met him, either, but it might well have been through a Masonic connection.

On the other hand, and digressing for a moment, there is a curious little essay that was written by Dion in 1931 which might have some bearing on the matter. In it she describes a trip to 'Poppyland' which she made in the months prior to the Great War.

Poppyland, despite the name's impact upon the psychedelic ear of the present age, was not some hallucinogenic haven on the inner planes but a precise area in Norfolk made famous at the time by the writings of one Clement Scott:

> On the grass of the cliff, at the edge of the steep,
> God planted a garden — a garden of sleep!
> 'Neath the blue of the sky in the green of the corn,
> It is there that the regal red poppies are born.

It is the area near Cromer, on a line between Overstrand, Sidestrand, and Trimingham. In places the cliffs along the coast exceed 200 feet in height. The sands are good and the countryside rich in bracken downs, cornfields, and bright with flowers. Sidestrand is the parish on the cliff made famous by Scott under the name of Poppyland. One day, leaving behind all the holidaymakers in Cromer who spent their time 'digging on the sands, playing lawn tennis, working, reading, flirting and donkey-riding', he rambled far enough beyond the lighthouse that marked the boundary of all popular explorations to discover 'the Cottage by the Mill'. It was at this cottage that he came to stay, having glimpsed something of an older and unspoiled world. It was at this cottage too, which because of his published writing became enormously popular and famous, that what must have seemed like the entire artistic world of England came to stay; including the mad and marvellous poet Algernon Swinburne whose contact with the elemental powers Dion was later to comment upon in several places.

At its height (or nadir) there were even special trains laid on to bring jaded city-dwellers down from the industrial Midlands to indulge in the sunspoilt peace.

It was here, in company with some friends, whom I would guess to have been the Allen sisters, that Violet came and made an important contact of an undefined sort that was later to work itself out in most unusual ways.

> A chance invitation took me up to the Norfolk coast. It was the summer before the War and never had Poppyland been so sheeted with its scarlet flowers, a fit omen for the scarlet flood that was so soon to

follow in 'Flanders Fields'. The friends with whom I was staying had a pony cart and our chief amusement was to go junketing off along the cliffs in this somewhat incommodious craft. One of my friends being of an archaeological turn of mind used to inspect any church that came in the way of our wanderings. I, who did not know the pulpit from the font, was usually quite willing to remain in charge of the pony during these researches.

One day however we came to a great church standing upon a spit of land running out into the sea. It was so big and the little village huddled about it was so tiny, that even I was interested and enquired about its history. I was told that a busy agricultural population once dwelt in sparsely populated Norfolk, but the Black Death came, and the towns were swept away. The churches however remained. Built to the orders of the Great Architect whose eyes see everywhere, they endured when the houses the rich burghers had built for themselves had mouldered to low mounds beside the causeway.

We passed up the sandy churchyard where the coarse sea grasses grew upon the graves and tanned netting hung to dry upon the low wall, and entered the church. A vast expanse of grey flag stones stretched before us, for there were no pews, and only a few rows of chairs at the east end of the nave. The pillars ran up and disappeared into the darkness of a lofty roof; not a soul stirred in the great building, there was dead silence, yet the emptiness was alive, warm and glowing. A little lamp burnt dimly before the altar. I did not know then, but I know now, that the Sacrament must have been preserved up there in the dark emptiness.

I stood motionless, fascinated, listening. I knew I was in the presence of something that was alive. There was a force in that church that seemed to key my soul up out of the ordinary pitch of life. My friends were looking at the tombs, but I walked about the church, 'feeling' the atmosphere. These things are hard to describe, one can only interpret them in terms of their effect upon the soul. But I felt like one who long suffering from homesickness in exile, at last finds himself back in the house of his birth and wanders through the rooms, soaking in the sense of welcome. The house is his and yet in some subtle way, he also belongs to the house.

I do not know what church it was, for we ranged far afield in our wanderings, I only know that it stood upon the sea shore and a light burnt in the darkness of the chancel. Not many souls could have made use of it, yet some man, working alone, had the devotion to keep the lamp burning before the altar. How far his parishioners appreciated his efforts I do not know, not much possibly for the chairs

> were few, and these things are not usually liked in country parishes, but he had served faithfully in the few things over which he was made ruler, and prayer and faith had filled his church with power so that I, a pagan, wandering with a picnic basket under my arm, was struck dumb by the presence of an unknown force, and did not forget.
>
> Where a sanctuary is made, there the homing soul will come. Does it matter that I never knew the unknown priest who ministered to me? Does it matter that he never knew that I had come, eaten spiritual bread and departed? Like crumbs put out for the birds, the spiritual food lay upon the neglected altar, and a wandering soul was fed.

She was describing Sidestrand Church, dedicated to St Michael. This had been built from the materials of an older church which stood at the edge of the cliff until 1881, when one by one the stones were removed from the old site to the new. The tower, for years a solitary landmark, was rebuilt in 1848 when the upper portion was destroyed in a tempest. But in 1916, the year that Moriarty was said to have come to England, the mass toppled over into the sea.

It had as much impact upon her senses in those warm young days as did the similar tower atop Glastonbury Tor. At Sidestrand however, St Michael, who presided over and came to over-rule the ancient and pagan places, was for once swallowed up by the great sea-powers of the awakening Goddess.

The connection with Moriarty via the Allen sisters might already have been laid down, if not made, by the time of Dion's visit to Poppyland. On the other hand, she could well have met him during one of the lectures he gave in the large shed at the bottom of Ursula Allen-Williams' garden in Inverness Terrace. This is quite possible because Dion's father was living not very far away in Kensington Gardens Square.[1]

On the other hand she could have met him at The Orchard, in Eversley, where Elsie Reeves ran a sort of commune for his pupils. Arthur Firth had, at that time, some connection with the nearby village of Crowthorne, where one of his friends lived.

Or else, taking time off from her arduous work on Monks Farm, Dion may have enrolled in the Science Arts and Craft Society that was run from Gwen Stafford-Allen's house in Bishop's Stortford, and which was a genteel front for the occult curriculum that Moriarty taught there.

Whichever way, the initial link between Dion's 'Dr Mirabilis' and herself, seems to have come through one of these three sisters.

The man's deeds, as recounted by his pupil, were extraordinary. While other men were coming to terms with the war on the home front, or in the trenches, the Irish mage was busy dealing with vampires. Or so

Dion tells us. Her very first short story, written in the early part of 1921, was a dramatized account of this encounter. Appropriately, it was entitled 'Blood Lust', and was set within the walls of the mythical nursing home as run by the legendary Dr Taverner. Nearly a decade later she revealed that this had really taken place in the Medico-Psychological Clinic, where she was at that time doing tutorials in abnormal psychology.

One of the other students took counsel with her concerning a case that had come to her in private practice, of a youth in his late teens: 'One of those degenerate but intellectual and socially presentable types that not infrequently crop up in old families whose blood is too blue to be wholesome.' This lad was taken as a boarder in the flat which Dion's student shared with another woman. Soon, they began to be troubled with curious phenomena:

> At about the same time every evening the dog in a neighbouring mews began a furious outcry of barking and howling, and a few moments later the French window leading on to the verandah would open. It did not matter how often they got the locksmith to it, nor how they barricaded it, open it would come at the appointed time, and a cold draught sweep through the flat.

At this point Moriarty was invited to deal with the happenings. Accordingly, one evening when he was present, he declared that an unpleasant invisible entity had entered the room. On lowering the lights as he bid, they were all able to see a dull glow in the corner where he indicated; when they put their hands into this glow, Dion at least was able to feel a tingling sensation 'such as is experienced when the hands are put into electrically-charged water'. She was harking back here to one of the exotic water treatments that the clients had once known at the Craigside and Limpley Stoke hydros.

Moriarty then proceeded to despatch the presence after finally pinning it down in the bathroom by means of a magic circle. When he had finished, so much energy had gone out of him that he fell over backward, unconscious.

Although the Doctor was very secretive about his methods, Dion soon came to learn enough to understand that he used the very difficult and indeed sublime method of absorption to deal with the malign creature.

> Now absorption is a very high-grade method, and its successful use depends upon the state of consciousness of the user. Each individual has to decide for himself whether in any given case at a given moment he is in a fit state to attempt it. Unless he can completely steady his

> own vibrations and arrive at a state of perfect serenity and freedom from all sense of effort, he should not attempt it.

She goes on to say that the adept who proposes a magical absorption has to reach the point where he had clearly realized the nothingness of the evil he proposes to absorb, and no longer has any feeling toward it but pity for an ignorance that thinks it can gain any good thing for itself in this way. As Moriarty was busy absorbing this vampire — opening his aura and literally sucking it in — he would have been almost overcome by blood-lust. Nevertheless he would immediately revert to his meditations upon the opposite qualities, maintaining these until his vibrations were once more fully harmonized. The end result, immediately prior to his collapse, would be a tremendous sense of spiritual exaltation and power, an enormous surge of *rightness.*

This was the method of an advanced occultist 'keyed up to the highest pitch.' It was the method of Moriarty.

Dion gives this remarkable tale even greater depth by the background details:

> The boy, whom we will call D, was in the habit of going to sit with a cousin who had been invalided home from France suffering from alleged shell-shock. This young man was another scion of a worn-out stock, and it transpired that he had been caught red-handed in that unpleasant perversion called necrophilia. According to the story elicited from the parents of D, this vice was not uncommon on certain sections of the Front, as were also attacks on wounded men. The authorities were taking drastic steps to put it down. Owing to family influence the cousin of D was able to escape incarceration in a military prison, and was placed in the care of his family as a mental case, and they put him in the charge of a male nurse. It was while the male nurse was off duty that the unfortunate young D was misguidedly employed to sit with him. It also came out that the relations between D and his cousin were of a vicious nature, and on one occasion he bit the boy on the neck, just under the ear, actually drawing blood.
>
> D had always been under the impression that some 'ghost' attacked him during his crises, but had not dared to say so for fear of being thought mad.
>
> What may have been the exact percentage of neurotic taint, vice, and psychic attack, it is difficult to say, nor is it easy to decide which was the predisposing cause that opened the door to all the trouble, but one thing stood out clearly to all beholders, that with the dispatch of the psychic visitant, not only did D's condition clear up immediately,

> but after a short, sharp upheaval the cousin also recovered.

Moriarty gave it as his opinion that some Eastern European troops had been brought to the Western Front, and among these were individuals with the traditional knowledge of black magic for which south-eastern Europe has always enjoyed a sinister reputation among occultists. These men, getting killed, knew how to avoid going to the Second Death, whereby the astral body disintegrates and allows the core of spirit to go on to higher levels. Resisting this Second Death they maintained themselves in the etheric double by vampirizing the wounded.

> Now vampirism is contagious; the person who is vampirized, being depleted of vitality, is a psychic vacuum, himself absorbing from anyone he comes across in order to refill his depleted resources of vitality. He soon learns by experience the tricks of a vampire without realizing their significance, and before he knows where he is, he is a full-blown vampire himself, vampirizing others. The earth-bound soul of a vampire sometimes attaches itself permanently to one individual if it succeeds in making a functioning vampire of him, systematically drawing its etheric nutriment from him, for, since he in his turn is re-supplying himself from others, he will not die from exhaustion as victims of vampires do in the ordinary way.
>
> Z was of the opinion that D's cousin was not the primary vampire in the case, but was himself a victim. Being a youth of unstable morale, he speedily acquired the vampire tricks, and the earth-bound soul of some Magyar magician exploited him. Through his act of biting and drawing blood from the neck of his cousin, this entity became transferred to young D, preferring pastures new to the depleted resources of its previous victim. Probably it alternated between the two, for it was not constantly with D.

She knew how to tell a story, did Dion: enough details to give a three dimensional quality to her writing, but stopping just short of giving away too much. Had she described her adept-mentor as a retired Civil Servant of indifferent health, by the name of Theodore Moriarty, it would also have been harder to swallow. But she called him Z instead, left out the mundane details, and allowed those who came later to imbue him with mystery by means of those mythophiliac qualities within us.

The vampire occurred when she was just a novice, magically speaking — a mere neophyte. We must, as Dion insisted, make of it what we will. As always, she offered such anecdotes for what they were worth.

But, true raconteur that she could have been, she did not stop there. When the rational senses are still trying to take in the possibility of such a thing as vampirism of this sort, she caps it all with another tale, and one in which she was directly involved. This was the tale of the werewolf.

It was not, alas, one of those splendid examples from Hollywood wherein a flesh and blood man undergoes a physical transformation into lupine form. The werewolf was from her own self. It was part and parcel of her own vital, 'etheric' energies.

> I had received serious injury from someone who, at considerable cost to myself, I had disinterestedly helped, and I was sorely tempted to retaliate. Lying on my bed resting one afternoon, I was brooding over my resentment, and while so brooding, drifted towards the borders of sleep. There came to mind the thought of casting off all restraint and going berserk. The ancient Nordic myths rose before me, and I thought of Fenris, the Wolf-horror of the North. Immediately I felt a curious drawing-out sensation from my solar plexus and there materialized beside me on the bed a large grey wolf. It was a well-materialized ectoplasmic form . . . grey and colourless . . . and it had weight. I could distinctly feel its back pressing against me as it lay beside me on the bed as a large dog might.

Although she knew nothing about the art of making Elementals at that time she had accidentally stumbled upon the right method — the brooding highly charged with emotion, the invocation of the appropriate natural force, and the condition between sleeping and waking in which the etheric double readily extrudes itself.

(In magical terms this is not so unusual. Every magician has some tale to tell along these lines. Once, when I was fifteen, a similar thing happened to me. Virgin, intense, pent-up with adolescent energies and thoroughly soaked in the atmosphere of magic as gleaned from a manic absorption of Dion Fortune's books, I came-to one morning after some fevered half-sleep and found a grey, cold, lifeless female figure next to me. It never stirred, the eyes never opened. Before the terror came on, I had just enough sense to take it back into myself.)

Dion goes on:

> I stirred slightly, and the creature evidently objected to being disturbed, for it turned its long snout towards me over its shoulder and snarled, showing its teeth. I had now 'got the wind up' properly; but I knew that everything depended on my getting the upper hand and keeping it, and that the best thing I could do was to fight it out now, because the longer the Thing remained in existence, the stronger it would get, and the more difficult to disintegrate. So I drove my elbow into its

> hairy ectoplasmic ribs and said to it out loud:
>
> 'If you can't behave yourself, you will have to go on the floor' and pushed it off the bed.
>
> Down it went, meek as a lamb, and changed from wolf to dog, to my great relief. Then the northern corner of the room appeared to fade away and the creature went out through the gap.

It was not the end of the story. Members of her household had nightmares about wolves; one of them woke in the night to see the eyes of a wild animal shining in the darkness. At this point, knowing that she was getting out of her depth, she went off to consult Moriarty. His advice was that since Fenris was really a part of herself extruded, she must at all costs recall and absorb it back into her psyche, at the same time forgoing any desire to revenge herself upon the person who had injured her.

It was an important moment in Dion's magical career. She was at the dividing of the ways. If she was not careful she would end up taking the first steps down the Left-hand Path of the black magic she detested. She knew instinctively that were she ever to use this werewolf to attack her enemies, the wolf-form would sever the psychic navel cord that connected it with her solar plexus, and it would no longer be possible to absorb it.

At first dusk she summoned the creature . . .

> It came in through the northern corner of the room again (subsequently I learnt that the north was considered among the ancients as an evil quarter), and presented itself upon the hearthrug in quite a mild and domesticated mood. I obtained an excellent materialization in the half-light, and could have sworn that a big Alsatian was standing there looking at me. It was tangible, even to the dog-like odour.
>
> From it to me stretched a shadowy line of ectoplasm, one end was attached to my solar plexus, and the other disappeared in the shaggy fur of its belly . . . I began by an effort of will and imagination to draw the life out of it along this silver cord, as if sucking lemonade up a straw. The wolf-form began to fade, the cord thickened and grew substantial. A violent emotional upheaval started in myself; I felt the most curious impulses to go berserk and rend and tear anything and anybody that came to hand . . . I conquered this impulse with an effort, and the upheaval subsided. The wolf-form had now faded into a shapeless grey mist. This too was absorbed along the silver cord. The tension relaxed and I found myself bathed in perspiration. That, as far as I know, was the end of the incident.

Moriarty would have been proud of her.

As mentioned, Dion's contact with him was via the platforms offered by the generosity of the Allen sisters. Most of his teaching was done at The Grange, Bishop's Stortford, owned by Gwen Stafford-Allen, but it was Elsie Reeves' house, The Orchard, in the village of Eversley, which has come down to us imbued with as much stuff of legend as any of the characters in the drama. She owned the house between the years 1920 and 1922, at least. Prior to that it was in the hands of a Mrs St Leger Harrison. This would be unimportant if it did not trigger off comparison with the name of Leo St Leger Stokes, who was a member of one of the lodges in the magical organization that Violet would eventually join — and thus become for all time *Deo, non Fortuna.*

Eversley is an unimpressive little village today on the border between Hampshire and Berkshire; more of a London overspill than anything else. When Moriarty was there the Hampshire Barrens, as the rolling levels are called, would have seemed just that — bare and wild, with Eversley an island sanctuary within it all. It was reached, from London, by means of the London and South-West Railway, the nearest stop being at Winchfield some 5½ miles north. From there the Leversuch Brothers would transport visitors the rest of the way by means of a fly. During the years in question the population was not more than 1,000, bolstered a little by the Morecote Sanatorium for Consumption, and centred around the parish church dedicated to — inevitably — St Mary the Virgin.

The village's only claim to fame is in its association with Charles Kingsley — the Reverend Charles Kingsley — who wrote a series of novels including *Westward Ho!*, an Elizabethan adventure story, and *Hypatia*, a forcible picture of life in the fifth century at Alexandria when the Christian Church and the Roman Empire were struggling for mastery. But it is for *The Water Babies* that he is best known, this being a delightful parable about young Tom the chimney sweep (who is thus an explorer and cleaner of dark channels) who uses his innocence to explore a strange and aquatic world.

Moriarty and his pupils would be doing much the same thing, for the true study of Magic depends upon the ability to sit down before the Mysteries like a little child.

In those days Violet was a water-baby. Thanks to Theodore's tuition she would soon become a Sea Priestess.

It is an old saw that behind every Western teacher is either a brothel or a boarding house, and this is not without some degree of truth, at least as regards the latter. Moriarty paid for his keep by means of his Science, Arts and Crafts Society, which offered a rigorous course of study in all those disciplines, lasting almost four years and including written exams. My informant, who prefers to be known only by the name that

Moriarty gave her, 'Lucius', confirms that certain occult exercises were taught, but would not specify what.

Dion, less secretive but far more able to tantalize, evokes some more drama from her own experiences at The Orchard.

> I made the acquaintance of a woman who was interested in psychic matters. She was a person of the most extreme sensitiveness to anything unclean or ugly, fastidious to a degree in her personal habits, living almost exclusively on uncooked vegetarian foods, even refusing eggs as too stimulating. Although not an animal lover, she was morbidly humanitarian, reading with gusto those papers which give lurid and detailed descriptions of vivisection experiments. Had I been older and wiser I should have recognized the significance of her ultra-cleanliness and ultra-sensitiveness as marking the abreaction of a sadistic temperament — sadism being a pathology of the emotional nature in which the sex instinct takes the form of an impulse to inflict pain. Not having learnt then many things I now know, I looked upon her characteristics, as indicative of an exalted spirituality.
>
> At the time I knew her she was verging on a breakdown which was alleged to be due to overwork, and she was very anxious to get away from cities and back to nature. I was just leaving London to take up my residence at an occult college which was hidden away in the sandy fastnesses of the Hampshire barrens. In the innocence of my heart I suggested that she might come down there and help with the domestic duties. The suggestion was acted upon, and a few days after my own arrival Miss L joined us. She seemed quite normal, made herself agreeable, and was well liked. One incident, however, in the light of subsequent events, was significant. On getting out of the ancient fly in which she had driven from the station, she immediately went and patted the still more ancient horse that drew it. That beast, usually sunk in an apathy from which he was with difficulty roused when action was required of him, galvanized into life at her touch as if she had stung him. He threw up his head, backed, snorted, and nearly turned the equipage over in the ditch, to the amazement of his jehu, who declared he had never been known to do such a thing before, and viewed our visitor with disfavour.
>
> Miss L, however, appeared quite normal, made herself agreeable, and was given a friendly reception by the humans at any rate.

That night Dion had a nightmare. She did not usually get nightmares. She had a great weight upon her chest and the room was pervaded with a sense of evil even when she was fully conscious. This was not the sort of circumstance that demanded any of the high-grade methods of absorption just described (in any case she did not have the know-how) but she coped as best she could with a simple 'banishing formula' which probably involved tracing the five-pointed star in the air before her.

She was not alone in her disturbed sleep. Six or seven of the community had also experienced nightmares. They continued to have them over the next few days, but put it down to indigestion caused by 'the village baker's version of war bread'.[2]

Whenever this was discussed however, Miss L (whom I have reason to believe was a certain Miss Leete) became very agitated, and refused to join in the discussions.

Soon, matters came to a head.

> Then one day I had a quarrel with Miss L. She had conceived a 'crush' for me; I have a constitutional repulsion for crushes and give them scant politeness, and she complained bitterly of my lack of responsiveness. Whatever may be the rights and wrongs of the case, I had roused her resentment in good earnest. That night I was afflicted with the most violent nightmare I have ever had in my life, waking from sleep with the terrible sense of oppression on my chest, as if someone were holding me down, or lying upon me. I saw distinctly the head of Miss L, reduced to the size of an orange, floating in the air at the foot of my bed, and snapping its teeth at me. It was the most malignant thing I have ever seen.
>
> Still not attaching any psychic significance to my experiences, and being firmly convinced that the local baker was responsible, I told no one of my dream, thinking it one of those things that are better kept to oneself; but when the members of the community came to talk matters over in the light of subsequent events, we found that two other people had had similar experiences.
>
> A night or two later, however, as it came to bed-time, I was overcome with a sense of impending evil, as if something dangerous were lurking in the bushes around the house threatening attack. So strong was this sensation that I came down from my room and went all round the house, testing the catches of the windows to make sure that all was secure.
>
> Miss L heard me, and called out to know what I was doing.
>
> I told her of my feelings.
>
> 'You silly child,' she said, 'it is no use latching the windows, the danger is not outside the house but in it. Go to bed, and be sure and lock your door.'

> She would give no answer to my questions except to reiterate that I should lock my door. This was the first night I had slept in that house, previously having been in a cottage on the opposite side of the road.

Nothing happened that night. She slept quietly. It was the next morning that the storm broke. As she and Miss L were working peacefully in the kitchen the latter suddenly caught up a carving knife and started after her, 'as mad as a March hare'. To defend herself Dion had in her hands a large saucepan full of freshly boiled greens which she kept before her as they danced around the kitchen table, slopping hot cabbage water in all directions. It was all done in silence; Dion fending her off with the hot and sooty saucepan, Miss L slashing at her with an unpleasantly large carving knife.

This was the moment for Moriarty to appear. He took in the situation at a glance and dealt with it by scolding them both impartially, telling them to get on with their work.

Miss L finished what she was doing with the carver; Dion dished up the cabbage. The incident passed off quietly.

During the afternoon, when Miss L had retired to her room completely prostrate with exhaustion, Moriarty gave Dion a glimpse of his talents in ritual magic. He went up to the bathroom and filled a soap dish with water from the tap, made certain passes over it (which she described in some detail later on in *Psychic Self Defence*) and, dipping his finger in the water, proceeded to draw a five-pointed star upon the threshold of Miss L's room.

Miss L, like the vampire in the bathroom, was unable to move. Forty-eight hours later Moriarty had to go and fetch her out himself.

After long talks, and other types of unspecified occult treatment, she became comparatively normal, although during that time in which she learnt from Moriarty that she had been a malefic witch in a previous life, two curious incidents occurred.

> The house in which she had a room was a very old one, and the front door exceedingly massive. It was secured at night by two enormous bolts that extended right across it, a chain that could have moored a barge, and a huge lock with a key the size of a trowel. When the door was opened in the morning it acted as an alarm clock for the entire village. It creaked, it groaned, and it clanged. Yet night after night we came down in the morning to find this door standing ajar. We all slept with our doors open on to the small landing. To go down the ancient, creaking stairs was like walking on organ stops. The back

Charles Webster Leadbeater

Dr Theodore Moriarty

Dr Moriarty with Hyksos and Peter

'Dr Taverner', from *The Royal Magazine*, 1922

Moriarty's pupils *c.* 1920. Elsie Reeves is standing on the right with 'Lucius' next to her. Gwen Stafford-Allen is seated looking at the camera. The men are members of the Sotu family from America and the remaining three women have not been positively identified.

McGregor Mathers painted wearing magical regalia by his wife, *c.* 1895

door was a modern affair, which could have been opened easily. The windows were modern casements of the most gimcrack description. Who opened the heavy front door, and why?

We exchanged recriminations several mornings at breakfast as to who had left the door open the night before, but no one could ever be convicted of the blame. Finally the matter came to the knowledge of the head of the group.

'I will soon put a stop to that,' he said, and each night he re-sealed Miss L's room with the pentagram. We had no more trouble with the front door coming open after that.

While he was dealing with Miss L he made a practice of sealing the threshold of his own room in the same way, only in this case he drew the pentagram point outwards, to prevent Miss L from coming in; whereas when he sealed her room, he put its point inwards, to prevent her coming out. She did not know this, nor was it likely to reach her ears indirectly, for he was very uncommunicative, I only knew that he was sealing his room because I chanced to see him doing it.

Nevertheless, one day I heard a knock at my door, and there was Miss L with her arms full of clean linen. She asked me if I would be good enough to take it into the room of the head of the community, and put it away. I asked her why she did not do so herself, for I knew he was out, and it was her work to put away the linen. She replied that she had been to his room for that purpose, but there was a psychic barrier across the threshold that prevented her entering.

It must be said that Dion was by no means as credulous about these incidents as these edited extracts from *Psychic Self Defence* might suggest. She had a very real understanding as to the type of woman that Miss L was, and was fully aware of the parts that could be played by auto-suggestion and imagination, but in the light of such spontaneous reactions as Miss L showed, she could not but accept such things as evidential. Miss L herself had had life-long dreams of being a witch, and the talent to ill-wish people. Several independent psychics had confirmed her own memories of practising black magic in previous lives, and she had made something of a habit of projecting malignant force at her mother and sister.

Regardless of all the Freudian explanations that can be dragged up to explain away all this in relation to Miss L, Dion became aware, as so many people do, that there really are people in this world who do have such dark talents as Miss L, and such bright ones as Dr M.

By 1921 the whole group moved to Gwen Stafford-Allen's home at Bishop's Stortford. This was situated to the north-west of the town, a short walk from the railway station. It was not, to the extent that The Orchard was, a residential place, although there were a few rooms for those who had come long distances. Moriarty had, for example, several American pupils, although it is not clear how they came to join his group or how long they stayed with it.

Nor was The Grange, as it was called, thrown over completely to the Science, Arts and Crafts Society, but was indeed largely used as a home for unwanted babies, under, I believe, the supervision of the Essex County Council. This is the basis of the nursing home in that tangled skein of fact and fiction known as the Dr Taverner stories.

It was not run by Moriarty, but by Mrs Stafford-Allen herself, with the help of Frank Seymour and wife Ida Mirrielees Seymour, Irish and Scottish physicians respectively.

Dion's first novel, *The Demon Lover*, written in 1927, is set in part in a house called The Grange. Once again she is using actual but disguised backgrounds, in this case placing the dwelling in the village of Beckering. For Beckering read Bishop's Stortford. As we have already noted *The Goat-Foot God* uses the same area for its backdrop.

Bishop's Stortford itself is a market town some thirty miles north-east of London. In the late Saxon and early Norman days it was the property of the Bishop of London; the ruins of the so-called Bishop's Prison are still to be seen. In the early decades of this century the chief employment was brewing and malting.

To the remarkable stories about Moriarty as gleaned from *The Secrets of Dr Taverner* and *Psychic Self Defence*, can we add one more drama as extracted from *The Goat-Foot God*? Can we believe that, in company with Moriarty, Dion visited the remnants of the Bishop's Prison and nearby Tilty Abbey and picked up the echoes of events that were to form the basis of her novel?

I think so. With a little effort we can picture them, old mage and young enchantress, seeing the earth-bound spirit of the deposed Abbot Roger Beverley, wandering from cell to cell, giving perpetual succour to his earth-bound brethren. Here, written up with no little skill, was the germ of the idea for Ambrosius, the heretical abbot who in her novel had been jailed for his invocations of Pan.

And did she, in those days at The Grange or during her time at Monks Farm, really invoke the Great God Pan?

Probably not. At least, not in those days. She and Moriarty were both very much Christians, despite the Gnostic overtones of their Christianity. Pan would come later, in his own good time.

At this time too — 1921 — Dion seems to have been riding two horses. For one thing she was a regular attender at Moriarty's lectures and deeply involved with his esoteric activities. For another, she had by this time been initiated into the Hermetic Order of the Golden Dawn, a potent and legendary magical organization that we will look at later.

It is not clear if the same applied to Moriarty. Lucius felt that it was unlikely that Moriarty was ever an initiate of the Golden Dawn. And although he espoused what he termed 'Universal Theosophy' there are no records of him ever having been a member there either. Once, she recalled, Moriarty sought permission from his Masonic lodge to admit and initiate women, organizing it all himself, and keeping it independent of any of the Co-Masonic groups. This, he told Lucius, was refused.[3]

Despite this we do have some fairly comprehensive accounts of what he believed, what he taught, though not what he practised in the occult sense. If I might coin a phrase, then it might be summed up as being 'Atlantean Christianity'.

Moriarty lectured extempore. In the copies of his talks that have survived we get the impression of his students hurriedly taking notes, recording all the grammatical errors, conferring together afterwards to ensure that all pearls had been gathered. Joan Cyprian Williams did much of this, along with Eleanor Whittall, Gwen Stafford-Allen and Pat O'Brien, an Irish nurse who was also employed within The Grange to help look after the orphaned babies.

Moriarty's lectures are studded with references to Atlantis, yet this is mentioned in passing, as though it were so well known to the speaker that it did not require detailed comment or explanation. We learn about the cataclysms, the first of which occurred around 800,000 BC, and the last — the fifth — at exactly 9146 BC. He sketches in the great Atlantean emigrations of the Tlavatli sub-race which went to India and gave rise to the Gymnosophists; the band of Atlantean Toltecs who went through Egypt to Asia, leaving colonies behind in Greece, Ireland, Spain, and Egypt, from which branch arose the Egyptian and Brahmanistical religions. We learn of the four rivers which flowed through Atlantis, in the form of the first cross ever known, and which formed the basis of the Garden of Eden. He mentions the fountain in the King's courtyard at the top of the hill, and outlines the classes and castes which existed on that hill in descending tiers, and makes reference to the Chronos pole in one of the courtyards, surmounted by the sacred serpent. And he speaks almost casually about the city of Glwn ('sometimes called Glaun') which lay some forty miles south-east of the city of Golden Gates, down the mighty river Naradek. Glwn, he tells us, was famous for its sacerdotal college.

Dion did not entirely agree with the visions of her mentor. Her own memories came back *en bloc*, following her contacts with the Master

R, and the Master Jesus, and these show some differences. On the other hand Atlantean history, if we are to believe the seers, covered enormous periods of time. It would be surprising if the accounts did not differ.

It must be said, however, that not every magician believes in the historical existence of this continent. These men and women, possessing formidable psychic talents of their own, are openly scornful in some cases of the classical beliefs about a great and lost civilization. Nowhere in their own visions or cosmologies can they find any room to accommodate the places and events that were so important to the occult doctrines of Dion and Dr Moriarty.

It does not matter. The truth about Atlantis is this: whatever the physical realities, the continent exists within the psychic geography of that group of magicians which eventually centred itself around our subject. It is fully explorable.

To Moriarty the well-springs of his Christianity were here. 'The Bible is a compilation of the Universal Theosophy which was first taught in Atlantis, and to gain its truths initiation is essential, for if you know the Mysteries you can find out what the Bible means, irrespective of the order in which the books are given.'[4]

The seed of this teaching was brought down through the ages by a variety of 'Pagan Christs', among whom he includes Horus, Mithras, Quetzalcoatl and Buddha. Each epoch, he felt, produced an exemplar of the Christos Principle whose task it was to manifest a state of consciousness just ahead of the prevailing human consciousness of that epoch. In each stage of evolution, he insisted, the Christos Principle was manifested and displayed to humanity through these advanced individuals of the epoch. 'These individuals are also found within the Mysteries as adepts, and the adept, functioning as the Christ, becomes the exemplar of the Christos Principle for that certain period.'

He, as an adept 'if ever there was one', was no doubt in some ways just such a manifestation of the Christ Principle.

It was here that he differed from his pupil.

In *The Demon Lover* the author describes the two ways in which occult power can be achieved: '. . . by placing oneself in the van of evolution, where force has not yet been confined in form but lies loose, as it were, free to enter whatever channel is opened to it; or by retreating to the rear of the race, where unabsorbed force is again available.'

Picture the magical current as it left Atlantis to sweep down through the aeons, like the last wave from the final cataclysm. Moriarty, with his tremendous capacity for compassion and his talents for using the varying 'Christ-energies' of each period of evolution, sailed ahead of the wave at all times, its great weight firmly behind him. Dion, who had a lot of trouble with the Christ in one way or another, chose, in the final years of her life, to go back to the rear of the race again, to take up her Atlantean powers.

Besides which, every magician has his own particular deity under whose aegis he or she works. With Moriarty it was the Christ. When he was fully functioning as priest he was, in a very real sense, not just a channel for the Christ-force, but a manifestation of Christ himself.

With Dion, in contrast, she was never truer to herself or more potent on magical levels, or more influential within this world than when she assumed the qualities of the Great Goddess herself, when she became priestess of Isis.

Christ or Isis . . . behind them both lay the drowned but timeless hierophants of a sunken land.

We can catch a glimpse of this in her descriptions of Moriarty dressed in his full ceremonial finery, which would only have been during the performance of high-grade rituals.

> Taverner opened his suitcase and took out the most wonderful robes I have ever seen in my life. Stiff with embroidery and heavy with bullion, the great cape looked like the mines of Ophir in the shaded lighted of that sombre room. Taverner put it on over an emerald green soutane and I fastened the jewelled clasp upon his breast. Then he handed to me, for he could not raise his arms, the head-dress of Egypt, and I placed it on his head. I have never seen such a sight. The gaunt lineaments of Taverner framed in the Egyptian drapery, his tall figure made gigantic by the cape, and the jewelled ankh in his hand . . . made a picture which I will remember to my dying day. Every time he moved, the incense of many rituals floated from the folds of his garments, the silk rustled, the gold-work clinked; it seemed as if a priest-king of lost Atlantis had come, in response to an invocation, to claim the obedience of his worshippers.

Whether Moriarty was a priest-king or not, Dion never lost herself within his spell. She was seen by the others in the group as rather bumptious at times, a little too forceful and presumptuous. Then again she was still a young woman; and few young women had ever had the vistas of past lives revealed to them as she had achieved within her own self, without help from anyone.

She was not above attempting her own magical experiments when the Doctor was not around. In one of these the case-history is less interesting than the solution, involving the destruction of an elemental that was being directed by a woman with no more than a rule of thumb knowledge of magic. At this time Dion had the arrogance that is common to all young magicians until they get their fingers burnt. She got some of the group from the Grange to lend a hand, and set the appointed time and place. 'To be frank, our attitude was that of a party of small boys going ratting.' They got together, formed their circle, and she went to work.

> The method I meant to use made it necessary for me to leave my body, and the group was really there to look after it while I was out of it, and see it came to no harm. I got on to the astral readily enough, did my job, and returned, feeling very pleased with myself, for it was the first time I had operated entirely on my own, without the supervision of my teacher.

As she began to recover physical consciousness she had the sensation as of machinery running, and felt as if she were lying on something very lumpy. She opened her eyes and saw something brown towering above her to an enormous height. In fact she was lying on the floor, close to the skirting, across the feet of a man whom she had pinned against the wall. It was the uncontrollable shaking of that hapless wretch which had seemed to her like machinery vibrating. Various other members of the circle slowly appeared from behind the piano and sofa and other heavy articles of furniture.

She learned that after she had gone out on to the astral they had experienced a good deal of phenomena in the way of bells and voices outside the circle. As everyone knows, all they had to do was keep very very still and not leave the circle. Unfortunately, they lost their heads and scattered.

What happened then was bizarre. Dion began to perform deep-trance acrobatics, arching up on her head and heels, juddering across the room until she came up against one of her terrified companions.

Nor did it finish then. They were just gathering themselves together and getting back to some kind of self-control when a force alien to anything yet experienced rushed around the whole circle and seemed to concentrate itself against one member in particular. 'He went flying across the room and landed, fortunately for him, face downwards in an armchair, and was ill in bed for three weeks.'

While all this was going on the father of one of the people taking part became uneasy about her and walked across from where he lived at the far side of Bishop's Stortford to see what was happening. 'Like most little country towns this one usually went to bed early, but he told us that as he came along he saw innumerable windows were lit up, and he heard the sounds of children crying all down the street.'

After this experience Dion began to feel that there was a special providence that looked after not only fools, drunkards, and little children, but inexperienced occultists too.

Moriarty's magical potency might well have been on the wane by now, in the last year or two before his death. He was not a well man. The Gods bestow few favours upon the physical health of the channels they use. The magus, expecting no favours, goes on with his Work as best he can even though age or illness tends to diminish the levels of power he can now bring through. By this time, 1921-23, the roaring years of his magic were gone, but there were still a few echoes, still some marvels.

One of his pupils at The Grange woke up one morning with some questions to ask the Doctor that had been puzzling him from the previous night. There waiting for him, in the first delivery of the day, was a letter that was stamped and post-marked from Portugal, yet bearing that previous day's date. The latter, of course, answered the very questions he had been about to put. Shades of HPB and all her precipitated missives from the Masters . . .

When the letter was shown to Moriarty, no doubt with shaking hand, the man just shrugged; he could not explain it and had no interest in even trying. The rest of the pupils, the more senior ones, were equally blasé. Things like that were always happening; inexplicable things, trivial little miracles.

Like Blavatsky — like Dion to some extent — Moriarty certainly had the talents of a materializing medium. This might well be a partial explanation of the Russian woman's Masters apparently appearing in the flesh: they were as real as Fenris had been; entities made tangible by the raw and malleable energies exuded by the medium. In every century there are periods when the Mysteries make their presence felt by the means of crude phenomena: apparitions, materializations, manifestations, apportations, and physical wonders of the fakir kind. They come like sledgehammers to break down the brittle casing of the rational mind.

Moriarty was like Blavatsky, was like the earlier and controversial Daniel Dunglas Home, who had levitation as one of his many well-attested and hotly disputed talents. They were special, they were different. In the light of modern knowledge their cosmic revelations might, in part, seem wrong or even rather silly, but it does not diminish to any degree the sheer magnetism, the marvellous singularity of their personalities.

Dion's final story about Moriarty from *Psychic Self Defence* gives us a glimpse of his materializing abilities. In some ways it draws together many of the strands of the foregoing chapters: Fenris; the appearance of the Master KH before Colonel Olcott's rapt gaze; the malevolent and disembodied head of Miss L; as well as themes that we will take up later.

It seems that after his return to England Moriarty's tuberculosis began to reassert itself. This despite the fact that he believed he had wiped it out completely with the help of a congenial climate and 'mind power'. It is a disease which has always had a peculiar association with the more visionary members of the artistic society. It has been speculated that the very nature of the disease releases toxins into the bloodstream which can produce an intensified vision of life; although war or adulation can have similar effects. But in Moriarty's case, being who and what he was, some rather bizarre side-effects took place.

In discussing the mechanism of the extrusion of the etheric double, Dion remarked how the Doctor was able to perform this operation. He would go into deep trance, after a few convulsive movements, and would then lose about two thirds of his weight. He weighed little more than a child on these occasions. She described what actually became of this missing weight too, for during one of his deliriums his ectoplasmic body found its way into her bedroom, presumably because it was she who had had the lion's share of the nursing — particularly the night work.

> He was plainly visible in the moonlight, clad apparently in his dressing gown, or so I took the muffling folds of the material to be that swathed him about. Both his face and wrapping appeared grey and colourless in the moonlight, but there was no question in my mind as to his solidarity, for not only could I see him, but I could feel his weight resting upon my feet. But at the moment I moved he vanished, and I was left staring in amazement at the smooth fold of the blankets over the end of the little camp-bed on which I lay . . .

By the year 1923 his senior students had succeeded in compiling his seminal work *Aphorisms of Creation and Cosmic Principles*. It is a dense and difficult piece with strong Theosophical overtones, but still an essentially original vision of the cosmos and its spiritual machinery. It tells us of the seven Principles 'without which the world of manifestation could not exist as manifestation', namely those of: Correspondence, Law and Order, Vibration, Rhythm, Cyclicity, Polarity, and Sex. We are left in no doubt that he was an Initiate in the Order of Melchisedec, and that this was no earthly Order.

Here, we get very close indeed to the core of Dion's own magic. In fact Dion's equivalent work *The Cosmic Doctrine*, which was supposedly communicated from the inner planes during the winter of 1923-24, bears such a strong resemblance to the *Aphorisms*, that we must discuss this in detail in a later chapter.

Theodore William Carte Moriarty died of angina pectoris in the Duke's Head Hotel, King's Lynn on 18 August 1923. No one now knows what he was doing there. Perhaps he was on a trip to Poppyland, where that by now ruined tower had once overwhelmed the pagan inclinations of the woman who was still then known simply as Violet.

A sample of his handwriting has survived, which David Annwn analysed as follows:

> This person is talkative (yet holds secrets), energetic, attractive (and knows it) and cannot understand why the world is not totally taken in by his own brand of grandiloquence and occasional pomposity. On the positive side there is warmth and humour, supportiveness and charm, but also a bad and almost vicious temper when he is not happy, or else not the centre of attention. Spirituality is shown and pronouncedly so . . . but even in the spiritual realms this person has not found the great rewards he deemed his by right. He is a king, a mage, and a great teacher — and the world hasn't recognized him. However outwardly humble this man was, his disciples cannot but have noticed his respect for his own work, systems and cultured character. Urbane, interesting, proud and even arrogant, he could be mistrustful but also approachable and enormously helpful when asked. A conservative by name and nature, he believed in hierarchy and the allocation of power to the elite, to the knowledgeable few.

Many of his lectures have survived, though as yet unpublished; and amongst them all is a piece called 'The Wayfarer's Prayer':

> *Master of Quiet and Memories* — Open to me the Gates of Wisdom; Restore unto me the memory of Divine Things; Watch over me in the hour of temptation that I may return to Thy Presence in Peace.
>
> *Master of the Just and Joyous Mind* — Kindle in my heart the Fire of Thy service. Remove from my eyes the vision of sorrow. May the seven lamps be trimmed and ready. Grant me Thy Power before the setting of the evening star.
>
> *Master of Keen Thoughts and of Courage* — I invoke Thy Power to direct my desires; I pray that I may walk with steadfastness the path of regeneration that Thy Strength may be my shield through the hours of darkness.
>
> *Master of Magnificence and Kingly Thought* — I recognize Thee as the source of my life. Vouchsafe unto me the knowledge of Thy Divine

> Law that I may walk the hidden ways of beauty, conscious of Thy Presence until the rising of the morning star.
>
> *Master of the Laughter of Lovers and of the Flowers of the Wood* — At the beginning of the dawn I raise my thoughts to Thee; Grant unto me Thy gifts of healing. May I be a Messenger and Interpreter of Love and live humbly among men adorned in Thy Splendour.
>
> *Master of Pleasant-sounding Words* — Every wise act is from Thee. With Thy word of power still the tempest within and without. May I speak and act with true understanding. Quicken my imagination and enliven the work of my hands from the rising of the sun till noon.
>
> *Master of Indolence and of Devout Hearts* — Remove the veil from my vision that I may look upon the seven lights with perfect eyes. Temper justice with mercy; teach me to walk humbly in Thy sight and may Thy Power be with me till the setting of the sun.
>
> *Masters of Silence* — Descend upon me. Purify my thoughts. Strengthen my Purpose. Lead me as a wayfarer to the Ancient Fold, as it was before the making of the worlds. *Amen.*

It is indeed very lovely in parts, yet the most striking thing about it is the fact that there is not a single supplication to any female source.

It is partly, one suspects, a matter of semantics, and the way these rubbed up against the prevailing mores of the Victorian and Edwardian eras. Blavatsky and anyone else could talk as long and loudly as they wanted about Masters, without anyone turning a hair, morally speaking. But in those times they could hardly use the obvious corollary and talk about their Mistresses, even if they did immediately point out that these were simply entities on the Inner Plane. The absurdity of the term 'Masters' came to strike Dion too, in later years. And of course it is partly a matter of training, Moriarty having spent a large portion of his inner life devoted to the exclusively male atmosphere of the Masonic lodges.

He was indeed a wayfarer, sometimes a very lonely one, making his path through the ages just ahead of the wave, the rest of us following on behind and trying to glimpse him above and beyond the crest as he made his stately progress — the progress of a priest-king from lost Atlantis, drawn to the lands at the people's call.

5.

THE WARS BETWEEN WOMEN AND THE GOLDEN DAWN

> Some ten years before I came in touch with Mathers' organization there were wars and rumours of wars.
>
> Dion Fortune

In the middle of June 1890, as Sarah Jane Firth walked along the shore of Llandudno Bay during the last quiet days before the start of the tourist season, she was becoming aware of many things. A landlocked girl all her life, she was learning about the sea and the tides of life, 'ebbing and flowing, waxing and waning, building up and breaking down.' She was learning about those processes which were turning her body ever more daily toward the shape of those round-bellied fertility goddesses whose figurines and images had now become curios, so divorced had the world become from their worship. Her clothes were becoming too tight for a start, but that was easily solved. More peculiar was the feeling in her stomach like the flicking of tiny fishes, the darkening of her nipples and the unpredictable pangs of morning sickness. There was the odd line which she noticed down her abdomen, too, which her in-law Dr John Chambers (who was also resident physician at the Hydro) told her was called the *linea nigra*, and which would soon fade after her baby was born.

For those who had eyes and permission to see, these signs marked her as a mother just as surely as the initiation marks emblazoned in the aura would show the adept to anyone who had the sight of Two Worlds. On inner levels, in this case physiological ones, the amount of blood circulating through her body was approaching something of a high tide; her uterus was increasing at a regular and noticeable rate; while inside the womb the foetal Violet Firth was turning and twitching in the moist dark comfort of the amniotic fluid. She was perfectly formed by now, with eyebrows and even some hair, able to drink some of this fluid when required and pass urine. This was the month when, according to occult philosophy and medical science, life most certainly had begun.

In the middle of that same month in that same year, on the 16th to be exact, a thirty-six-year-old curator and librarian with Freemasonic interests, married a twenty-five-year-old artist in the village of Chacombe, near Banbury. The man was called Samuel Liddell Mathers, and the woman Moina Bergson, whom everyone immediately explained was the sister of the famous philosopher Henri Bergson. They were married by the Reverend William A. Ayton, also a Freemason, who studied alchemy in his cellar and once believed he had discovered the Elixir of Life — although he was afraid to use it — and who could evoke the mighty Planetary Spirits, but declined to do so. The Mathers, like the Firths, would have only one child, although theirs would be no earthly creature and would bear many names. In many ways theirs was a marriage of necessity, for they were busy giving birth to their child at that very moment. Unlike the Firths however, theirs was a fearsome conception and gestation: difficulties in breathing; loss of blood from nose, mouth and sometimes the ears; cold sweats and the sensation of being close to a lightning flash. It made the Firths' purely physical mating seem rather dull. Still, we could not have wanted the Golden Dawn to be conceived and born in any other way.

The story of the Hermetic Order of the Golden Dawn, to give it one of its full names, has been told exhaustively elsewhere. In brief, a trinity of Freemasons belonging to the Societas Rosicruciana in Anglia used some mysterious cipher manuscripts that had been discovered, to form the basis of an occult society independent to their own craft — and which, moreover, admitted women. Although the manuscripts gave only the bare bones of a system, Mathers turned his genius into putting flesh on them, and creating an entity of great life and no little power. Although the Golden Dawn at its height never possessed more than a fraction of one percent of the members admitted to the Theosophical society, it would in the generations to come make the whole edifice of the latter look soft.

The genius of the Golden Dawn was the genius of the Mathers: both of them. In fact they can scarcely be considered apart. They formed a *syzygy*, which might be defined as the conjunction of two organisms without loss of identity. Together, by means of clairvoyance, clairaudience astral projection, and even such disturbingly crude methods as table-rapping and swinging a dowsing-type pendulum over letters of the Hebrew alphabet, they brought through from their Secret Chiefs a body of magical techniques which have only now, a century later, become outdated.

If Moriarty, who at that time in 1890 was presumably sailing back and forth between the Emerald Isle and the Dark Continent, was to mak

Dion Fortune into everything she was and wanted to be, then the Mathers might be held in the same regard by generations of occult students since. Dion actually owed them a greater debt than she ever acknowledged. Without their wisdoms she would have lost herself in some quasi-Theosophical Spiritualism, if such can be imagined, with no drive and no direction saving vaguely Eastward.

It was said that Moina had met her husband in the Egyptian Room of the British Museum. Or else in the Reading Room of the same, where he was hard at work upon the rituals of the Outer Order. It is easy to see the attraction they had for each other: 'So might Faust have looked in his changeless aged youth' said the poet Yeats of Samuel Mathers as he commented upon that man's perfection in voice and looks. He certainly had a peculiarly other-worldly air about him, something that Blavatsky recognized when she asked him if he might help organize the Theosophical Society within England. Although a nominal member at that time he refused, having a great dislike of the Oriental bias. He was a lean, strong, handsome and hard man — a boxer — passionate about magic and war, and with the sort of behaviour that made other magicians point out (rightly) that 'the planes are separate'; meaning that exalted spiritual attainments need not always be reflected in the earthly personality.

Moina was a perfect match for him. She was a thinking mage's object of desire even though she herself, like her husband, had no capacity for such. Crowley thought her learned, beautiful and gifted, even if he did accuse her of prostitution (he was always accusing someone of sex-orientated crimes); Yeats, who had known very many great and fascinating women, remembered her with affection and wonder to the end of his days; Langford Garstin pronounced her as being the greatest clairvoyant of the century; while Dion, coming along much later, always believed she was a murderer.

A photograph survives of Moina from her days at the Slade, where the bright young things, swept by the new tides of art, all tried to go. Moina was there from 1880 until 1886, and the photograph probably dates from that period. It shows someone startlingly modern, with carefully tousled hair, a natural face, and wide dark eyes which look easily and knowingly down the passing of time. In dress and mien she presents an image far removed from the stilted poses in stiff dark clothes so common to Victorian women. If her husband had seemed other-worldly then she, to the men of the time who could still remember when women were all buns and bustles, must have seemed unearthly.

Moina, by virtue of the fact that her clairvoyance had helped create it, became one of the first initiates of the Golden Dawn and later the dominant member after the ruling triad of Wynn Westcott, a London coroner, W. R. Woodman, a clergyman, and Mathers himself. As an Order it grew rapidly, although at best its membership was in the low hundreds, spread over many years throughout a variety of temples. The temples had names like Isis-Urania, Alpha et Omega, Amen-Ra, Osiris, and Horus. Unlike Theosophy, whose members could drift along with large portions of faith and dogma, the Golden Dawn demanded an extremely high level of academic ability. It demanded discipline, commitment, imagination, and no little flair for the psycho-drama of ritual. Initiates were expected to be competent in the Qabalah, to have a working knowledge of Hebrew (because it was felt, wrongly, that this was essentially a 'magical' language); to be able to show abilities in the direction of psychometry and skrying, clairvoyance and some of the more sophisticated varieties of mediumship; to be able to make and charge with power a wide variety of magical implements and talismans; and generally show all of those moral and spiritual qualities which might be dignified by the title of Adeptus.

Once they had progressed through the Outer Order, through a system of grades which equated with planetary influences — Earth, Moon, Mercury, and Venus, in sequence — and been initiated into the sphere of the Sun as an Adeptus Minor, then they found that a Second Order was open to them, far more potent and based upon the mythos of Christian Rosenkreutz, in which they could go even higher, through Mars and Jupiter, to Saturn and beyond — to achieve Union with God or the Gods.

Or so they believed. Very few ever claimed to rank higher than Adeptus Exemptus, or the sphere of Jupiter, at which level all karma had been paid off and there was no future need to reincarnate.

Samuel Mathers expanded his name in due course to become Samuel Liddell McGregor Mathers, and bore the title Le Comte de Glenstrae. From being a Hampshire man he now assumed the persona of a 'braid Scot' as he and Moina, now removed to Paris and the Ahathoor Temple they founded there, made the Rites of Isis a semi-public performance in a variety of chic and not-so-chic locations. Not that Paris was particularly concerned. The Mathers were just another pair of sorcerers in a city that was full of them, many of them intimately connected with the art world, calling down Isis and Hathor and, at Moina's behest, many of the Celtic pantheons.

Mathers became increasingly autocratic; which is a polite way of saying that he became slightly mad. Removal from the occult scene in England meant that many of the Adepti dared to rebel against him in his absence. Chief among these was the tiresome Arthur Edward Waite, who had no time for the purely magical demands of the Golden Dawn's curriculum and who created some instantly forgettable variations of the rituals in those temples which rallied behind him.

The Order began to fragment. People began to point to the formula of the card known as The Tower (See p. 236), with the two falling people, blasted by the lightning flash.

No matter that Mathers now spoke about a Third Order behind the other two, ruled by the Secret Chiefs whom he would occasionally meet in the flesh, à la Blavatsky, but more usually on the Astral Plane. Many of the members, lacking vision, could never accept this. The mighty ceremonies which had once drawn patterns of Light within the air and in men's souls became little more than wavings of hands. Only a few could see behind it all to the real Magic that was still aglow.

It was in this organization that Violet Firth died and Dion Fortune was born. It was by initiation in this Order that the rent made in her aura by the Warden of the 'educational establishment' was now repaired. If nothing else, she no longer leaked prana, as she put it.

She was initiated into the London Temple of the Alpha and Omega in 1919. Although this was under the leadership of the novelist J. W. Brodie-Innes, her immediate teacher seems to have been Maiya Curtis-Webb, who later became a Mrs Tranchell-Hayes.

According to Bernard Bromage, Maiya was a walking encyclopaedia of occult knowledge, who possessed a massive and discerning collection of books and manuscripts on sorcery, necromancy and all other kinds of ungodliness, and who held benevolent sway over a flat in Kingston House and also Kensington Square — rooms bedecked with witches' rosaries, occult amulets and charms, and numerous potent mandalas. She had known Dion since she was a girl — presumably they were neighbours in London — and had seen in her from the start 'an individual of strong and talented personality, a poetess of great charm and distinction, and a potential occultist of discernment and cultivation in her chosen province.'[1] She was also the widow of an eminent psychiatrist, and, while residing with him in a big mental home near Northampton which he ran, she had availed herself of studying the types of derangement with a view to expanding her own ideas about the body-mind relationship.

Obviously Dion began to model herself upon her new teacher to some extent, even to writing her up as a character in her two last novels. If Maiya had known Dion as a girl, say from the time the Firths arrived in London, it must have been she who arranged her entry into the Alpha and Omega. It might even have been Maiya who introduced Dion to Moriarty, for she was known to indulge in little salons, or discussion groups related to occult topics.

Crowley, showing his usual venom and cattiness, accused the woman of being a 'Sapphic': 'Mrs Webb does what she can/As a lusty lesbian . . .' went a poem of his. No doubt she had done no more than spurn his advances at some time. It was because of this, and an inherent mannishness in Dion's own personality, that rumours have come down as to the latter's own sexual orientation. But Dion was no lesbian, as we shall see.

And if Dion was not erotically attached to Mrs Webb, neither did she feel any deep rapport with this new manifestation within her young life. The whole Golden Dawn was rather boring compared to what she had known with Moriarty.

> Practical teaching from official sources was conspicuous by its absence, and unless one was lucky enough to have a personal friend among its members with a gift of exposition, one was left high and dry. One was put through the ceremonies, given the bare bones of the system in the knowledge lectures and a few commentaries on them called side lectures, for the most part of very inferior quality, and left to one's own devices. The glory had departed . . . for most of its original members were dead or withdrawn; it had suffered severely during the war, and was manned mainly by widows and grey-bearded ancients . . .

One of the grey-bearded ancients was the saturnine J. W. Brodie-Innes, who had been one of the few to support Mathers in his apparently manic assertions, and whom they believed was a reincarnation of Michael Scot, the mediaeval wizard, while one of the widows was Moina Mathers, who had come back to run her portion of the Golden Dawn's empire after her husband had died of Spanish influenza in 1918. The dislike was immediate on Dion's part. 'The cloak of Elijah did not necessarily descend on Mrs Elishah' she commented tartly, before going on to add: 'Nevertheless, anyone with any psychic perceptions at all could not fail to realize that there was power in the ceremonies and formulae; and anyone who had made a study of them also speedily found out that in the system of correspondences taught in the GD they had got something of inestimable value.' Indeed they had.

It was at this time, then, that she took on the Magical Motto of *Deo, non Fortuna*. The motto was meant to be a technical device to be used in conjunction with the Body of Light, which was the astral form of the magician modelled to his highest standards, imbued with his noblest aspirations, and brought into operation by means of this new name during moments of ritual or ceremonial magic. Likewise the robes used by the magi were seen as a means of knocking the consciousness out of the personal and mundane and allowing this spiritual essence (an analogue of the Higher Self) a few ritual moments of potency.

Ideally the motto would be an expression of one's secret aspirations, but in practice, because of the snob appeal, many simply used mottoes that had been in the family for generations. Where an occultist had no imagination and no family traditions, he would cast around the names on the distaff side with the aid of a book such as *Elvin's Mottoes* until he found one with the right ring to it. Brodie-Innes, for example, was Sub Spe, which means 'Under Hope'. In *Elvin's Mottoes* it is given to the Duffas, Dunbar, and Cairns families — one of these names almost certainly was to be found on his mother's side. Even Mathers, who understood the principles of the Magical Name or Motto, used S Rioghail Mo Dhream, or SRMD, meaning 'Royal is My Race' from the motto of the Clan McGregor. Moina, showing much more knowledge and originality became Vestigia Nulla Retrorsum, 'I Never Retrace My Steps'.

Although Moriarty had a temple of sorts at 26 Sinclair Road, London, it is not clear how or where he fitted into all this. No trace has yet been found of him having been a member of the Order, although Dion tended to imply that this was so. On the other hand if he were a GD initiate it is unlikely that she would have stayed in the Alpha and Omega for such a short time. Like herself, he may have been a maverick.

Looking back at it all with an outside eye it is easy to be dismissive about the idea of a group of people in robes and bearing items of ritual equipment, perambulating about a room with serious intent. We are so used to the modern age with its projected two-dimensional entertainments, electric lighting, double-glazed and centrally-heated lives that we have forgotten the impact of the great rites. We have forgotten the effect of candle-light and shadow, chanting, incense, ritual and invocation, when each member is robed and masked, unknown, a pair of glittering eyes expressing power in a throbbing room. Used to the cult of the personality we have forgotten the awe that such obliteration of the face can bring, forgotten the way that we ourselves, when cloaked in anonymity, can become something other than our normal selves, momentarily greater and truer to our higher natures, no longer tied down by physique or physiognomy but pure expressions of energy. In such rites the magician feels himself and his world charged with immanence, with the sense that some great door is about to open between the worlds, and the gods pour through; he feels as though his mind is peeling open like a flower, revealing the jewel glowing within, glowing with the *spiritus mundi* that dwells inside, awaiting its call.

We have forgotten how to make this call. We have forgotten so much.

As Dion said, even the least psychic person could pick up the sense that these regular ceremonies involved more than mere words and empty gestures, more than a piece of cathartic play-acting. They can and invariably do degenerate to that level in time, of course, but when that happens the participants soon cease to come. What is obvious on reflection, but what modern magicians have never quite made clear, is that each rite involves more than purely human participants, and that to the psychic perceptions of those present the room is filled with the august spirits under whose aegis they work. The skin prickles, a curiously sensual emotion is aroused which yet has no link with any genital responses. The neophyte and the magus alike become aware, in their differing ways, that gods are present — or representatives of the gods. The temple shimmers; it becomes alive.

No camera, no film, no video, and no recording could ever capture any sense of this.

Each temple of the Golden Dawn would have its own set of inner contacts, or Chiefs. These would be the manifestations of the peculiar type of power expressed by the God or Goddess to which each temple was dedicated. By the time that Dion progressed through the Alpha and Omega temple, and finally found what she sought within the Hermes Temple of the Stella Matutina (the latter referring to those portions of the GD which had rebelled against Mathers), she would have attained the grade of Adeptus Minor, equating with the Sun. Having taken this solar initiation then ideally the intuitive, inspired, and radiant potentials within her psyche would be fully functional. She would have become a figure of status within the lodge, a presence as tangible as a flame, a figure with Gods and Goddesses crowding behind her.

Often, at this point, the adept would be given a charter by the Secret Chiefs to form his or her own lodge and interpret the magical current in his or her own way. Before very long Dion would do just that. It was inevitable, really. She was too strong a character to take second place to anyone.

Perhaps the best thing that Dion was ever given by the Golden Dawn on intellectual levels was knowledge of the Qabalah. This philosophy was the basis of everything that Dion believed or taught. Hebrew, which has no vowels, spelt it as QBL, pronounced (and once spelled) as 'kabbalah.' As a philosophy it has several aspects, one of these being known as Gematria, which is like a sophisticated version of numerology but which Dion described as being akin to doing mensuration with an elastic ruler. That was typical of her: she had a marvellous talent for seeing right through the more tedious aspects of so-called 'traditional' occultism. This was the branch of the Qabalah that Moriarty knew best, although he seems never to have gone as deeply into it as, say, Crowley. Few did.

Few went into anything as deeply as Crowley. No, the Gematria was not for Dion. What fascinated her was in the system of Correspondences. These Correspondences were based upon the *otz chaim*, or Tree of Life.

It is a simple glyph. It is capable of infinite interpretations on an infinite number of levels. One of her pupils described it as 'the mighty all-embracing glyph of the Universe and the soul of man.' Surprisingly it is exactly that. Once planted within the psyche it grows and grows, almost impossible to uproot. It links heaven and hades and leads mankind up or down, only to find that one is the same as the other. We can make it grow exactly how we want, give it any slant and make it bear any fruit.

It comprises three columns, like three rays of light. The columns are positive, negative, and neutral. Upon these columns lie ten spheres. Each sphere equates with a planet. Each sphere has certain key-symbols and qualities with which it is linked. Thus the sphere of Yesod, meaning Foundation, links with the Moon, with the number nine, with the symbol of the cup and the mirror, and the 'beautiful naked man, very strong', and certain specific colours. After these basic symbols and just a few others, the neophyte learns to make his own associations until eventually he will be able to relate every aspect of his existence, every happening within him and without, with the inter-related symbolism of the spheres upon the Tree. The magical virtue of this means that in due course Dion could take up her magical staff (which she might, for example, relate to the sphere Chockmah) and by means of the system of Correspondences link herself through that with all the dynamic, thrusting forces of the universe.

The glyph of the Tree, built into the aura as she would believe, would act like a circuit diagram: it would link hitherto separate compartments of her mind into a functioning whole.

At a time when she was probably still watching things grow in that quiet room run by the Ministry, listening to the first whispers from the Masters Rakoczi and Jesus, and when she was still sharing memories of Atlantean days with Moriarty, the body of knowledge which Mathers and his wife brought to Western consciousness was just being planted in the centre of her brain. It would grow and blossom throughout the marvels of the years to come.

Despite her later status, which few would deny, Dion was by no means the Great White Hope of the Golden Dawn. There were many people who did not think she was very good at magic at all, although they seem not to have made any allowances for her youth. As noted, she was not especially popular within Moriarty's group, and members felt she often presumed a little bit too much, on many levels; while one member of the Golden Dawn with whom she did not empathize was Moina

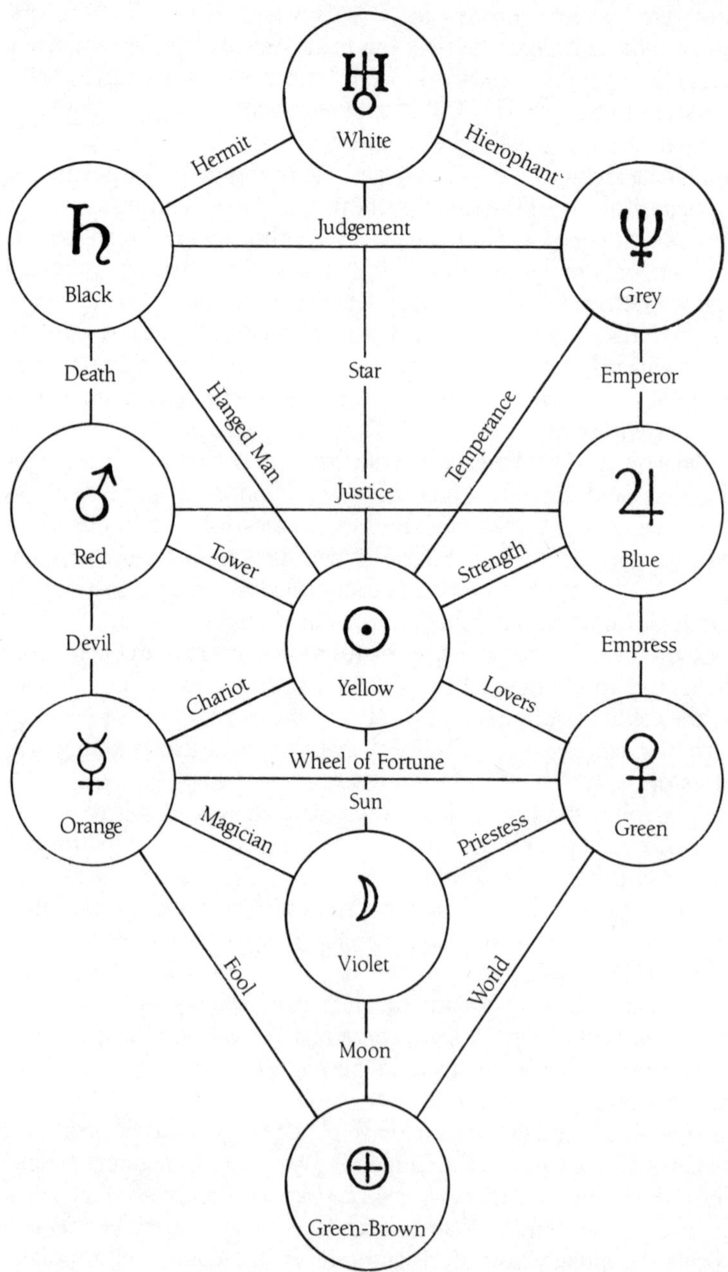

The Tree of Life and the Tarot

Mathers herself. In fact Moina actually expelled her, as Dion was the first to admit. 'She nearly turned me out' she wrote, 'for writing *The Esoteric Philosophy of Love and Marriage*, on the grounds that I was betraying the inner teaching of the Order, but it was pointed out to her that I had not then got the degree in which that teaching was given, and I was pardoned. She suspended me for some months for writing *Sane Occultism* and finally turned me out because certain symbols had not appeared in my aura — a perfectly unanswerable charge.'[2]

Edward Langford Garstin, a fellow initiate of the Alpha and Omega, had another tale to tell as to why she had been expelled. According to him, Dion and a certain C.T. Loveday showed to Moina the rough draft of what was to become *The Cosmic Doctrine*, the seminal book of her philosophies. After considering it Moina pointed out that the contents were hardly in accord with GD teaching. She then gave the two enthusiasts the choice of setting aside their revelations while continuing as her students, or leaving her lodge to follow their newly discovered path. They chose the latter.

Gastin had been astonished that Dion had set herself up as a teacher after little more than a year's study, during which she had not progressed very far up the ladder of grades. He insisted that she had but slight magical expertise at the time.

What seems to have happened is that while Moina had no doubt as to the reality of the inner contacts Dion had made within the GD, she felt that these same contacts did not accord with those that the majority of her lodge used. Whatever the cause of her expulsion, it was not sudden and not dramatic. Indeed, as Dion wrote in *The Occult Review*:

> 'The Fraternity of the Inner Light' was founded by me in agreement with Mrs Mathers, to be an Outer Court to the Golden Dawn system. All went well at first, and I was in high favour; but presently I fell from grace; why I never knew. No specific charges were levelled against me save that of not having the proper symbols in my aura. Finally I was turned out without reason assigned, save the ridiculous one above.

According to some magicians, it is not such a ridiculous reason. They would argue that whenever they came into everyday contact with someone else who had made links with the same inner sources as themselves, they would *know* this beyond any doubt. They would recognize a kindred spirit — in more than one sense — a fellow initiate of a peculiar and entirely compatible sort; another member of their magical tribe, in fact, even though a complete stranger. To some of them this would show within their psychic vision as just such symbols in their aura; others might have no more than a feel in the gut. In many ways the developed magicians recognize each other, and can pick fellow flame-bearers from out of a crowd, including those who have the potential and as yet no conscious interest.

In other words, Moina felt that Dion's own Secret Chiefs were incompatible with those used within her temple. This often happens. Ideally the parting should be amicable but there were two very formidable personalities involved here. In the classic sense it was a confrontation that was as old as time, between the old sterile woman and the young fertile girl — although Moina was not so old, nor Dion so very young. It involved more than the mere parting of the ways in this case, for what developed was, in a very real sense, a cat fight.

One of Dion's best friends in the late 1920s was Netta Fornario, who wrote many articles on occultism under the name Mac Tyler. Miss Fornario was something of an artist and one who (rightly) felt that Britain had gone wrong in the seventh century in choosing, at the Synod of Whitby, to follow the Pauline Christianity of Rome rather than that of Columba in Iona. She went up there in the winter of 1929/30 because she had a 'terrible case of healing on' as she told her servants. She was found not very long after, nude on a bleak hillside, her body covered in scratches. Round her neck was a cross secured by a silver chain, and near at hand lay a large knife which had been used to cut a large cross in the turf. There were rumours on the island about blue lights having been seen in the vicinity where her body had been found.

'She was half-Italian and half-English,' Dion recalled, 'of unusual intellectual calibre, and was especially interested in the Green Ray elemental contacts; too much interested in them for my peace of mind, and I became nervous and refused to co-operate with her.'

Dion then became very careful in the next paragraph when she speculated that death may have been caused by an astral expedition from which she never returned: 'She was not a good subject for such experiments, for she suffered some defect of the pituitary body. Whether she was the victim of psychic attack, whether she merely stopped out on the astral too long and her body, of poor vitality in any case, became chilled lying thus exposed in mid-winter, or whether she slipped into one of the elemental kingdoms that she loved . . . who shall say?'

She said. She said very clearly if cleverly, although she waited for another few chapters in *Psychic Self Defence* before she did so. She talked about the ire that she had aroused in the occult fraternities over some articles she had written in *The Occult Review*. These articles had apparently upset a number of the Adepti within the Golden Dawn, for she and her compatriots began to come under a peculiar form of psychic attack. They became most desperately afflicted with black cats — real cats, not hallucinatory ones — which bunched up on the doorstep of her house in 3 Queensborough Terrace, blocking up the windowsills. The whole house became filled with the feline stench; it followed them about wherever they went.

They attributed this siege to natural causes at first and thought nothing much of it. But as the Vernal Equinox approached — 'always a difficult time for occultists' — there was a sense of strain and tension in the atmosphere.

> Coming upstairs after breakfast one morning, I suddenly saw coming down the stairs towards me, a gigantic tabby cat, twice the size of a tiger. It appeared absolutely solid and tangible. I stared at it for a second and then it vanished. I instantly realized that it was a simulacrum, or thought-form that was being projected by someone with occult powers . . . Feeling decidedly uncomfortable, I asked one of my household to join me, and as we sat in my room meditating we heard the cry of a cat from without. It was answered by another, and another. We looked out of the window, and the street as far as we could see was dotted with black cats and they were wailing and howling in broad daylight as they do on the roofs at night.

She was not having that. Gathering together all the ritual paraphernalia that she had made and charged with power during her training in the Golden Dawn, Dion did an exorcism there and then. When they looked out of the window again these was not a cat in sight, and they never saw them again.

It was only the beginning of the onslaught. When the Vernal Equinox arrived it signalled the time for 'certain meetings which take place on the astral plane' which were necessary for her to attend while out of her body. She knew that this was the time that her attacker would choose to make a direct assault, and so she gathered together her own little group and sealed up the place with the usual ceremonial.

> These astral journeys are really lucid dreams in which one retains all one's faculties of choice, will-power and judgement. Mine always begin with a curtain of symbolic colour through whose folds I pass. No sooner was I through the curtain on this occasion than I saw my enemy waiting for me . . . She appeared to me in the full robes of her grade, which were very magnificent, and barred my entry, telling me that by virtue of her authority she forbade me to make use of these astral pathways.

That was the worst thing anyone could have said to Dion. She denied her enemy's right to close the astral paths and thence a battle of wills ensued in which she experienced the sensation of being whirled through the air and falling from a great height, to find herself back in her body again.

She came to shaken, knowing that if she did not get up and complete her journey she would lose her powers, and the Otherworld would be barred to her for the rest of that life at least.

The group, which had been disorganized by her convulsions during the onslaught, re-formed itself and she went back on to the astral planes. 'This time there was a short sharp struggle, and I was through. I had the Vision of the Inner Chiefs, and returned.'

The fight was over. Her opponent never troubled her again.

But when Dion took off her clothes in order to go to bed her back felt very sore. Looking in a mirror she found that she had been scored with scratches from neck to waist, 'as if clawed by a gigantic cat'.

They were exactly the same kind of scratches as those found on Miss Fornario's body.

And in her article in *The Occult Review* entitled 'Ceremonial Magic Unveiled' she states quite categorically that all this happened as a direct result of her quarrel with Mrs Mathers.

A typical Dion tale that, told with style and force. A typical magician's tale, too, in not being quite accurate. What Dion does not seem to have known was that by the time Netta Fornario chose to commit suicide on that lonely and haunted isle, Moina had been dead for eighteen months. Had Moina chosen to rule the Order after her death, too? Magically this is not unknown. McGregor Mathers was appearing as one of the Chiefs in at least one of the temples some twenty years after *his* death. Or had Dion simply got it all wrong? Yet the occult world in Britain is so small that it would be unlikely that Dion had not known of Moina's death. Perhaps it was another member of the GD who wreaked such havoc on the inner planes, and merely acted as an enforcer, taking it upon herself to attack Dion (and others) after she had broken with Moina and upset everyone with her articles.

In that case one possibility was Annie Horniman, whose wealth did so much to support Moina and her husband during their early days. She was one of those wealthy women who helped make all things possible within the GD. Moina and McGregor might have been channels of the Gods, but like anyone else they needed money to survive. Annie Horniman was the daughter of a wealthy businessman who had made a fortune marketing tea. She arranged the couple's posting as curator and librarian in her father's Horniman Museum, at Forest Hill. Brought up an Anglican, she met Moina at the Slade, where they both studied, and while progressing through the grades of the Golden Dawn she branched out to help build and equip the famous Abbey Theatre in Dublin, later the Gaiety Theatre in Manchester, and helped Yeats found an Irish National Theatre. She was a precise, meticulous, and occasionally prudish woman, with no little capacity for magic and a talent for divination. The only reason for labouring the point in this instance is because of her nicknames within the GD, these being 'Tabbie' and 'Puss'.

Whatever the identity of the mysterious cat-woman, the magical combat which Dion won marked the effective end of her relationship with the Golden Dawn as it had existed until then. She had proved something to herself in this victory. No longer would she be a pendant to any other man, woman, or organization. From that time onward, 1929, she became her own mage and no one else's.

Her journey toward this singular status was by no means as clear-cut as she tended to imply, however. It was not simply a matter of leaving Moriarty's group after his death to concentrate on the GD's system and then, in 1927, form her own Fraternity of the Inner Light which had been intended, 'in agreement with Mrs Mathers, to be an Outer Court to the "Golden Dawn" system'. During this period also she had been the shining light in a group which now seemed to embarrass her, but which was the direct precursor of her Fraternity, and which in many ways refused to die. This was the Christian Mystic Lodge of the Theosophical Society.

The only detailed account of her time within this group was found by Mr Leslie Price in an old issue of the 'O. E. Library Critic', which he kindly sent to me. The lodge in question was founded by Daisy M. Grove who wrote books on Esoteric Christianity, with titles like *The Apocalypse and Initiation*, and *The Mystery Teaching of the Bible*, and who was quite well known at the time. The Lodge seems to have been formed in 1923 and published monthly journals. These publications, which would provide a mine of information about a little-known period in Dion's life, have apparently disappeared off the face of the earth; no private or public reference library in Great Britain possesses any set; neither does the present-day Society of the Inner Light; the headquarters of the Theosophical Society does not have any records dating from much before 1934 and knows nothing about either the Christian Mystic Lodge or its monthly *Transactions*; the world headquarters of the Theosophical Society at Adyar, Madras, while professing that there is no religion higher than Truth, has consistently failed either to answer or acknowledge my enquiries in this direction. Because of the dearth of information about this time, I reproduce the article in full.

The Christian Mystic Lodge of the Theosophical Society, with headquarters in London, was instituted with the object of 'Interpreting Christianity in terms of Theosophy, and Theosophy in terms of Christianity,' this being not only in harmony with the objects of the Theosophical Society, but also with the policy of freedom of thought professed by Mrs Annie Besant. Its first president was Mrs Daisy M. Grove, a somewhat well-known theosophical writer. The Lodge published a monthly *Transactions*, which by July, 1927, had reached the number of forty-eight.

Meanwhile, in 1924, Miss Violet M. Firth, now Mrs Penry-Evans, who is the author of several psychological and occult books under the name Dion Fortune, received 'instructions from the Inner Planes' to join the Theosophical Society. Of the exact nature of these instructions I am not informed, except that Dion Fortune claims, with what evidence I am not able to state, to be in touch with the Master Jesus, one of the Masters recognized by the Theosophical Society, but supposed by neo-theosophists to be the original Jesus of the New Testament who surrendered his body for the use of the Christ at the time of the baptism in Jordan. With regard to these instructions Dion Fortune herself says in a personal statement (*Transactions of Christian Mystic Lodge*, No. 48, July 1927, page 4):

'Three years ago, just a year before the announcement of the Coming of the World Teacher, I received instructions from the Inner Planes to join the Theosophical Society, and as is usual when instructions are received in this way, I asked for a sign to be given in confirmation so that I might know that my imagination was not deluding me. The sign appointed was that the two signatories of my application form should be Mrs X, a well-known Theosophical worker, whom I had once known slightly, but had lost sight of some years previously, and Mr Y, who was known to me only by name and reputation. I was also told the time at which the signing would take place. The sign appointed was thus a triple sign, difficult of fulfilment by coincidence. As is customary in such matters. I told no one except those who were assisting me in my esoteric work.

'When the time arrived, I was reminded from the Inner Planes of the Instruction, and told to hold myself in readiness. Within three days of receiving the second intimation the sign was fulfilled in every detail without any initiative on my part. It was fulfilled in no less than five particulars: 1 and 2, the sponsors named appeared spontaneously; 3, at the time appointed; 4, they appeared in the order in which they had been named; and 5, the exact words the Master had made use of were employed by Mr Y in writing to me. I therefore took it that the message of instruction had been properly signed and counter-signed and that I had received my credentials for the mission to which I have been appointed, and for the same reason I give the incident in these pages so that those whose support I seek for the carrying out of the work entrusted to me may know that the Master who gave the order was also able to give the "signs following".'

This is remarkable enough, take it as one may, and the recipient of the instructions felt herself under obligation to work in the interest of the Master Jesus within the Theosophical Society, following in the footsteps of Anna Kingsford. Ultimately she was chosen president of the Christian Mystic Lodge.

As president, Dion Fortune attempted to cultivate friendly relations with the Liberal Catholic Church, under the impression, apparently, that this church was likewise interested in the Master Jesus. In this she was mistaken, however, the regionary bishop, the Right Reverend Pigott, informing her that his church was not in the least interested in the Master Jesus, but rather in 'the new outpouring of the Christ'. Clearly she had not informed herself beforehand as to the actual facts regarding this church and its inspiring spirit Leadbeater. This led to a discussion carried on in the pages of *The Occult Review*, and finally to controversial articles in the *Transactions of the Christian Mystic Lodge*, and the eyes of Dion Fortune were opened to the corruption in the TS, which she had not discovered until brought face to face with it.

These controversial articles gave offence to some of the Lodge members, who claimed that the *Transactions*, while intended to expound Christian Mysticism, was becoming the personal organ of Dion Fortune and was being used by her to attack the policies of the TS. In a spirited reply to her opponents (*Transactions*, July 1927, page 7) she says:

'Nevertheless, I feel that I can do no otherwise than stand up in the Name of the Master Jesus, relying upon Him for protection, and raise my voice in protest against conditions which "sin against the Light." I ask those who are in sympathy with what I am doing to remember that thought power is potent for protection and support, just as it is for attack, and to lend me their help on the Inner Planes. My task is not a light one. But as long as I am responsible for the conduct of this magazine I will follow the example of our Master, Who, while He had compassion for those who fainted by the way, had a scourge for the backs of those who made His Father's house a den of thieves.'

The final outcome was that Dion Fortune resigned not only from the Lodge, but from the Theosophical Society, acting upon instructions received from the Inner Planes that she should do so upon receipt of a certain sign, which was fulfilled in every particular. Whereupon she established the Community of the Inner Light, which is devoted to Esoteric Christianity according to the 'Western Esoteric Tradition,' untainted with Krishnamurtyism or Leadbeaterism. This Community publishes Transactions in line with those of the Christian Mystic Lodge, which still exists, although there is another Lodge of the TS in England, the Christian League, which also issues its own publication and is apparently devoted to Esoteric Christianity as it is in Leadbeater.

To go into the details of the extended and interesting controversy would take too much space. The whole matter may, however, be summarized thus:

Dion Fortune (whether actually in communication with the Master Jesus or not need not concern us) is a believer in what the Quakers likewise call The Inner Light. It has nothing whatever to do with the ideas of Mrs Besant or Mr Leadbeater, but is based upon the possibility of communion on the Inner Planes. This did not please the Leadbeaterites, who permeated the Lodge, and who desired that its teaching should conform to those of the Liberal Catholic Church, even if the ceremonies were omitted. One of the active spirits in opposition to Dion Fortune's plans, and in support of Leadbeater's ideas, was Mrs Grove, who had been president. As to Mrs Grove's views, the reader is referred to her booklet on Esoteric Christianity reviewed in the December *Critic*. The contest was really between those who defended the Western Tradition, and the backers of Leadbeater.

In the course of her attempts to guard the interests of the Lodge Dion Fortune met with persecution aimed at driving her not only from the Lodge but also from the TS. Her letters to the editor of *The Theosophical Review* never reached him, but were confiscated and opened by officials of the TS and their contents betrayed to Dr Arundale and the General Secretary, Mr Gardner. Further, *The Theosophical Review, The Herald of the Star* and *News and Notes*, the organ of the British TS refused to publish the announcement of the Christian Mystic Lodge lectures, with the obvious motive of crippling the Lodge activities. Another TS Lodge, the Christian League, an appendix to Leadbeaterism, likewise threw obstacles in its ways.

All this is natural enough. The treachery and shameless dishonesty of the officials of the TS in Great Britain on various occasions is a matter of record and fairly smells to heaven. The opening of letters by spies to whom they have not been addressed and the refusal of publicity to dissenting members is an old story. It is a deliberate attempt to force the vagaries of Mrs Besant on the Society and to prevent by fair means or foul any attempt to oppose them. No one can be in good odour in the TS in Great Britain who does not stand for these. Those who will not endorse the absurdities of the Leadbeater cult are subjected to ostracism if not to actual persecution. I am no advocate of retiring under such conditions, but as the talented president of the Christian Mystic Lodge believed herself the recipient of orders to withdraw, and to carry on her mission independently, perhaps she was right, even at the cost of leaving the 'thieves' in possession of the Father's House. Nevertheless, I regret it.

While there may be differences between the Western teachings and the Eastern, these are matters of detail and of phraseology rather than of fundamental conceptions, at least so it seems to me, and while one may be a follower of the Masters who are responsible for the existence of the Theosophical Society, he may study with profit and sympathy the Western teachings based upon the Christian traditions. But the teachings of the Liberal Catholic Church as set forth by Leadbeater in his book, *The Science of the Sacraments*, are repugnant both to the followers of the Master Jesus and to those of the Masters M and KH. How can anybody reconcile the words of Jesus: 'But thou, when thou prayest, enter into thy closet, and when thou hast shut thy door, pray to thy Father which is in secret' with the teaching that communion with the Spirit is to be secured only through the agency of a priest, innoculated with the serum of apostolic succession, clad in fantastic garments and performing gestures to the odour of burning drugs? 'But when ye pray, use not vain repetitions, as the heathen do, for they think that they shall be heard for their much speaking.'

The above is not intended as an unqualified endorsement of all views held by the Community of the Inner Light or its warden, Dion Fortune, but rather as a defence of the general principle that one may be a disciple of the Master Jesus as well as of any other Master of the White Lodge, the aims of the Masters of this Lodge being identical, even though the methods followed by the different Masters may vary and be adapted to mentality, requirements and antecedents of different races and cultures, and as opposing the idea that there needs to be, or can be, an intermediary between man and the Spirit, or, if you prefer, the Inner Self, or the Christ within.

The Community of the Inner Light publishes under the editorship of Dion Fortune, a monthly, *The Inner Light*, at 6/6 per annum. This, and information as to membership, can be obtained from the Secretary at *3, Queensborough Terrace, Bayswater, W. 2, London.*

This article, dated February 1928, proves once more that Dion, who never particularly liked animals, should have been a horsewoman — one who could ride two mounts at once. Indeed we can see her at this time within the card The Chariot, drawn by two sphinxes, symbol of Mystery, with opposing polarities. She sits resplendent in a block of stone — the philosophers' stone — and is heavily armoured for the fray or for any crashes she might have. The cubic stone itself represents all those occult edifices in which she was imbedded: The Science, Arts and Crafts Society, the Alpha and Omega Temple, the Christian Mystic Lodge of the Theosophical Society, and the Hermes Temple, and finally the Fraternity of the Inner Light. As a physical vehicle this particular chariot would go nowhere in the linear sense. Lao Tzu, whom Dion admired, put it thus:

The further one goes, the less one knows.
Therefore the sage knows without going about,
Understands without seeing,
And accomplishes without any action.

Keyed to the path between intellect and intuition, this is what Dion would do all her life. By 1924 at the latest she had acquired her own house off the Bayswater Road and turned it into a temple; she would never leave it except to form at least two similar: one in Glastonbury and one in West Halkin Street. In the outer world she never did very much at all; but in the inner world, mastering the opposing forces which provided her motive power, she travelled long and hard.

She also did so because there were things she wanted very much to outdistance; not least being the belief she once had in the World Teacher, as shown by the article.

The World Teacher was a coy Theosophical attempt to avoid the term Messiah — for that is in fact what the Theosophists believed their young protégé, Jiddhu Khrishnamurti, to be. The Messianic vision is a tempting one, especially coming after a period of international trauma such as brought on by the Great War, and during times of social unrest as the 1920s proved to be. The World Teacher to Dion was like a great strong man coming to put all things right — a Master, but on an immeasureably greater scale.

The hapless World Teacher in question had been discovered by Charles W. Leadbeater in April 1909, when he, along with some pupils, Ernest Wood, Johan van Manen, and B. P. Wadia, walked to the beach on the Theosophical Estate for a swim. One of the Indian boys following the party was a thin and unhappy looking child whom Wood, his teacher, considered to be something of a dim-wit. Leadbeater, who had been looking closely at the boy's aura, was nevertheless quite certain that this youth (he was then fourteen) would one day be greater than them all — that he would indeed be the vehicle for the Lord Maitreya, as the spiritual ruler of this world was known, at least to Theosophists.

The boy's past lives were researched — they were exalted; the rumour began to spread among the Theosophists — they were ecstatic.

In 1911 Mrs Besant, who had taken over from Blavatsky as President of the TS started the Order of the Star in the East, of which Krishnamurti was made the head. The hierarchy of Theosophical Masters, who had been comparatively subdued after HPB's death, began to inundate Besant and Leadbeater with telepathic messages for Krishna, as his intimates called him. The boy, who truly did become an extraordinary individual, unhappily submitted himself to what was virtually a life of occult brainwashing, bolstered by the atmosphere of intense reverence and adoration which surrounded him. It was during this period that the TS attracted its highest membership. It was during this period also that a few people, less Messianic in temperament and more clear-sighted, began to express grave doubts as to the spirituality of Leadbeater himself.

Leadbeater was in fact nothing less than a pederast of the kind that is quintessentially English, mixing fond words on Lord Jesus with the lordly fondling of little boys, and managing to find some divine justification for it all. Fiercely misogynistic (except for Mrs Besant whose Presidency of the TS allowed him his platform), he probably did more harm to the occult cause this century than anyone. Possessed of undoubted powers he completely dominated Mrs Besant, who had been such a formidable personality herself in the days when she had been a labour leader, and managed to survive the increasing scandals about his sexual activities long after any lesser man in that era would have gone under in despair.

What proved his undoing was not the onslaughts by outraged former members of the TS, or articles such as appeared in the *O.E. Library Critic* attributing to him and his satanic associate James Wedgewood such publications as *Sex Hygiene for Boys, Practical Uses for Choirboys,* and *Buggery* and *Humbuggery in the Church* — for he survived every slander that could be and was thrown at him. What proved his undoing was the fact that in 1929, to his eternal credit, Jiddhu Krishnamurti dissolved the whole organization which had been built around his role as Messiah. He renounced the estates and riches, the jasmine and rose-filled railway carriages, the camps where thousands had listened to his every word and would have died for him, and maintained that truth was a 'pathless land.' He asked his followers to put aside all religious practices and instead look within themselves for the light. Without saying it outright he made it clear that he scorned the increasing follies of Leadbeater and Wedgewood, who held the reins of the Liberal Catholic Church, Co-Masonry, and Theosophy itself, and who preached that great initiates like themselves forwent all sexual activity (while themselves indulging in a variety of sodomitical practices).[3]

Many of the people who had invested so much faith in this Second Coming never recovered from the scandals that arose around the revered Bishop Leadbeater; still less did they get over the effect of Krishnamurti's renunciation. Dion did so by advocating support for the 'Back to Blavatsky' movement, which was an attempt to bring Theosophy back to the integrity it had had in the pre-Leadbeater days. She followed this up by attacking Leadbeater in print in a variety of sources, accusing him of being a black magician. Not content with this she also had another of her many psychic battles with one of the men who had been with Leadbeater on that day when he had first dicovered the World Teacher: although this was some years before her total disillusionment.

B. P. Wadia had come to England shortly after the Great War to found an occult school of his own. He had seen what Leadbeater had achieved over the previous decade, and was quite sure that he could do as much

Moina Mathers

J.W. Brodie-Innes

Lord Erskine

Thomas More as portrayed by Holbein

Anna Kingsford

Aware that he was deeply involved with Mrs Besant in the politics of Indian nationalism and wanted nothing more than for the British to leave his country well alone, Dion was under no doubt that he disliked the English and all their ways very much indeed.

Even so she was willing to find out what he had to offer. And, still resonant no doubt with the inner contacts she had made just before the War, she went along with him as far as she felt able. She went so far that she actually made contact with those Himalayan Masters that she would eventually and so forcefully reject.

> When Mr Wadia, once a worker at Adyar, and later founder of the United Lodge of Theosophists, was in England shortly after the War, trying to make a start with his scheme, he gathered together a small group of people, of whom I was one, and put us in touch with the Himalayan Masters. For what my testimony is worth, I can vouch for the genuineness of these contacts; I certainly got in touch with something; but although it was not evil, it was to me alien and unsympathetic, and it seemed to me that it was hostile to my race, but that is another story. Anyway the rapport came to an end so far as I was concerned. Whether I was cast out or walked out, I cannot be certain, anyway, the parting was simultaneous and by mutual agreement.[4]

Looking around at the little group, Dion felt that she was the only pure-blooded Anglo-Saxon present, and began to take issue with him over his idea that he would pour the regenerative spiritual force of the East into the group-soul of the British Empire, which he felt was in a very bad way indeed.

It is here that the only motherliness Dion would ever feel arose. It is unlikely that she ever felt any constant longing for a child of her own; and while she would protect — and right fiercely — any of her pupils whom she felt might be hard done by on any level, it was only in relation to her country that she felt any of the maternal qualities of protection and nourishment. This man Wadia, with his intense spiritual pride, as she saw it, and his nasty little idea that England must acknowledge the spiritual supremacy of India and take her spiritual inspiration from the East, was not going to get all his own way. The group-soul of Great Britain, she maintained, was not dying, but only very tired by the War.

Wadia, being a good psychic, detected her uneasiness and asked her to withdraw from his group.

A few days later she was sitting in her room one afternoon chatting with a friend. It was dusk; they chatted by the light of a gas-fire. Suddenly they were both aware of a hostile presence in the room, and both turned in the same direction. Dion, being the more psychic, perceived Wadia's form within an egg-shaped sphere of misty light. As her friend was not particularly advanced upon the path of High Magic, Dion bade her to wait outside for a while, while she in turn attacked the phantasm by means of the pentagram and certain names of Power. Immediately the appearance in the corner by the door shattered and vanished while at the same time a resounding crack was heard. This crack had been caused by one of the door panels splitting in two.

Not surprisingly she began to feel something quite sinister was going on, and something not at all congenial to the health of her race. Not being at that time an advanced occultist herself, all she could think of doing was to invoke her Masters upon the Inner Planes. The reply came back quite clearly: 'You are to go to Colonel Y.'

Or so she wrote in *Psychic Self Defence*. Colonel Y was actually Colonel J.F.C. Fuller, who is remembered today as 'Boney' Fuller, an *enfant terrible* in military theory, champion of tank warfare, and politically somewhere to the right of Ivan the Terrible. In his later life he was very close to Oswald Mosley, head of the British Fascists; in his early manhood he was a pupil of Aleister Crowley, the Great Beast. A genius in the art of warfare, he also had a profound knowledge and expertise in Magic.

Dion was taken aback by this information, for after having been introduced to him once, he was the last person in the world she would want to trouble.

Quite reasonably, she demanded a sign. The inner voice of the Master insisted that Fuller would be at her next lecture. To her surprise he did indeed appear, and was fully expecting her information as he had had an inner voice of his own telling him that Dion was about to come and ask his help, and that he was to give it.

Quite what he did she never knew, but a few days later Wadia left the country.

On the surface it seems odd that Dion in 1919 or thereabouts should be so vehemently opposed to Wadia's own espousal of Theosophy while, a few short years later, she should be so eagerly referring to the coming of the World Teacher. But the difference was quite simply this: Leadbeater was a champion of King and Country, and Empire, as was Dion; and until she learned the truth about the old prophet's unnatural vice, and became shattered by the World Teacher's rejection of his own role, she followed the wicked Bishop with the full and happy knowledge that he was, above all things, an Englishman.

Of all the confusing strands of her philosophies, of all the contradictions suggested by the various groups with which she affiliated herself, the only consistent strand that carried right through was the one in which she rejected the Eastern Masters. In 1926, when she was an initiate of the Golden Dawn and President of the Christian Mystic Lodge with eyes that turned to the hope expressed by a young Indian gentleman, she was nevertheless crying out in *The Occult Review*: 'Do not let it be forgotten that our traditions are racial. What that great initiate Rudolph Steiner did for the German-speaking races someone must do for those who use a Latin-root language and the Anglo-Saxon tongue.' She meant herself of course. Referring to the TS she noted: 'We have in our midst a wide-spread organisation that has an open platform. The Eastern Masters are working through it, but where are the Western adepts?' She knew full well. Her frustration was in not being able to tell anyone. She had found these Western adepts in the form of Brodie-Innes and Moina Mathers, in Maiya Curtis-Webb and Hope Hughes, who ran the Hermes Temple.

And she had already, in the winter of 1923/24, made contact with her own Secret Chiefs, and had written her own cosmology based around their collective wisdoms. These were entities very different in style and tone to Rakoczi and Jesus, utterly removed from anything within the Oriental bias of the TS, and probably even completely different to any of the Chiefs used by Moina and her fellow-adepts within the Golden Dawn.

With them she began to break away from everyone, although it was a slow process. With them she began to get her power.

6.

THE MASTERS — AND THEIR MISTRESS

> I don't know the names of my own Spirit Guides. I wouldn't believe them even if they told me.
>
> AFA

There is a picture by William Blake which almost happens to portray the structure of the Magical Orders. It is called 'He Encompasseth the Heavens'. The mighty and muscled figure of God looks down from on high; from his hand streak two rays of pure light which do just what the title implies. It *almost* fulfils our needs: ideally there should be three rays, like the druidic *awen*, burning out from a single point.

The inner pattern of Dion's own little cosmos is a complex one. And although no person will ever resolve it with a single diagram it can be suggested, at least loosely, with this image of the three rays emanating from a single source. As will be seen the outsider (in this case everyone except Dion herself) will encounter Mysteries when it comes to analysing her Secret Chiefs. What must be remembered is that these were, and are, living beings. They cannot be parcelled and sorted into neat units, appearing and reappearing at specific and expected times, in a regulated manner. The inner contacts come and go, they overlap, they assume greater and lesser prominence at different and unpredictable times, just as can be said about the flesh-and-blood companions in any person's life. As Langford Garstin pointed out, the Fraternity of the Inner Light was something of a melting pot. The trinity of Chiefs that are most dominant in Dion's magic was not the only trinity she used.

And so, to start at the point where all begins and all ends, we must look at the one contact that is not in dispute, whose role is quite clearly recognized, and from whom the three rays began: Melchisedec of Salem.

This should not be taken psychologically, as should be obvious by now. This is not a matter of archetype — whatever that might be — but of divinity. Not a matter of symbol, but revelation. Like Moriarty before her, who made many references to that being, she achieved direct psychic contact with Melchisedec presumably when her teacher was still alive, and probably just after her disastrous romance with a man she felt sure was not human.

It is a name which appears in many of her books, as though she were gasping to tell the world. In *Training and Work of an Initiate*, written in 1930, she writes: 'In the same way the archetypal ideas were brought to mankind by the Manu Melchisedec, who was a Lord of Flame and also of Mind . . . and therefore it is that the highest of our Initiates are referred to as "High Priests after the Order of Melchisedec", that is to say they trace their spiritual lineage back to a primordial Initiation.'

In the visions of two later magicians that she worked with and partly trained — Charles Seymour and Christine Hartley — Melchisedec was a simple enough soul whom they would meet on the Inner Planes by going to the 'House by the Wall', a description which conjures up some Old Testament dwelling of whitewashed clay, where the leader of the Order was available for teaching.

According to the esoteric theory espoused by Dion (but not necessarily accepted by other magicians) Melchisedec came to Earth from Venus, bringing the life-wave with him. This is not to be understood in terms of space-ships and primordial astronauts, but more in the context of the Theosophical idea that the life-force of humanity travelled like an electric current around the solar system, energising each planet systematically.

Melchisedec brought with him the three substances of wheat, honey and asbestos, which were felt to have certain parthenogenetic qualities representative of Melchisedec himself, and also provided links between the present day and the Mysteries of the unimaginable past: 'The reason why these three things — the Corn, the Bee, and the Asbestos — were used so universally', wrote Moriarty, 'is that they all came to earth from other evolutions. That is, they have no archetypes on this planet but have been brought over to us in order to teach definite lessons. For this reason they are called "Manu manifestations".'

If Dion and Moina shared any contact in common it was probably this. In Dion's own group the candidate after initiation was then granted the status of High Priest after the Order of Melchisedec. After that, what contacts he or she might make was an individual matter, although they usually tended towards those used within the main body of the lodge. The tutors of the trainee magician would be able to tell whether he was heading in their own direction either by their psychic perceptions, or by the tone of the essays each pupil had to submit.

By no means all of the adepts who came to practise with Dion used the same trinity of contacts as she did within the mainstream of the group; nor did she restrict herself exclusively to those which she termed 'The Watchers of Avalon'.

Melchisedec, then, was the beginning. Whatever came after, whatever the complexities and apparent contradictions of the contacts Dion came to use, all were resolved within that being.

We must imagine him sending out the three rays. These were known as the Hermetic Ray, which was connected with the philosophy and practice of ritual and ceremonial magic; the Orphic, or the Green Ray, connected with a passionate and sublime devotion to the Earth Mysteries and the world of faëry; and the Mystic Ray, the hardest of all, resolving all opposites and antinomies within the Mysteries of the Son and/or the Sun.

Each ray had its representative within the inner side of the lodge, although it is by no means certain which equates with which. And the representatives in question were: Socrates, Lord Erskine, and David Carstairs. These were her Secret Chiefs. These were the entities that she made psychic contact with at Glastonbury in the winter of 1923/4. She had been staying there with her friend Charles Loveday, a keen Christian Mystic whom everyone thought of as being her boyfriend but was probably no such thing — at least from her point of view. She had achieved this contact via Melchisedec, by standing atop the Tor and visualizing an amphitheatre under the earth, where red flashes filled the darkness, and the faint sound of a hammer on an anvil was heard, faintly at first, but coming nearer with a hard, strong and simple rhythm. And as the sound came nearer, vast and dim forms began to appear before her inner vision — forms from the cthonic depths of inner earth.

Socrates needs little introduction. He grew to manhood at a time when Athens was at the height of its glory. In the year 450 BC or thereabouts, at the age of 19, he seems to have become interested in the Ionian philosophy that had just been introduced into Athens by Anaxagoras, and accordingly attached himself to Archelaus, the latter's successor. It seems, further, that he became disillusioned with physical science and was compelled to strike out on his own, although the teachings of Pythagoras undoubtedly had an impact upon him. He next appeared serving as a hoplite in the army at Potidaea (430 BC), Delium (424) and Amphipolis (422), where he won renown for his valour and powers of endurance. He had become well-known by this time, and attracted the satire of Amipsias and Aristophanes, who burlesqued him in *Clouds*. Nevertheless, in 406 BC he allowed himself to be elected to the Council of Five Hundred, although it did not take him long to fall from grace. After taking an unpopular stance on an obscure issue he was charged with impiety and corruption of youth. The latter indictment amounted to Socrates' encouragement to the young to criticize the existing order. He was found guilty by only a narrow majority, but his attitude after the verdict so enraged his judges that he was sentenced to death. Although supporters had made plans for his escape he refused to take advantage of these and took the hemlock in the spring of 399 BC.

The value of Socrates' contribution to philosophy is disputed, as Socrates himself denied that he had any positive doctrines to teach, and most of the information about him has depended upon the records of others. Nevertheless we know that he defined the soul as that in man which had knowledge, and also ignorance, good and bad. For the first time a distinction had been made, therefore, between intelligence and sensation, and the soul identified with the normal consciousness or character of man. Moreover Socrates declared the immortality of the soul, and it was but a step from this to the doctrine that goodness is knowledge. The Socratic method of 'examination in arguments' or 'Socratic irony' was in itself not new, but via its application to questions of ethics and aesthetics, he believed that he had something of a divine mission. The nature of this mission was to convict men of sin (ie, ignorance) by question and answer, systematically examining those fundamental assumptions from which discussions of conduct and morality arose, and insisting on a strict definition of terms. In this method Socrates may be regarded as the founder of formal logic.

If Socrates was the 'world-famous philosopher' who dictated *The Cosmic Doctrine* (and this is by no means certain) he was aided and abetted by a much more interesting entity which presented itself as Lord Erskine, former Chancellor of England.

Thomas Erskine, who became first Baron Erskine, was born on 10 January 1749 in an upper flat in a high house at the head of Gray's Close in Edinburgh. As a youth he always wanted to study mathematics or philosophy and enter some appropriate profession, but his father could not afford the expense. So, despite the fact that he loathed the sea, he became a midshipman on board the *Tartar*, commanded by Sir David Lindsay. After several years in the West Indies during which he studied botany, practised drawing, and was struck by lightning, he returned home to take up a commission in the 1st Royal Regiment of Foot, of which John, Duke of Argyll, was Colonel. His first station was Berwick-upon-Tweed, his second St Helier, Jersey: all this before his twentieth birthday. Coming back to London he made some impact upon Society. Boswell noticed him and described him as a young officer who 'talked with vivacity, fluency, and precision so uncommon that he attracted particular attention.'

In 1772 Erskine studied law at the suggestion of Lord Mansfield, and six years later he was called to the Bar. In 1783 he took silk, as they say, and within a few years he was earning £10,000 a year – an unbelievable sum.

Thomas Erskine was a striking man, as Boswell had first perceived. His figure was elastic and erect, his eyes brilliant and captivating, his voice sharp and clear and without a trace of Scottish accent. His oratory in court was sharp and relevant, and he was famed for his wit.

The only really flabby part of his character that anyone could see in those early years of ascendancy was that he was terrified of Pitt, the Prime Minister, before whom he was 'awed like a schoolboy at school'; yet there were moments when Erskine achieved an almost superstar status within the country which we might find hard to credit today. When he successfully and brilliantly defended Horne Tooke and other advocates of parliamentary reform against the charge of treason, bonfires were lit throughout the land, crowds dragged his carriage in triumph to his house in Serjeants' Inn, portraits and busts were sold all over the country, and tokens were struck bearing his effigy.

On the other hand he took up cudgels against causes with which we would all sympathize today, in such acts as prosecuting a bookseller who had done no more than sell Paine's *Age of Reason*.

Erskine developed a colossal ego after all this success and was indeed often satirized as Counsellor Ego, who ranked 'very little lower than the angels.' And although he proved eminently unsuited for the post, in 1806 he was entrusted with the great seals of the realm, and appointed Lord Chancellor. He took his title, Baron Erskine of Restormel, from the ruined castle of that name in Cornwall, as a compliment to the Prince of Wales. From this time, which should have been the start of his greatest years, he sank into comparative insiginificance, and lost the Chancellorship to his old rival Lord Eldon, from whom he had taken it in the first place.

In his final years he lived the life of an idler and man-about-town, sometimes melancholy in private, but invariably vivacious and sprightly in company. The only political question in which he interested himself was a Bill for the prevention of cruelty to animals, while on the literary scene he kept himself amused by writing an imitation of More's *Utopia*.

Thomas Erskine died on 17 November 1823, and was buried in Linlithgow in his native land.

Who remembers him now? Who but an extreme specialist in history would have known much about him even fifty years after his death? And how, out of the plethora of well-known historical figures, did Dion Fortune come to seize upon him as her most important Secret Chief, or Inner Plane Adept as she came to term it?[5]

But Erskine was, in many senses, far more than he seemed; for one of the great secrets behind Dion's Fraternity lay in the belief — the knowledge — that Erskine was no less than a later incarnation of someone immeasurably more famous, of someone undeniably exalted in the realm of the spirit.

Thomas Erskine's previous manifestation upon this earth had also been as a Chancellor. It had been as True Thomas, the greatest Englishman of all. It had been as Thomas More.

It is not known whether Dion made an immediate identification of More with Erskine. The contact itself was referred to by her and her pupils as Lord E or as The Chancellor. They were all forbidden to mention his full name or his real name. It is quite possible that Erskine did not reveal his more dominant aspect until 1935, the year that Thomas More was canonized and also the year that Dion published her masterpiece *The Mystical Qabalah* — an act which she feared would result in the loss of her contacts entirely, and provoke some sort of punitive current from the egregore of the Golden Dawn.

More was born on 6/7 February in the year 1478, in the Cripplegate ward of the City of London, within the hearing of Bow Bells. He became a man of many parts: 'citizen of renown, man of law, man of learning, man of affairs; Secretary to King Henry VIII; High Steward of both Oxford and Cambridge Universities; Speaker of the House of Commons; Lord Chancellor. Prisoner of conscience, confessor, martyr, saint.'

He made a lasting friendship with Erasmus, the scholar who was a living legend within Europe, and built a name for himself in Parliament by his bold opposition to Henry VII's demand for a grant on the occasion of his daughter's marriage — as a result of which the Commons reduced the subsidy considerably.

When Henry VIII acceded to the throne More soon came to the attention of both him and Wolsey, the Cardinal. In 1518 he was appointed master of requests and made a privy councillor, and found himself sent on various embassies to the Low Countries. It was while in Flanders that he began to write his most famous work, *Utopia*, which was based upon a Sparta-like island set like Atlantis beyond the edge of the known, in the centre of which lay the town of Amaurotum, 'City of Dreams', where the elders of the island would gather to discuss affairs of state once a year.

In 1520 More accompanied the king to the Field of the Cloth of Gold, and in the following year he was knighted and made treasurer of the Exchequer. In 1529 he succeeded Wolsey as Lord Chancellor of England. As the supreme judge within England he became famous for his fairness, promptitude, and incorruptibility — which could not be said about every Chancellor.

Although within his Utopia he had declared for tolerance of religious creed within an ideal state, he did not, in practice, extend such tolerance to the new heresy of Lutherism that had begun to sweep Europe. He used all his influence to oppose a bill intended to relax the severity of the heresy laws.

A cloud appeared over his friendship with the king, too, because of the latter's new marital plans and his intention to take to himself the powers of the Church of England held by the Pope. When Henry forced the rest of the clergy to acknowledge him as 'Protector and Supreme Head of the Church of England' it became the first push towards More's resigning his Chancellorship.

The final crisis came over the Act of Succession, with its inevitable implications. While the nullity case of Henry's marriage with Catherine of Aragon was still being decided at Rome, Henry married Anne Boleyn, who was then crowned Queen. More refused to attend her coronation. In 1534 the Act of Succession required the king's subjects to recognize the offspring of the marriage of Henry and Anne as successors to the throne; also that the previous union with Catherine of Aragon was no true marriage, but that the union with Anne was a true marriage and that the authority of any foreign prince or potentate should be repudiated.

More was ready to agree to the first part of the oath but not the rest, as only a little while before Pope Clement VII had at last pronounced the marriage of Henry and Catherine to have been valid. As opposition to the Act was declared high treason, so More and John Fisher were sentenced to death.

More was beheaded on Tower Hill on 6 July 1535, his last words being that he was dying for the faith of the Holy Catholic Church and was 'the king's good servant, but God's first'.

The 'King's Good Servant' has entered the popular consciousness of the twentieth century as a completely benign and lovable man, devoted to his family, incapable of lies, fair and honourable to a fault, liberal and wise. He is most perfectly embodied in the superb portrayal by Paul Scofield in Robert Bolt's *A Man for All Seasons* (which, interestingly, was written in the Glastonbury area). This is the view that Dion held of him, although of course she knew him on the Inner Planes long before Bolt ever dreamed of the play in question. It is also the personality that many of her magicians at the time, and in the years since, have experienced in contacting him.

It is also a personality that no modern, objective historian would countenance. Increasingly today, More is seen as a cold, narrow and dark man, who made cruel jokes in public about his wife's ugliness and stupidity, but made them in Latin so that the poor woman would not know why the learned company was laughing at her; he cared little for any of his family but his daughter Meg Roper, who was the only person who knew the secret of the hair shirt he wore under his clothes; and if, as the Protestants swear, he did not actually tie heretics to the tree in his back garden and whip them unconscious, he certainly used his authority to pursue and torture heretics with implacable and unforgiving zeal; an arrogant man, he was so treacherous and duplicitous as to make the name True Thomas a masterpiece of irony.[6]

In fact there are many points in common between Erskine and More: the wit, the ego, the private melancholy . . . the major difference is that one had the immeasurable benefit of martyrdom. It was only at this time, say the modern commentators, that More really did redeem himself and show some of the qualities with which he is associated.

This is a view that Dion would not have known. It is one that she would have been unlikely to accept.

The third of the Chiefs was David Carstairs. In many ways he is the most interesting of the trinity. He came to Dion when she was in full trance, gave his name, and the information that he had been a young officer killed in action in the Great War, at Ypres (which everyone pronounced 'Wipers'). After a brief career in the Midlands (Coventry, it was felt) where he had been something of a worker for the downtrodden, his light had been snuffed out as so many others had been, and upon his death he had determined to do what he could to ensure that such folly would not happen again.

Carstairs had humour. Once, on taking over a medium, he was heard to exclaim with mock ire that she smelled like an old boot. On another occasion, again taking over Dion in full trance, he made her walk outside into a motor-car, and controlled her as she drove it through the crowded streets of London — something she had never done before and never did again.

Many others made the Carstairs contact. He was very popular, being so eternally young and vital. They called him, with affection rather than reverence, the Master David.

The story of Carstairs is extraordinary and rather moving — a young and yet great soul becoming so intimate with the earth-world so soon after his death. But it gets more extraordinary still:

David Carstairs did not exist.

No officers of that name, or with different first names, were killed at Ypres in the Great War, or on any other salient for that matter. The only David Carstairs in the entire British Army was a private in the Black Watch, a native-born Scot.

What are we to make of this? Depending upon one's stance, a great deal. Those who take the anti-Magic attitude will see it as a means of denying the validity of the whole concept of inner contacts. Those who are pro-Magic fall into two categories: the great magicians, who have almost no interest in defending themselves or their art, wishing to do no more in life than what they were born to do, which is to create Light; and those lesser magicians, would-be Adepti, who seek to defend magic by means of psychology, yet end up destroying it. Even among the more advanced practitioners of magic there is sometimes a tendency to indulge in internal squabbles: in Dion's day the trend was to accuse another magician of being 'black'; nowadays, when the lines of good and evil have apparently been blurred, one magician is likely to suggest of another that his contacts are 'impure', sullied, or in some way not quite what they seem. I have met several people for example, who have made the Socrates contact yet distrust that of More; at the same time I have met others who swear by the decency and wisdom of the More contact and yet cast aspersions at Socrates.

Which, of course, does not take us any nearer to understanding Carstairs. He, I believe, was an image of the man Dion would have married had not the War taken the chance away. He was, I believe, an ideal specimen from that lost generation of menfolk which would have been all that she wanted for herself: strong, young, earthy, humorous, kind and wise — a helper of humanity. David Carstairs never existed, but the form and vital image did. Something energized that image and made it live — not only in Dion's mind, but in the minds of some who came after her.

I discussed this knotty point wth Basil Wilby, who has written some influential books on magic under the pseudonym of Gareth Knight. I think his off-the-cuff reply touched upon something important.

> It could be that DF got the name wrong — and with this in mind one wonders if it was this that caused the communicator to discourage them from trying to contact his family. Names are difficult to get mediumistically — though I believe DF was working in full trance, which should have made it easier.
>
> To anyone not accustomed to this kind of work it might appear strange that the 'wrong name' should continue to be used. But these types of contact are never summoned by name, nor addressed by name. Images are used, plus blocks of intuitive realization, but certainly images as a contact or call-sign.
>
> I have in the course of my experience picked up two names of new contacts at this level and they have in each case been encoded in 'signs following'. One used a nickname I didn't know about until I saw it in a reference work; the other used the image of a name in an important novel.

> Alternatively Carstairs may have been a convenient 'mock-up' by an Inner Plane communicator as a means to make contact. (I have in mind the oft-quoted phrase in the *The Cosmic Doctrine*: 'The Masters as you picture them are all "imagination". Note well that I did not say the Masters were imagination: I said "The Masters as you picture them . . ." What we are you cannot realize and it is a waste of time to try to do so, but you can imagine us on the astral plane and we can contact you through your imagination, and although your mental picture is not real or actual, the results of it are real and actual.')
>
> I have never taken the identities of the Masters too literally — in fact I couldn't tell you what they really are — but acting on the 'suspended disbelief' that they *were* real I have found them to have served me very well over the years.
>
> Apropos of this Roma and I have recently picked up a contact that uses the persona of a well-known author . . . An interesting technical point is that he sucks and taps at a pipe. And he said as an aside during a recent communication: 'This is not real tobacco of course, and it doesn't taste of tobacco. It is a useful device to concentrate the mind of the mediator.'

The art of making an inner contact, then, is the art of achieving some empathy with the target. It is less a matter of faith or the proper application of some exquisite technique from the so-called 'science' of occultism, than the talent for achieving some sort of rapport via the imagination.

As with Carstairs, so with Thomas More. It does not matter that the reality of More might well have been diametrically opposed to the benign martyr that has come down to us in history. When Dion set her cap at him, thinking he was the greatest of Englishmen, she was aspiring toward the highest spark of English character, she was reaching toward the bright spirit of the race itself. Which is why she got Erskine first, because she touched upon the reality of More seen within this 'Counsellor Ego'. She could not have sustained the More contact if she had been aware of his real character; but by seeing this dark side as a later incarnation, as Erskine, she could look beyond both of them, out towards the brightest star of English manhood.

These were the contacts which gave her the charter to form the Fraternity of the Inner Light, via the Christian Mystic Lodge of the Theosophical Society. These were the Secret Chiefs that she would treasure and protect throughout her life. It has still not been resolved whether they had any antecedents within the magical workings of the Golden Dawn.

In many ways, despite her obvious debts to Blavatsky and the Mathers, the true precursor of her group was to be found not so much within

The Theosophical Society or the Golden Dawn, or the inner clique of Moriarty's pupils, but more within the Hermetic Society of Anna Kingsford.

Anna Bonus Kingsford, to include her maiden name, had all the things that Dion would come to admire: she had the peculiar power that arises from charisma; the wisdom that comes from courage; and above all else she was beautiful. Everyone said that Anna was beautiful. They always commented upon how young she was to have achieved what she had. She was a woman as clothed in sun as Dion would be in moon.

Anna was born at Maryland Point, Stratford, Essex, on 16 September 1846. In 1867 she married Algernon Kingsford, who was then vicar of Atcham, Shropshire. She wrote stories for the *Penny Post* and was received into the Roman Catholic Church by no less a person than Cardinal Manning, in 1870, thence adopting the splendid and incantatory Christian names: Anna Mary Magdalen Maria Johanna. A fierce opponent of vivisection, she purchased and edited in her own name *The Lady's Own Paper*, in 1872, in order to propagate her anti-vivisectionist attitudes. Two years later she went one step further when she went to Paris to study medicine. Her belief was that she would fight the vivisectionists in their own back yard, and use medical science for her own ends.

Although she had an active practice as a fully qualified physician in London following her return from Paris in 1880, she had also felt the first impact of the Otherworld. She began to have visions of the past, and was inclined to accept these as past lives: Mary Magdalene, Joan of Arc and Anne Boleyn jostled for space within her busy psyche. They may have been ether-inspired but they had their impact upon her, and beyond her to others. She was, not surprisingly, elected President of the Theosophical Society in England, and the members who had elected her were enormously proud of their leader. Their choice of this free-thinking woman reflected well upon themselves, they all felt. After all she had a superb mind, no little talent for writing, was a pioneer in the cause of higher education for women, and had excellent credentials — both professional and social. The only drawback was, as the members came to discover, that Dr Kingsford had not the slightest interest in the Eastern Masters, and was not at all impressed by the Theosophical arguments for their existence. Westerners, she insisted, would do far better to look for their inspiration within Greek and Christian sources of occultism.

At an emergency meeting that was held in London to debate this point, Madame Blavatsky herself appeared, sweeping down the hall and past those members of the audience who had tried to kneel at her feet, before confronting this, the first of her heretics. Anna's only supporter in this and in other causes was Edward Maitland, who was then her vice-president. According to him Blavatsky tried, quite blatantly, to mesmerize the pair of them and force them to do her will. It was dear old Olcott who saved the situation, coming in between them and using his charm to defuse it. Having recognized her match, the Russian priestess gave in, and agreed to a charter whereby Dr Kingsford and Edward Maitland would found the Hermetic Lodge of the Theosophical Society — which in fact bore very little relationship to the parent organization.

I am not in any way suggesting that Anna Kingsford was in some way a 'pre-incarnation' of Dion, or that she had any conscious link with the same Chiefs, but when one thinks about Dion's vegetarianism, her anti-vivisectionist stance, her regret that she never received formal recognition from the British Medical Society for her work in psychoanalysis, and her own impulses toward the Catholic Church at one point, one cannot help but think that the spirit behind them was the same.

Perhaps the glyph which best expresses the link between them is that of the caduceus. At a time when Dion was still Violet and a Christian Mystic herself, Moriarty was using the image of the caduceus to describe the way two differing currents balance each other. The caduceus, as is well known, being the symbol of Hermes and thus the Hermetic Arts, was badly drawn by Moriarty: he missed out the centre-line. And although the glyph has a multitude of meanings, we might add one more of our own: the *three* lines represent the intertwining of three occult movements — the Golden Dawn, the Theosophical Society, plus the Hermetic Society of Anna Kingsford down the centre. Three separate and fluid movements that part company and re-join again at various points throughout the years, sometimes losing their identities in each other before separating once more; three separate lines of light that curve — as light does — move apparently parallel for brief moments, come together, and speed away. Unto the ages of ages.

Although the Hermetic Society continued after Anna's death in 1888, it was still just a child, magically speaking, when it died. And magically speaking again, it was reborn soon afterward and found another kind of achievement in the Christian Mystic Lodge, and finally the more truly Hermetic fraternity which sprang from that.

Dion and Anna never knew each other, their organizations had no earthly connection, but in their deepest beings they were sisters.

All of which brings us to the year 1927 and a consideration of the mysteries surrounding *The Cosmic Doctrine*, that revelation which had been given Dion by the Chiefs in the winter of 1923/4.

Somehow, Moriarty is the figure which resolves all of the above, a manifestation of one of those nodal points on the caduceus, absorbing and re-issuing all three currents as described.

Quite simply, *The Cosmic Doctrine* bears such similarity to Moriarty's *Aphorisms of Creation and Cosmic Principles* that we have to wonder just what part her former teacher played within the formulation of her own great illumination.

The obvious, natural, and yet rather cruel assumption is that Dion did not so much 'receive' her doctrine from discarnate Masters as crib the information from a man who had just recently left this bourne.

A superficial glance at Moriarty's *Aphorisms* would tend to support this assumption: there is a similarity in tone; there are certain terms peculiar to him which reappear in those portions of the work which might be described as 'early Dion'; the breakdown of the planes, as experienced by Moriarty, is used by Dion without a quibble; and several statements made within the *Aphorisms* immediately take the eye:

> The Christ is essentially the Power, Love and Wisdom of the Son (the Sun) made manifest . . . and thus from the initial aspect of the Eternal Principle ever unmanifest and the Logos in duality comes a threefold aspect, the Three-in-One. This Initiatory Three comes into manifestation as three Powers — called in this philosophy the Lords of Flame, Form and Mind, the Lords of Form and Mind being the reflection of the duality and the Lord of Flame the reflection of the entitial three of the highest level.
>
> The Law of Correspondence is briefly summed up in the ancient Canaic saying of the Order of Melchisedec — 'From one, know all.' . .

On the other hand *The Cosmic Doctrine* is better written. It is less verbose, less psuedo-scientific, and denser in terms of insight. It is almost as though Dion took the symbol of the caduceus, upon which Moriarty's philosophy was based, and twisted it about into a figure of three dimensions, to create her own image of the Ring-pass-Not. On top of which we should notice that in terms of pure philosophy — whether we take to it or not — it is incomparably superior to anything else Dion wrote throughout the rest of her life, and this tends to support the statement that the work was indeed received from intelligences of vastly superior wisdom.

The fact that the winter of 1923/24 is given as the date of transmission is significant. Dion was trying to tell us something here, for it was in August 1923 that Moriarty died. Given her mediumistic talents, can we really believe that Dion did *not* make some sort of contact with her marvellous and lamented teacher? And given the similarities between the two works, can we really believe that Moriarty did *not* have any part in this?

The argument might go that she and he shared the same inner contacts, but that she, being a woman, English, and from a different generation, would focus the light from the Chiefs in a slightly different way. It might also go that Moriarty was in fact the 'world-famous philosopher' in question, rather than Socrates or More. But Dion and Moriarty would point out that none of this is important; that the vital thing was the doctrine itself, however it was received, however it was created, by whomever.

The Cosmic Doctrine is something that the reader either takes to or not. Francis King, a former initiate of the Inner Light in the post-Dion years, felt that there was a great deal of value therein for the Christian occultist; but Ithell Colquhoun, who had met Dion, believed that it was a worthless tome from any esoteric standpoint, and obviously incompatible with the spirit of the Alpha and Omega temple. Either way it is a difficult book, and a far cry indeed from the dreary platitudes of the Spiritualist Guides that were marketed as revelations of world importance.

Dion was very proud of *The Cosmic Doctrine*. It was the best event in her life. This, she felt, would survive long after she was dust. Blavatsky had her *Secret Doctrine* to provide the TS with a core book, a central spark of revelation, but she, Dion, had given the West this tiny gem which fairly rippled with life and light.

Dion was right. The book has indeed survived her. People today buy it and look through it. They look through it not for the philosophies – which are passé even if they are eternal – but for the glimpse they might catch of Dion herself, as if peering into a deep and distorting pool. They look through because, in the long years since her death, a sense of wonder, affection, and even love has grown up around a woman who knew so little of the latter in her final years.

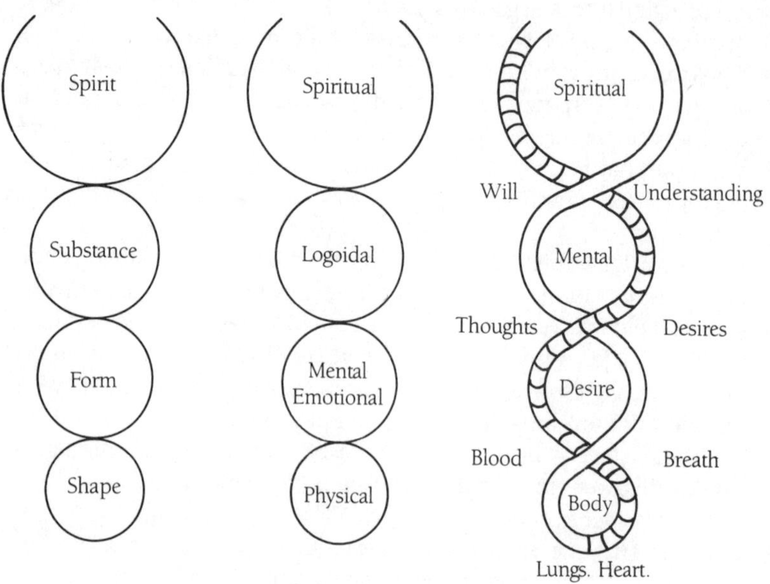

The caduceus twisted into a three-dimensional unit to give Dion Fortune's three primary rings.

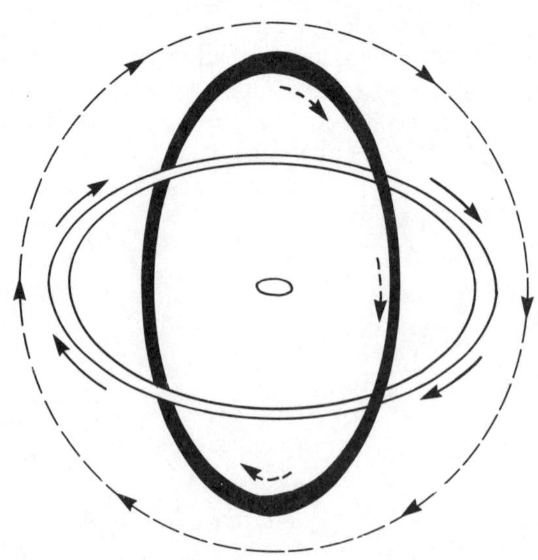

Moriarty's caduceus and the different levels of interpretation

7.

THE INCUBUS, BEAST, AND WINGED BULL

> If those upon whom circumstances force celibacy would rise into the higher air of spiritual activity instead of fretting behind the bars, they would find that they have attained an inner fulfilment, and, being in circuit with the universe, they were no longer incomplete.
>
> Dion Fortune

There is a card in the tarot known as The Lovers. It shows a naked couple on a bare plain, with a mountain peak in the distance. It shows a fiery being in the heavens, who is often described as the Archangel Michael, but who might as well be a Lord of Flame, Melchisedec himself. The man is looking at the woman; the woman looks to the heavens. This is the formula of the priest and priestess, and of human love. Only through woman (the woman within) can man find the higher realms.

The figures have names: the man is Thomas Penry Evans and the woman, of course, is Violet Mary Firth. The empty plain behind is the state of the latter's psyche when the Star in the East, the troubled Krishnamurti, had quietly extinguished himself. In the distance, across emptiness, the desolate mountain peak rises to the heavens. In the card, because of perspective, it rises no higher than the couples' genitals.[1]

The woman is scarcely aware of the man; she is too busy in some converse with Melchisedec. She is probably only aware of him at the periphery of her vision — a disturbance in her consciousness.

This all took place in the year 1927. This was the year that the man appeared who would drop Violet's eyes down from on high and make her become aware that there is — and always will be — Another Way.

She was ready for it, too, if not consciously aware of the fact. If the Light of the World was not about to manifest itself in the world, then the time had come to look for it elsewhere, in some untouchable source. She would find it within herself; she would find her Inner Light. The man, the strange, naked, and barely perceptible man, would help her.

Looking at her writings in *The Occult Review* at this time and noting her various references to the renegade version of Theosophy as propounded by Rudolf Steiner, the founder of the Anthroposophical movement, one can almost see Dion casting around the manifold altars of Christianity in search of something more nourishing to her soul — something that Socrates, Carstairs, and the Chancellor could never provide. To the astonishment of everyone, perhaps even herself, she found exactly what she was looking for. The prophecy embodied in the image of Carstairs was made manifest in a man who really had done bold things in the war, who really was bent on helping his fellow man, and who was earthy, good, strong, dynamic, with a voice like Taliesin and the glow of a real magus. When he came into her life the Christian Mystic Lodge suddenly began to look more and more like the tower of St Michael at Sidestrand: only the smallest of lights remained, while the great and cold waves smashed at the cliffs below, crumbling it away.

Her Christian mysticism did not actually die — it would never do that. But it did retreat. The man she married woke her dormant paganism and drew it, Lazarus-like, to the mouth of the cave, toward the light. This was the man whom she portrayed by images of the winged bull and the sacrificial priest. This was Penry, whom the juniors came to hold in awe and whom they all called — although never to his face — Merl.

Even today, because the rumours of Dion's sexual ambivalence still hang around like an earthbound spirit, people are surprised that she should have made such a catch as Penry. Physically she had qualities which yielded great feminine beauty, even despite the obesity of her last years, but there was never anything warm about her, rarely anything sensual. She could never have played the vamp.

Whenever anyone who knew Dion spoke to me about her marriage they always in some way raised a doubt about the couple ever having shared a bed. That is to say, there was never any obvious warmth between them which would make people take this for granted. And although sex was all-important to Dion, there is the constant impression that actual coitus was distasteful, and indeed rather an inferior mode of making contact with one's partner.

This was partly an attitude of the time among the so-called adepts such as Mrs Besant and Charles Leadbeater, both of whom publicly forswore the necessity of sexual activity. This was something that Great Initiates just did not do. A stainless-steel purity was the prerequisite for the advanced soul. Every neophyte knew that. And many lonely people, taking to occultism as a means of justifying their rather sad lives, took great comfort in this.

Nevertheless, in her young womanhood Dion wrestled with the beast of the libido as much as anyone. She even devised a method of, in effect, 'magical masturbation' to relieve the worst of the tensions engendered by celibacy.

'Next,' she wrote in *The Problem of Purity*, 'visualize the spine as a hollow tube and make a mental picture of your hand encircling it, and then, with this *imaginary* hand, begin to massage the spine with an upward, squeezing action. Supposing you had a length of soft rubber tubing that had become blocked by some sediment, you could get rid of the obstruction and empty the tube by drawing it through your fist, squeezing it as it went, and so pushing the substance it contained on ahead of the constriction in the tube made by the pressure of your fingers. It is the same process that you are to use in imagination on the spine . . . by repeated pushes, gradually working your way up the spine with a stroking action . . .'

As soon as this energy entered the brain, she advised, it must be directed to the intellectual centres in the forehead, where the celibate was then to visualize the famous 'third eye.' This done she had to imagine herself looking out on to the world from a great height; and then she had to choose some philanthropic movement, making a mental picture of the organization at work (she suggested the Save the Children Fund) and projecting the energy that had been dragged up from the base of the spine in a radiant stream on to that little mental picture, willing this energy to be a driving force behind the movement.

Perhaps it worked: the Save the Children Fund still thrives today.

There is nothing very unusual about any of this, for most people in her class in that era were preoccupied with the 'sex question' as they called it. Most people had their own nostrums to cope with their sexual frustrations — using methods that were far more bizarre and punitive than this little technique of Dion's. It would be some time yet before the world discovered that masturbation was in itself an outlet, utterly harmless, and not at all injurious to health.

The concept of 'free love' was bandied about a lot in that era. It was something that appalled Dion. She was all in favour of waiting for the right man, and then making that right man wait until marriage: 'As soon as a woman yields herself to a man in an unsanctified union, she loses caste in his eyes, and as soon as a man asks this sacrifice of a woman to whom he cannot offer the protection of his name, she feels that his love is selfish and his character contains the elements of weakness.' Thus did she condemn the sort of illicit affair that found expression in the ancient British penchant for the 'dirty weekend'.

Dion was a prude. At least by today's lax standards. In the years immediately before her marriage she railed against pre-marital intercourse, against sexual perversions such as masturbation and homosexuality, and brought down fires against those wretches who, having fallen, abort their unborn child.

On the other hand she made a strong plea for clemency towards those women who, having fallen and given birth to an illegitimate child, were nevertheless willing to confront their error and 'come up from the depths'. She could admire this kind of courage. Regardless of a man or woman's crimes, she was willing to forgive all if an honest admission of error was made, and stand by them against the calumnies of the ignorant mob.

Look, she was telling the world in *The Problem of Purity*, it is possible to conquer sin and rise from evil. There are battles to be fought along the way, but they are battles which can be won.

There is so much more in love than desire for the beloved, she tells us. There is so much more in sex than physical passion, she insists. 'Unless love can be experienced in its entirety and beauty it is better forgone' she advises from the depths of her experience.

They are sad words, lonely words, but she goes on to assert that this need not be the case, for love should be offered up as a voluntary sacrifice by the lower self to the higher self, which will bring not only peace but power.

> The magicians of old always invoked their gods with sacrifice, and it is by sacrifice that we invoke the higher powers of the soul; the love that is cast aside may bring the bitterness of regret, but the love that is laid upon the altar of noble living brings a light that is all its own.

And her final injunction to womanhood was to live in such a manner that the noblest soul might seek incarnation through her body and come into the world undefiled.

These are the words of a woman in the grip of some overwhelming epiphany, the sort of exultation that comes to the single and/or the lonely during those infrequent but inevitable moments when it seems that their condition is justified by some divine plan. They are also the words of a woman who was still, in her late thirties, a virgin.

There is a curious thing about her writings in this period: up until that year of 1927 the tone was that of someone far younger than her years. An intelligent but unawakened twenty-one-year-old, say, who was looking at the 'love experience' from the outside, with only a disastrous minimum of personal knowledge; but by 1930, when she wrote *Psychic Self Defence*, she was showing the wisdom and depth of a sixty-year-old, rather than someone only two-thirds that.

The difference was that she was a married woman by this time, and as happy as she was ever likely to be.

One of the dominant aspects of Dion's emotional life was her struggle to come to terms with an inherent mannishness in her personality. She confronts this in several places in her writings, notably in her novels *The Sea Priestess* and *Moon Magic*, when she describes the peculiarly masculine aspects of her heroine's character — aspects which neverthless did not detract from her allure. As neither they should. She was only too aware, alas, of the attraction she had for women of a certain persuasion, and patiently explained that where the leader of a magical group is a woman, then that person will get a lot of unstable people of her own sex abreacting their passions for her. She even noted, with some amusement perhaps, that she had once been accused of being a man in disguise, and that the charge had found believers. It has also been implied that she may have had a lesbian relationship with Maiya Tranchell-Hayes, whom Aleister Crowley accused of having Sapphic tendencies. But there is nothing within her work to indicate that she had any actively lesbian impulses. Dion was aware to a healthy degree that we are all two-sexed beings — an extraordinary concept at that time. She knew that it was part of the Mysteries to look for the woman within the man and the man within the woman. Had anyone dared press her to describe her own orientation she would just have implied that she found more of the opposite sex within herself than most. As she wrote in *The Sea Priestess*: 'But the ancients did not concern themselves with anomalies, but said that the soul was bisexual, and that as one or the other aspect manifested in the world of form, the alternative aspect was latent in the world of the spirit.'

Without doubt, if anyone was to put rumours about the small world of occultism regarding Dion's sexual preferences, it would have been Crowley. He circulated rumours concerning everyone, and some of them took root. The *bête noire* of the Golden Dawn, and the first to release its material to the outer world, he was a real tantrick, as he would have termed those practitioners of Sex Magic. To him the sexual energies and processes represented sources of power that could be tapped. Dion was always happier when coitus was on the Inner Planes, in a manner that made physical intercourse a mere analogue of the real and inward exchanges; but Crowley was one of the great priapics of our time. He would have sex with anyone, male or female, though he evidently drew the line at children and animals, of which he was quite fond.

Present-day Crowleyans, if we may call them that, affirm quite strongly but with no hard evidence that Dion once worked magic with the Great Beast, the Logos of the Aeon. She herself denied ever having met him, which was probably a fib, but the rumours are so persistent that we may as well examine the possibilities.

Much of it, I am sure, can be traced back to the name Loveday. Charles Thomas Loveday was the man with whom Dion was associated during that fell winter in Glastonbury when the Watchers of Avalon first appeared. Born on Hallowe'en in 1874 at 3 Roberts Terrace, South Road, Forest Hill, London, his father was Frederick Loveday, a house agent. This would make Charles forty-eight years old when Lord E first appeared. And this is the Loveday whom Edward Garstin described as being Dion's 'current boyfriend'.

There is no doubt that he was devoted to Dion, and far more uncritical than Olcott was towards his chum Blavatsky. He was the sort of slightly womanish man who tended to be drawn towards strong and large women, with the sort of princely (but inoffensive) mien which gained him the nickname 'his Nibs'. A darling in his own way, as everyone thought, he had the manner and bearing of some spiritualized scoutmaster.

Charles may well have loved Dion. He almost certainly did. When he died in 1948 he arranged to be buried next to her. If they never slept together in their lifetimes, they did so for an eternity after their deaths.

But what has confused the issue is that juniors within the Lodge began to call him, behind his back, 'Raoul'. Now *Raoul* Loveday was one of Crowley's most brilliant pupils. When he first came to the Old Master, as the latter was sometimes mockingly called, Raoul was already in possession of the very essence of magic — or 'magick', as Crowley rather charmingly wrote it. So very young, nevertheless he had 'every gift that a Magus might need'. Raoul's real name was rather more prosaic: he was christened Frederick Charles, and had been born on 3 July 1900, the son of George Loveday, a civil servant. If there was any relationship at all with Dion's scoutmasterish friend, it must have been as uncle and nephew. Raoul — the real Raoul — died in February 1923.

Even so, the rumour that Dion worked with Crowley, or worked some form of Crowleyan magick, has persisted. There is the comment in *Psychic Self Defence*: 'As a young girl, at the commencement of my interest in occultism, I came into touch with an adept whom I soon realized to be on the Left-hand Path, and with whom I soon severed my connection.'

Crowley? Not necessarily. The capital was crawling with black magicians of the self-professed variety, while those who were not were always being accused of being black in any case, by those with grudges or stricter morals. It happened to Dion, too, in later years.

What does seem to cry out from her earlier writings, however, is the probability that at some time before the great revelations in Glastonbury she had had some absolutely disastrous romance with a man whom she believed was not entirely human.

The Secret Chiefs themselves seem to have tried to show some light on her wounds, commenting:

> It may also happen that one who has made contact with the Elementals instead of being obsessed may be mated. Then will the Elemental aspect of his nature be linked to an Elemental and yearn towards that unseen lover who is not of human kind. There is sorrow for such, for they thirst with a thirst which cannot be slaked within the flesh; and to meet their lovers they must issue forth in the etheric form. Much might be said on this subject.

Much indeed. Ithell Colquhoun, taking up the Golden Dawn's teachings on the matter comments:

> Mathers' teaching dealt with sex in another, more recondite manifestation — that of the Elemental spouse. Both he and Wynn Westcott not only believed in the possibility of such a union but must have taught methods by which a partner from praeternatural regions could be attracted . . . While Moina disliked the idea of Elemental mates as much as human ones, she did not doubt the possibility of such, and one wonders how long she continued to resist it in the

> face of what she sincerely believed to be Rosicrucian teaching. She must in the AO have given instructions on such subjects as The Esoteric Philosophy of Love and Marriage if she banned, as too revealing, Dion Fortune's book of this title.

If Dion had known how, she would certainly have attempted to conjure up such a lover. And who can blame her? Lonely, frustrated, the idea of a faery marriage must have held a wondrous attraction. No longer need she wait until the right man arrived: by magic, she could have the one she wanted. No matter that there was no flesh and blood involved: she lived so much in the Otherworld that that was the least of her needs.

It is an intriguing concept, but it was not a faery mating she was looking back upon in 1926/27 when she wrote her first novel, but a very real romance indeed. The novel in question was *The Demon Lover,* an appropriately entitled work on the Sleeping Priestess theme about a wise virgin, Veronica Mainwaring, who leaves a hostile and class-conscious secretarial college and takes up employment with one J. Lucas. She becomes the secretary to, as she slowly learns, a rogue male in a powerful occult fraternity who uses Veronica shamefully, exploits her mediumistic talents in a manner akin to rape, and gains forbidden information. Ultimately Veronica's purity triumphs: her Christianity serves as a shield against his depredations, a barrier against his evil. None of which stopped the prim young maid from falling in love with the young demon, or making him fall for her in return.

'Unless his skin lied,' Dion wrote, 'there was Latin blood in him, and his temperament had the quick liveliness of the South.' In other places she tells us that he was of medium height and lightly built, adding that his skin was olive or perhaps biscuit-coloured. It was in describing his character that she came to touch upon his non-human aspects: 'His source of strength had been his complete freedom from all sense of obligation to his kind, and therefore from scruple or remorse . . . ' And elsewhere: 'You don't feel about things as we do,' Veronica tells him, 'I think you are going a different way.'

The Demon Lover is a first novel. It has some lovely moments and is also quite obviously based upon some very real and raw experiences. Dion was even so bold, within that book, as to describe the headquarters of the mysterious male-only fraternity in such detail that she can only have been describing E. A. Wallis-Budge's house at 48 Bloomsbury Street. It had long been rumoured that a lodge of the Golden Dawn was held in the basement of the British Museum, among some Egyptian antiquities, and, as Budge was the famous curator of the Egyptological departments, *The Demon Lover* goes a little way to either feed the rumour or partly confirm it.

Lucas was based upon a real person: that much is obvious. In her descriptions of the man and his character there is at least a specific experience — a 'love experience' — hidden away behind the narrative. It caused a pain that was not quite expunged by writing *The Demon Lover*, for four years later she returned to the theme in *Psychic Self Defence* where she warned us about 'the pathology of non-human contacts', saying:

> There are many of us who have met people who might well be described as non-human, soulless, in that the ordinary human motives are not operative with them, nor do the ordinary human feelings prompt or inhibit them. We cannot but love them, for they have great charm, but we cannot but dread them as well, for they spread an infinitude of suffering around them. Although seldom deliberately evil, they are singularly detrimental to all with whom they come in contact . . . Gratitude, compassion, good faith, morality and common honesty are utterly foreign to their natures . . . They are not immoral, however, but simply non-moral.

And on and on, repeating the refrain that gratitude is unknown to such a person.

Nowadays we would probably designate such a character as psychopathic, a state which is expressed less by sudden and mindless violence than by complete amorality coupled with sublime charm.

Whoever Justin Lucas was, he had shared a past life with Veronica/Violet in Ancient Rome, and later in Avignon, too, where he had been burnt at the stake. He was a real person who had stimulated great emotions within the heart of the woman who remembered him, but his identity is not important. The Crowleyans will have it that it *was* Raoul, even though their champion was ten years younger; even though he married the bitchy American artist Betty May before he died in Crowley's Abbey at Cefalu, trying to find his True Will but contracting acute enteritis instead; while those who abhor Crowley and venerate Dion will always deny it. The only certainty between the two poles is that at some time before the age of thirty-three, Dion, like most mortal women, loved a man and suffered.

As for the rivalry between the two factions, when all the little assertions and aspersions are cast into the open, like runes, the final divination will be as ambiguous as their separate sexualities. It will be this: Crowley was greater; but Dion will be better.

All of which brings us by labyrinthine paths around and between the speculations on men and non-humans, to the one solid figure in Dion's life. Regardless of how she may or may not have been connected with

Crowley, either or both of the Lovedays, and with the reality behind Justin Lucas. Thomas Penry Evans rose from the hard world of the Welsh valleys and came to be — in the eyes of Dion at least — higher than all of these.

He was born in the Air sign of Libra, on 27 September 1892, at an address simply given as Farmer's Field, Pontardulais, His father was Kercy Evans, who was a shearer in the local tin works; the maiden name of his mother, Elizabeth Ann, was also Evans. He was their first child, being followed shortly after by Raymond, who did not live very long, and by his sister Hazel. Penry was named after the enormously popular Congregationalist preacher who had died in Pontardulais in 1888, but who had been very active in nearby Llanelli. This was presumably his grandfather, but Evans being such a popular name and such preachers having enormous public appeal in that place and that era, the boy might simply have been named after his precursor.

Related or not, Evans the Preacher could not have begun to imagine the strange path that Evans the Magus was about to follow.

Pontardulais was, and is, a nondescript sort of town, with little myth and less history; a sort of void upon the border between Dyfed and West Glamorgan. Later on the family moved to Llanelli where Kercy had been offered promotion in one of the seven tin works established within the town by then, gaining it the title of 'Tinopolis'.

Llanelli was different. The miners here regarded themselves as the Lords of the Working Classes, Kings of the Underground, as they walked home at the end of each shift, the streets loud with the sound of their boots on the cobbles, their eyes glinting behind the masks of dirt.

There was, and is, nothing half-hearted about these men. They were Celts above all and beneath all, an influence which ran through whatever outward form of religion might be practised. Their soul, like any Celtic soul, had a particular universality of its own, life and the world being interpreted in terms of light and shadow, but with a generalism that has never enabled the Celt to achieve military conquest, overseas empires, huge wealth. All was concentrated in this self-pride, expressed through the voice and in the quicksilver nature of their spirit, the clarity and the brilliance of their language becoming their expression. Whatever mask they might assume for living in the world, they maintained the Celtic shadow as a secret background in which to treasure their deepest emotions. This was Penry all over; this was Merlin.

No one is certain what Llanelli means, although the standard interpretation gives 'the sacred enclosure of Elli' who was supposed to have been a princess, or else a long-forgotten saint. Some have tried to equate Elli with Elen, the beautiful Goddess of Light. Still others have suggested that it meant 'the sacred wells of Elli'. Legend has it that an underground stream runs from the town, under the Bristol Channel, to the reputedly cavern-filled world beneath Glastonbury Tor where Dion would hear the Lords of Flame pounding in the darkness.

Lords of Flame? Perhaps it was the tin-miners of Wales she heard. They would say so. Others might take up the theme that it was the tin trade which brought the Arimathean merchant and his luminous nephew over from Palestine in the first place, landing at the then major port at Brean Down before going on to learn the Druid-secrets of the land.

There is yet another secret link in Gwyn ap Nudd, the beautiful and seductive Lord of the Underworld, whose home was said to be in the dell near Stradey Park in Llanelli, and who can also be found, it is said, on that same Tor in Somerset, guarding the dark gate from which the Wild Hunt pours. Either way, through Llanelli and Glastonbury, Merl and Dion were linked by dark and subterranean means.[2]

There is a pattern in it all, somewhere. One which we can only glimpse in part or try to reconstruct during our rational moments. There is a justice too, expressed in a way that is almost a divine joke, though not in any sense a malicious one. For Dion, the granddaughter of a man who made steel, would one day marry the son of a man who cut tin. As is the way of magic, all would be reversed upon the Inner Planes.

In Penry she came hard against something she had long ignored or rejected: the fact that she had been born upon the good earth of Wales, to which she owed a debt that was never repaid in her lifetime. In Penry she met the incarnation of her dark side, for he was the Sacrificial Priest who featured in her last novel, a man who could take life in order to give it, a man who proved that the magical path was not one of Theosophical sweetness or dreary lamb-like platitudes.

In Penry, therefore, she met the quintessence of Welsh manhood, who forced her to recognize and take stock of the dark areas within her own psyche. In a word he had *hwyl* which, like something from the Greater Mysteries, can never be translated. He was also from the south of Wales, which meant he would have been brought up to mock, with varying degrees of sincerity, the supposedly snooty folk from places like Llandudno — the soft folk of the north coast whose manners were genteel to the point of effeteness; exactly as the industrialized communities in the north of England would poke fun at the their indifferent cousins in the south.

Male and female; dark and fair; recognized by the BMA and rejected by the same; south and north; Celt and Anglo-Saxon . . . the pair were doomed from the start. They were meant to be doomed.

No one could understand why Penry had married Dion. He could have had any woman he wanted, some felt — with no small degree of envy. The sort of envy which caused a few of his associates to whisper that he often did. Because of his obvious working-class background, which he made no attempt to hide, the snobbish assumption was made that he chose Dion in order to get on in the world. If nothing else his father, who cut tin-plate, would be deeply impressed by his son marrying a Firth — one of *the* Firths, as was always added. The rumour also went that it was Loveday who had discovered Penry, seen his remarkable qualities, and paid the full cost of his medical studies.

Both speculations are probably untrue. When Penry first qualified as an MD his address was given as Maesycoed, Bynea, Llanelli. It was not until the following year, 1925, that he reappeared in London as House Surgeon and Medical Registrar for Charing Cross Hospital, giving his address as 3 Queensborough Terrace, where he was renting one of the bed-sits. He became Tubercular Officer for East Ham; he became Medical Superintendant for a sanatorium in Hampshire; later still a Tubercular Officer for the Borough of Southwark and the south-east Buckinghamshire area, centred in Slough; all of which took place during the early years of his marriage. Had he married Dion simply to get on in the world he would have left as soon as he got his first post in Charing Cross. He did not: he stayed with her for twelve years; no small time for two such formidable personalities.

The truth is straightforward: Penry married Dion for the magic. And also because, behind all the rows, underneath all the antagonisms, there was a bond between them which was suspiciously like love, in its darker aspect.

Penry, it should be emphasized, was no mere shadow to his wife, as has often been implied. When the Great War started he was one of the first volunteers, being one of those high-spirited young men who looked forward to short conflict and easy victory over an obviously demonic nation. He joined the Artists' Rifles, which was something of an élite corps that had been formed by Lord Leighton and other professional men in 1869, re-forming itself in 1908 to become part of the National Territorial Army as the 28th Battalion of the County of London Regiment (Artists' Rifles). When the King visitsed the trenches, they provided the honour guard. They fought with clean and clinical distinction. In 1947 long, long after Penry had ended all his links with them, they were re-formed once more to become the 21st Special Air Services Regiment (Artists' Rifles) Territorial Army. Penry was no mere soldier slogging away and hoping for a mild wound to take him back to Blighty: he was a professional.

In 1917 it was obvious to the Generals of the British Army that the enemy had a conspicuous advantage in fire-power through the Maxim machine-guns that were being used against the Tommies with devastating and demoralizing effect. Accordingly the Machine-Gun Corps was developed, which Penry promptly joined, finding himself behind one of the tripod-mounted Vickers machine guns, pouring out hundreds of bullets a minute into the advancing lines of German soldiers, taking on the aspect of the Grim Reaper as the corpses piled up.

He served throughout the war, leaving the Army as a Second Leiutenant, the lowest commissioned rank. Like so many before him he must have looked for something in life that would atone for the suffering that he had caused and also ease the pain of the inner wounds that he now carried. The study of medicine was the ideal choice. He would put something back into the world; he would heal and give succour.

All of this meant that he understood life and death in a way that Dion never could. She had done no more by the age of forty than hold a dying rook in her hands[3]; Penry had mown down men by the hundreds and watched them twitch in the mud.

No one will ever know how they met. It may have been through Moriarty, with Penry having attended to his tubercular complaints at some point. It was quite possibly in connection with Dion's work on the fringes of the genuine medical field, Penry deciding, perhaps, to learn something about this newish branch known as psychoanalysis. It may well have been that he was going through his own Christian mystical phase to purge his nightmares of the war.

They were married on 7 April 1927 at Paddington Register Office. Kercy Evans' profession was given as tin-plate manufacturer, which indicates that he had got in to the industry by this time, while Arthur Firth was still describing himself as a solicitor, although he had long since ceased to practise. Dion's father was one of the witnesses; Penry's sister Hazel, who by this time was employed as a maid at 3 Queensborough Terrace while studying as a nurse, was the other. Penry gives his rank as a Member of the Royal College of Surgeons, while Dion, the Priestess of the Age, leaves her space a blank. The Priestess of the Age also shows a very lovely and very human touch by lying about her age, giving it as thirty-five and thus only one year older than her husband, instead of thirty-six as it really was.

No white wedding here: perhaps they both felt they were a bit past it.

The only surviving photograph of them together is a wedding photograph, taken at the Chalice Orchard, on what was presumably their honeymoon. There is an almost roguish look on Penry's face, as though he had made some *sotto voce* joke while the cameraman adjusted his focus. Dion, standing at his side but a little way apart, tries hard to be amused. There are spring daisies at her feet and a scattering of flowers, but the tree behind them looks dead.

The mating of an occultist, she wrote at this point, was so much more than an ordinary mating; which is true enough, but it is also often much less, too. Something is invariably sacrificed from one of the levels — physical, mental, emotional or spiritual — to achieve the tension necessary between priest and priestess in magical work. It is not often a deliberate sacrifice: the magician has little choice in the matter. Often, as with Moina and McGregor, it is the sexual aspect of their relationship which is jettisoned — at least upon the Outer Plane. People who are perfectly suited as mates can rarely work great magic together. Likewise in the field of art and literature. The most interesting artists are those who are, as Dion would put it, 'riding the whirlwind'.

She described the four levels as the Four Harmonies, namely:

The Material Harmony: in which duty is the key-note, a duty which can only be achieved through diligence, endurance, and self-sacrifice. They are Victorian values these. The modern generations cannot help but add a sexual gloss to this, and bring to mind all those supine ladies who survived intercourse by setting their thoughts upon England.

The Emotional Harmony, based upon a clear sense of justice, which causes each to face their own errors, admit them frankly and honestly, and co-operate in their redemption. This would give patience, and compassion for each other's weaknesses. (Evidently they had been rowing.)

The Intellectual Harmony, based upon the realization that it is impossible to force the growth of a soul, either by argument or admonition. There must be respect for differing viewpoints. This, indeed, was the plane on which Dion was happiest, for here was developed 'the friendship of marriage, which is a wonderful and beautiful expansion of its emotional aspect, wherein is found the aspect of the marriage relationship which is developed when two souls of intellectual capacity are mated.' Namely herself and Penry. This is the aspect on which she lavishes attention, asserting that an important aspect of this is courtesy, which tempers all relationships, 'and is the lubricant of life.' Courtesy restrains impatience, she tells us; gives the expression of disagreement such a form that it creates the minimum of reaction; observes the minor amenities of life which 'though trivial in themselves, indicate an attitude of mind, and are interpreted as such by the subconscious mind of another'.

And the fourth harmony, *The Spiritual Harmony*, was not very much described at all, being expressed in an attitude towards love 'which makes of its activities ceremonial sacraments'. It was the most important aspect, she knew, but unless the lower three achieved some sort of harmony then it would never function.

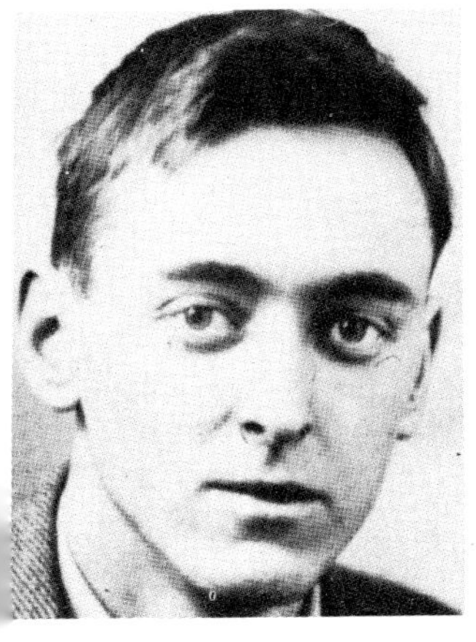

Raoul Loveday

Penry and Violet Evans

Christian Mystic Lodge

OF THE THEOSOPHICAL SOCIETY.

President : DION FORTUNE (Miss VIOLET M. FIRTH),
3 Queensborough Terrace, Bayswater, W.2.

PUBLIC LECTURES— Mondays at 5.30 and 8.15, the latter being a study group conducted by the President.

Read the Transactions of the Lodge, price **3d.** or **3/-** per annum post free, a monthly magazine dealing with ESOTERIC CHRISTIANITY. Editor: DION FORTUNE.

Sane Occultism, Independent Outlook, Active Practical Work. Specimen copy and syllabus of lectures free. Apply—*Secretary*.

COMMUNITY OF THE INNER LIGHT

Warden - - DION FORTUNE.

The Community of the Inner Light is a fraternity whose purpose it is to pursue the study of Mysticism and Esoteric Science. Its ideals are Christian and its methods are Western.

It maintains a Lecture Centre and Library in London at 3 Queensborough Terrace, Bayswater. Public lectures are given on Mondays at 8.15 p.m. by Dion Fortune throughout each term. Syllabus on application. Admission to all lectures and study groups is free, all contributions being voluntary.

THE CHALICE ORCHARD CLUB, Glastonbury, Somerset, is maintained as a hostel and pilgrimage centre. It is open from Whitsuntide to Michaelmas. Terms from £2 12s. 6d. a week.

"THE INNER LIGHT." Edited by Dion Fortune. A monthly magazine devoted to Mystical Christianity, Esoteric Science, and the Psychology of Super-consciousness. Price 6d. 6s. 6d. per annum, post free. Specimen copy sent free on request.

BOOKS BY DION FORTUNE

"Esoteric Philosophy of Love and Marriage." Rider. 3s. 6d.

"Secrets of Dr. Taverner." Fiction. Noel Douglas. A Study in Esoteric Medicine. Cheap edition, 2s. 6d.

"The Demon Lover." Fiction. Noel Douglas. A Study in the abuse of Occult Power. Cheap edition, 2s. 6d.

Syllabus of the lectures, tariff of Chalice Orchard Club, and all information may be obtained from the Secretary, 3 Queensborough Terrace, Bayswater, W. 2. Tel. Park 7217.

Two advertisements which appeared in *The Occult Review*:
top — before Dion's marriage; bottom — following her marriage.

Lady Caillard

The Belfry, West Halkin Street

\nne Mower White — the second Mrs Penry Evans

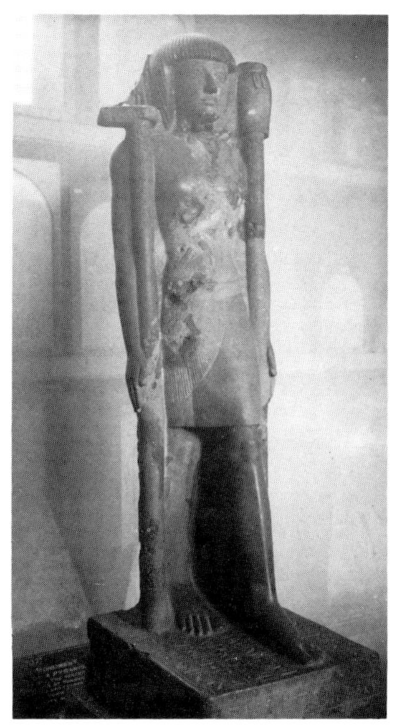

Kha'm-uast

Christine Campbell Thomson and 'Dair' Hartley, *c.* 1950

Lord Eldon

She describes the problems that can occur when partners begin to drift apart through a failure of one or both to understand these harmonics. She urges that we should never forget that overcoming imperfections is the essence of the Path, that each must look upon the faults of the other as sicknesses to be healed, and that tolerance and forgiveness should always be ready. Think mercifully of each other, she wrote, no doubt after another of their murderous rows; let each partner realize that they are bound in a mutual destiny, she pleaded, when she sensed that her mage might one day leave her. And she concluded with this final injunction, which was written not for posterity, not for the illuminations of her pupils or readers but simply and directly to Merl:

'There are two vital things in married life: love of each other and dedication to God's service. Let each adhere to these, even if the companion be lost sight of in the darkness, and they will surely find they are not far apart when the light dawns once more.'

This was 1933. She knew she was losing him.

Regardless of whichever Harmony was lacking in the Evans' marriage, there was abundant tension. As priest and priestess they were superb. As man and wife they fought with an apocalyptic intensity.

As always Dion looked for the magical explanation for this rather than seeing it as the sort of mismatch that mortals make. To her, a lot of it was to do with her inability to work with the Element of Air, for which she had little natural affinity.

> The Element of Air, as all occultists know, is a very tricky element to deal with. More initiates turn off the Path in the Grade of Air than in any other, and it is rare to see a Ritual of Air worked without something being dropped or knocked over. It is a quarrelsome element; when it is being worked, the operators are apt to bicker and squabble. It is also intimately associated with sex, as is revealed by its symbolism . . .

Penry, the Libran, would have been able to fan her own Sagittarian flames — or else blow them out. When she described an Air Ritual that was worked in 3 Queensborough Terrace she mentions how two of the principal officers, husband and wife, helped to maintain the contentious reputation of that element by having a 'family jar' in the middle of the proceedings. It is apparent that she is describing themselves.

For the next two weeks she lived amid a cataclysm of crockery. She smashed her way through two entire tea-sets and all the mantelpiece ornaments. The ornaments, as if gripped by a poltergeist, just fell off the mantelpiece one by one 'of their own accord'. She actually saw two of them do it. The smashing continued, until she was reduced to a tin mug and a tooth glass. She knew that the solution was to get into some sort of rapport with the Sylphs but she was in London at that time, and the Elemental contacts, with the exception of Fire, cannot really be worked in a city.

Finally, she went to Glastonbury, where she found herself on the Tor on a day of bright sun and high wind.

> The air seemed full of silver sparkles, which is always a sign that the veil is thin. There was no one present save some friends who were sympathetic. I faced into the wind and raised my arms in invocation. Suddenly we saw below us a figure bursting through hedges and leaping ditches and running wildly toward us . . . and when he joined us he told us that he had felt the sudden rush of power while in the valley and on an overpowering impulse started for the hill-top. Then all of us without any suggestion of leadership, began the Dance of the Elements, whirling like dervishes upon that hill-top. Fortunately nobody was about, but I do not know that it would have made very much difference if they had been, for we were caught up out of ourselves and the air seemed full of rushing golden flames, lying level in the wind. For days afterwards we seemed charged with elemental energy by that extraordinary dance.

She had never known a more glorious experience. For her, that peculiar sunwise dance, revolving on her own axis as she went, induced the divine inebriation of the Mysteries. After that there was no more smashing of crockery. After that, too, she may have come to terms with Merl's own elemental qualities a bit better.

That hill-top will reappear later on. It became as important to her as any living person, and was more enduring in her life and lives than even Penry. It was here, through the moon-gate, just above the orchard that had once been surrounded by a ring of oaks, that she gained access to the secret heart of Britain, and the spirit of the Goddess in her darkest and loveliest aspects.

8.
THE MOON AND THE MATED WOMAN

> Now I cannot tell what I said to the Moon, or what the Moon said to me, but all the same, I got to know her very well. She ruled over a kingdom that was neither material nor spiritual, but a strange moon-kingdom of her own. In it moved tides — ebbing, flowing, slack water, high water, never ceasing always on the move, and these tides affected our lives. They affected birth and death and all the processes of the body. They affected the mating of animals, and the growth of vegetation, and the insidious workings of disease . . . All these things I got by communing with the Moon.
>
> Dion Fortune

Things began to change from 1927 onward. The World Teacher may have renounced his mission, and Dion may have renounced her earlier ideas about the solitary life and the necessity of wrestling with the beasts of her own thwarted sexuality, but on another infinitely more trivial yet vitally important level something else had begun to change, too. The regular advertisement she had placed in the back of *The Occult Review* had begun to take on a different form.

Before her marriage her group was described as the Christian Mystic Lodge of the Theosophical Society, and jostled for space with the Brotherhood of Light in Penge, and enticements for the talismanic jewellery of W. T. Pavitt of Hanover Square. It stated that the President, Dion Fortune, would be giving public lectures on Monday at 5.30 and 8.15, and that the latter was a study group conducted by the President herself. The transactions of the lodge were also for sale at 3s (15p) per annum post free, and these were in the form of a monthly magazine dealing with Esoteric Christianity.

A year after her marriage, however, the group had become the Community of the Inner Light, and Dion was now the Warden. It was now seen as 'a fraternity whose purpose it is to pursue the study of Mysticism and Esoteric Science. Its ideals are Christian and its methods are Western. It maintains a Lecture Centre and Library in London . . . Public lectures are given on Mondays at 8.15 pm by Dion Fortune throughout each term.'

Note the new title. The Christian aspects which had been emphasized in large letters and heavy print in preceding advertisements were less prominent now. This was probably due to the increasing influence of Merl, as he must now be called. If anyone had ever thrilled to what Crowley called 'the lissome lust of light' from the goat-footed one it was he. His force, his energy, deflected the direction of the lodge. Although the ideals were still essentially Christian, the power that was now being tapped took on a more Celtic tone — the sort of Celticism that could happily absorb and transmit its own variants of the Lamb and the Goat.

Of the very few lectures that Merl gave within 3 QT there was a series of four given in 1933 on 'The Four Elements', 'The Celtic Gnosis', 'The Christ Within', followed and completed by his own favourite theme 'The Pan Within'. Thanks to him the Community became very close in spirit during these early years to the Hermetic Society of Anna Kingsford, which espoused an occultism based upon Greek and Christian inclinations.

The heyday of Dion's pagan period was still a few years ahead yet, though, for 3 QT, as they all called the Queensborough Terrace headquarters for convenience sake, was still being established. There was much work to be done.

The house had been bought in the first place by Charles Loveday whose father had left him some properties in London. Loveday, whose Magical Motto was *Amor Vincit Omnia*, as might be imagined, knew that if his friend's revelations were to make any impact upon the world then a steady base was needed, a permanent temple.

It became, very quickly, a real community. The basement contained the kitchen and the communal breakfast room. The ground floor had the administrative offices where AVO attended to such matters as the correspondence and the production of the magazine. The first floor had two large rooms that were used for rituals and public lectures, and the floor above was where the Evans lived. For outsiders there were two furnished guest rooms: a large double room at 3½ guineas (£3.68) per week, or 5 guineas (£5.25) for two; plus a small single room at 2½ guineas (£2.63) per week. These charges included everything except gas, coal, and personal laundry. There was a choice of vegetarian or ordinary diet. Dion chose the former. Merl ate meat.

Secure in this foundation, which had been bought in early 1924, and safe within a marriage to a professional man, Dion began to cast around for pupils now that she had jettisoned the Theosophical Society and knew that the Golden Dawn was about to do likewise to her.

In October 1927 she gave a series of five lectures: 'The Inner Light of the Higher Self', 'The Path to the Inner Light', 'The Work of the Inner Light in the World of Man', 'Preparation for the Dawning of the Inner Light', and 'Dedication to the Service of the Inner Light'. On top of that, on 16 October, she lectured and presumably demonstrated her mediumship at the Spiritualist Church, Grotian Hall, Wigmore Street, as well as at the Spiritualist Mission, 13 Pembridge Place, in Bayswater.

She herself disliked Spiritualism and regarded it as an essentially inferior art, subject to great error. In the crudest of senses the Spiritualist medium was 'taken over' by any old entity — usually a shell — which happened to approach the earth-sphere. The poor medium often attracted spirits of most questionable integrity, and even the bright spirits often found their messages distorted by the dense matter around, much as light is distorted when passing through impure glass. Her method, in contrast, was to 'rise up on the planes', taking her consciousness beyond the earth sphere and closer to the pure, free levels of the Masters.

She was not at all surprised to find her little group taking root and expanding. Initially they had printed 500 copies of their magazine and stacked them up high on the altar in their Sanctuary, whereupon they said a prayer of consecration over them and sent them out into the world. They sold out within a fortnight, and had to put the tattered stencils back into the duplicator to try and coax out a few more impressions for the interested enquirers.

This 'prayer of consecration' sounds innocuous enough, but what she was really doing was magnetizing the papers in the occult sense, creating a link between her and the readers, seeking to pull them in toward her. It is a common enough practice in the magical world even today — especially today. There was also the silly rumour that at the public lectures Dion would try to hypnotize the more affluent members into putting more money into the collection plate, kept near the door. Dion would not have done this even if she had known how; it was just a private joke between her and her associates which escaped into the world at large.

Which is not to say that she was lacking in hypnotic qualities. Far from it. From the moment the enquirer entered 3 QT between the two columns which formed the porch, and which Dion used like the symbolic Pylon Gate to the Otherworld — from that moment he knew that he was in an entirely 'different' place. 3 QT itself had an almost feline quality in those early days, the sort of quality a cat might show in contact with dead bodies and dead souls, bristling stiff-tailed with a sort of erotic delight, a passion consumed within itself by some sublime dream.

It is said that magical rituals attract entities from the Otherworld like moths to a flame. No less so do they attract people. On Monday evenings upward of thirty people would cram into the larger of the two rooms and sit spellbound while this tall and handsome woman would walk up and down before them, talking in her resonant, accentless voice, clad in bright red or blue kaftans which contrasted so nicely with the drabness of the fashions during this, the time of the Depression. They could not fail to be enchanted by this sorceress who was locked within her mystic house.

Those who came back for more were left in no doubt that what went on within her temple was Magic, and that far more was involved than mere philosophy and the sort of anaemic meditations that would have been practised within the Theosophical Society. Two types of ritual were worked within 3 QT: initiation and evocation. In the former the candidate would be put in touch with certain forces; in the latter, forces of different types were contacted, concentrated, and then used for whatever purpose may be in hand. The initiation ceremonies were performed for the purpose of putting the candidate in touch with the group-mind of the occult tradition on the Inner Planes which, in the Western tradition to which Dion belonged, was known as the College of the Illuminati.

Of course, without the psychic perceptions neither kind of ceremony would be worth very much at all. Without some talent for vision it would all be play-acting. 'But there is a technique,' she added, 'by which most people of reasonably good intellectual capacity can be rendered sufficiently psychic for ceremonial purposes.'

The rituals were always enacted in dim light because, she explained, bright light disperses the subtle forces, while it is also much easier to concentrate in dim light. This dim light is rendered even dimmer by dense clouds of incense, usually frankincense, which is supposed to assist the formation of the astral forms.

The altar was in the shape of a double-cube of the height of the solar plexus of a six-foot man. This was always placed at the centre of the temple — which in itself represented the universe and the soul of man. The symbols of the altar and the colour of the altar-cloth were changed according to the rite being worked. There was also always a light on the altar that was lit at the beginning of the ceremony and extinguished at the end.

The senior officers sat on a dais, in a row, across the eastern end of the room; the working officers had different positions on the floor according to the rite being worked, they being channels for the cosmic forces they represented.

The opening of the lodge was done by walking round and round in a circle chanting, building up a wall of psychic force. 'The first round is easy enough,' she wrote, 'but the second and subsequent rounds, as the power gathers, make one feel exactly as if one were wading in fast-running water, getting gradually deeper. It is no easy matter to keep one's feet where there is a good head of power in the lodge, and one will often see people who are treading the magic circle sway as if they were drunk . . .'

There was always an officer in the west, facing the magus across the altar, and to the psychic vision a line of power would be discernible, 'like a broad band of light' stretching between these two magi, while all around the working place where the magic circle had been trodden at the start, another line of psychic force lay like a rapidly-running band-saw.

The real heart of the rite lay in the next phase, in which the cosmic entity or entities would be invoked, who were the *real* priests of the rite. They would manifest in the astral forms constructed for them and interact with the officers in a piece of team-work between the visible and invisible worlds. 'No rite is effectual unless these invisible beings are present', she stated. 'It is the knowledge of who they are and how their presence is obtained which constitute the real secrets of a degree.'

There it lay, the true centre of magic. A centre which had been buried by decades of psychobabble, obscured by the fear of public ridicule. Ceremonial magic is really a highly developed form of seance, the effect of which is to develop extraordinarily dynamic personalities.

'There is no mistaking a trained ritualist. He is like an electric battery of psychic force.'

There was no mistaking Dion or Penry. No mistaking at all.

Loveday played his part in all this too. In terms of getting the Fraternity properly launched in the outer world he played a greater part than anyone. Having a responsible position in London Tramways he had great talents for organization and administration, as well as the funds to make it all possible. Although he had no real penchant for anything which strayed very far from the Narrow Gate of his own Christian vision, he had psychic talents of his own, and it was he who started the series in the magazine called 'Words of the Masters'.

Alas, well-meaning and inspired as he may have felt, the Masters as heard by AVO were rather dismal, full of peace and platitude, uttering nothing that could stretch the mind or spirit in any way. There is no doubting his sincerity, but the sad truth was that as mediator he was never in the same class as his friend. After a short time this feature was quietly withdrawn from the new issues. Loveday knew his limitations; he could only shine with the brilliance for which he was built, in the direction he happened to have been pointed since birth.

In contrast was a piece that was surely received by Dion herself, and based upon a diagram about the Rays.

'Think of the Rays,' she advised, 'as successive beams of light shining out as the Logoidal Consciousness turns upon itself, and you will conceive them as successive manifestations. So you get the three primary and four secondary Rays . . .'

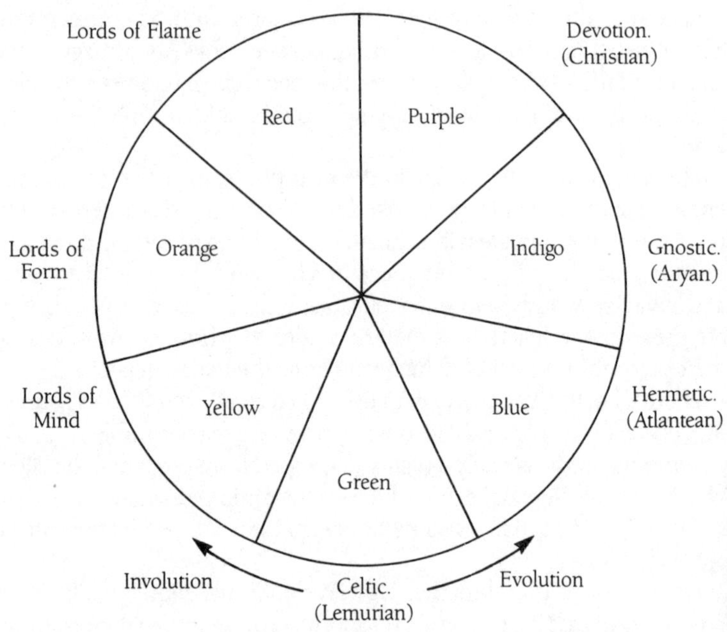

Diagram of the Rays

The clue to the Rays was in looking upon them as touching manifestation in an arc, not in a straight line — an arc with the Green Ray in its centre. The Red Ray of personal power is on the involutionary side, balanced by the Purple Ray of meekness, compassion, and spiritual power. The Orange and Yellow Rays are balanced by the Indigo and the Blue respectively, while in the Green Ray the involutionary and evolutionary aspects meet.

The Green Ray would become very important to Dion, although for a long time she was afraid of it. It is the Ray of Ancient Greece and also the Celtic Ray, for the twain are profoundly connected.

> On the Green Ray — the Celtic nature Ray — you will find the connection with the Purple Ray through the Celtic Saints, such as

> St Bride, St Columba, and many others. You will also find the link with the Hermetic Tradition also, through the Mage Merlin, who is very important, and is the Master of the Celtic Ray in these islands.

Remember that this was not Dion writing, even if it was coloured by her style. It is one of the Masters speaking through her.

Small wonder that in this refreshing blend of philosophy and practice, all expressed through a disarming candour and with an admirable directness, 3 QT had a steady stream of candidates.

Many people found that they could not attend the study groups, so by 1930 correspondence courses were arranged. No charge was made except for a small fee to cover the cost of producing the papers. Any contributions made towards the expenses of the centre were entirely voluntary. There was also an Associate Membership for those who, for various reasons, were unable to enrol in the Fraternity but were interested in its work. This cost them 10s 6d (53p) per annum and gave them five priviledges: a) they would receive the Inner Light magazine each month; b) they could enrol in the study classes; c) they could attend certain meetings not open to the public; d) they were allowed access to certain sections of the inner library; e) they received the annual report.

Those who chose to become full members of the lodge were first subjected to a study course that related, roughly, to Malkuth on the Tree of Life. This last nine months, the traditional gestation period in magical groups. It consisted of basic occult teachings, the reading of recommended texts (namely all of Dion's) and ground-work on *The Cosmic Doctrine*. At this time it was not yet a completed book but duplicated chapters which were handed out one at a time when students had proved that they understood the previous chapters.

The second part of the course was run by Edward Maltby, an old Etonian and former officer in the Royal Corps of Signals, who married Merl's sister, Hazel. Teddy, as they called him, had a real talent for magic as well as a typically military style of delivery. He taught basic visualization work, meditations, information on the planets and the occult anatomy of man; breathing techniques, esoteric histories, and basic Qabbalistic knowledge.

These first two parts of the study course were, by and large, theoretical, and corresponded to Malkuth and Yesod. It was only on the next level, at the sphere of Hod, or Mercury, that the student was allowed to participate in ritual work.

It is evident that not all of them would have stayed the course, which would cause little regret to any of the seniors. Anyone who wanted to practise magic — real magic — would have to work for it in harder and stranger ways than they had ever worked before. That much never changes.

Despite this it was clear very early on that some members of the original Christian Mystic Lodge were not too happy with the way things were developing, and had little enthusiasm and less talent for the more stringent aspects of the study courses. At Loveday's urging a group was organized 'for those who desire to follow the Mystic Way and study the esoteric Christian Tradition.' It is ironic that this, which had been the prime impulse during the pre-Merl days, was now just a side-issue.

The Guild of the Master Jesus, as it was called, had its true genesis in one sense in that solitary candle in the lonely tower on that Norfolk cliff, when she, 'a pagan', had found a spark of light within the outer darkness. It took her back, too, to the very first contact she had made during her days as an analyst, when the Master Jesus and Rakoczi had burst into her psyche. No doubt she felt that the time had come when she personally could take her leave of the Compassionate One and exercise her true bent at last. And so a group was formed within her group that would retain and foster this contact. Loveday, who had little interest in her increasingly pagan inclinations, made this into his own child.

The Guild offered 'adoration and service to Our Lord, and seeks to know Him as the Risen Christ, the Unseen Companion of the Heart, the Master of Love and Compassion, the Great Initiator of the West.'

This was Loveday writing, given his full head. It was what he had always wanted; the ideal compromise.

At the Sunday services held at 11 a.m. the Mystic Repast was celebrated, to which all were welcome — members, associates, or public. Its ministrants made no claims to Apostolic Succession but served, at its altar, in a spirit of devotion. Both men and women were eligible for this office.

What was performed was a simple variation on the Mass, but with deliberately magical overtones, and all preceded by a most potent prayer which had been given to the Guild by the Masters themselves:

> Prepare us O Lord, to drink of the living waters of Life, soon to be made manifest unto us; open our eyes that we may see, and our hearts that we may understand. Make the way plain, O Lord, that we fail not in Thy service.
>
> May we be a channel whereby Thy Holy Ones may approach the World. May we be the centre of radiation of Thy power. Teach us to travel light, as do all who travel upon the path; to give ourselves entirely to Thy service; to attune ourselves to Thy will; to suffer gladly for Thy sake; to play down the small personal life into the great Cosmic Life, and to love with the love of God.

This prayer was a means of 'bringing the soul to its knees' as Loveday thought, inducing a sense of humility and helplessness — both of which are prerequisites before the worshipper can truly begin upon the Path. It also had a hidden significance: the Unseen Companion of the Heart, the Living Christ, was really an invocation of the initiate who seeks his Master in the Hidden Church of the Holy Graal, for within the Guild it was the risen Christ who was adored, not the slain Christ. It was this risen Christ who would come to meet the communicants upon the Inner Planes, who was the Unseen Companion with whom the initiate sought contact.

There is a sadness about it all, somehow. An appeal to the lonely and the hurt who made their way to this highly unorthodox chapel down an undistinguished street in a lonely City on a Sunday morning.[1]

It was Loveday's gem. It was also a dumping ground. Privately Dion used it as a place to put all those earnest but rather dim souls who were unable to cope with the intellectual demands and self-discipline needed for the full magical curriculum, yet who would not simply go away.

This period of 1927-33 was probably the best time in her odd and pressured adult life. She was married, whatever the likelihood of success, to a man that all women seemed to admire; she was held in awe by very many people; her books were translated into numerous languages; she was known about town; she had her contact with the Otherworld and was making great magical strides; she had 3 QT and a Pilgrimage Centre at Glastonbury — of which more later; she was working by stages on her masterpiece *The Mystical Qabalah* and had completed *Psychic Self Defence*, which she knew (if no one else did) would become one of the most unusual books ever written; and she had started to touch upon the Green Ray magic which had hitherto scared her.

Gradually she began to enter the Green Ray as cautiously as Violet, her former self, had once dipped her toes into the cold waters of Llandudno Bay. Though she may have shivered at first, she would one day learn to plunge head first and explore the different world below. In 1930 she was warning against the glamour of the Green Ray, and the danger that a person could very well be drawn into the Otherworld for all time in a manner that was quite different from mere death. But in the years following she became more and more bold.

The contact which helped her in this respect was Lord E. They were all forced to call him this by now, for Dion forbade the mention of his full name within the lodge. She also suggested the title The Un-named Master, or the UM, in order to protect her Chief's identity. Odd as it might seem, Erskine/More was intimately bound with the Green Ray workings, although these were considerably more decorous and staid in the inter-war years than they would be today.

She'e was probably encouraged to do so by the role of Merl within her life. As a young and lonely woman, yearning for the sort of mating that no man could provide, the possibility of some faery love would have a wicked attraction. Were that achieved, then she feared, like so many people throughout folk-lore, that she would simply disappear from the face of the earth, into some world of perpetual youth and eternal stasis. But with her man behind her, tying her firmly to the everyday scene, she could go exploring in deeper waters than she had yet dared.

We can almost give a list of what she was like at this time. It is a list given in Robert Oinstein's *The Psychology of Consciousness*, describing the qualities of yang and yin, the bright male and dark female spirits, the left- and right-hand spheres of the brain, the sun and the moon, Merl and Dion. The list is not doctored, the parallels not forced. Those who knew both characters at this time confirm that each really was as 'specialized' as the other. They really were priest and priestess functioning as a single unit, but without losing their unique identities.

Day	Night
Time, History	Eternity, Timlessness
Intellectual	Sensuous
Explicit	Tacit
Analytic	Gestalt
Lineal	Nonlineal
Sequential	Simultaneous
Focal	Diffuse
Intellectual	Intuitive
Causal	Synchronicity
Argument	Experience[2]

It sums them up exactly.

Needless to say, Merl was not the only man in 3 QT at this point. There was William Knowles Creasy who had progressed to the grade of Adeptus Minor before angering Dion over some now forgotten issue to such an extent that she almost ejected him from the lodge. He only redeemed himself from perpetual obscurity by working his way back up the grades again from the beginning. Dion, who understood the quality of dedication, was willing to forgive very many things for qualities o that sort. Later, Creasy was to become one of the executors of her estate

There was Victor Yorke, whose approach was essentially mystical and who was so much in the grip of the gods that he wrote in the sort o purple and pompous prose that is the sure sign of a man having mad his first contact. When the gods first start to speak to a person, the are *always* pompous. Later on, as the mediator gains more wisdom and maturity, the tone becomes more natural. Yorke did not last long, but during his time at 3 QT he was something of the poor man's AE, contributing to the 'Inner Light' with articles of a 'Celticky Twilight' nature.

There was that curious little man Ernest Butler, who had been advised while in India to look for 'the lady with the roses'. The woman who so advised him was a Theosophist, at Adyar, who felt that the TS was not for him, and whose psychism gave him this image to dwell upon. Later he found the Rose Lady at the foot of Glastonbury Tor where Dion, arms full of them, looked at this stranger on his bicycle and said: 'I've been waiting for you.'

A wise and fearless man, Butler had the reputation of being a superb magician, a real priest. It was said that he left the Fraternity because Dion objected to him continuing as a Spiritualist medium, but it was also because he had had a vision of his own, of Anubis carrying the figure of Christ. It was this that made him feel quite sure — and Dion agreed — that his destiny lay elsewhere. He was one of those who, having made the Melchisedec contact, went on to find Chiefs of his own. More, Carstairs, Socrates, meant little to him, although he respected their wisdom and their power enormously.

W. E. Butler, as he is better known to the world through his books, was a great magus. Nevertheless his parting did not hurt Dion as much as it would have done in later years, because she still had Merl. No matter that their marriage was often under strain, no matter that she had a sense of doom about it, he was at least the best magician she had ever known and he was *there*, within 3 QT, while it lasted. He brought out her qualities and helped to stabilize them. He saw her as Priestess of the Moon and so she became just that.

She became a matrix for fantasy and dreams, a container and holder of life's energies. As Moon Priestess she represented the collective of the lodge and her race, on outer and inner levels. Her magic was based upon the formulae of the Child — that child seen upon the horse in the card known as The Sun. It is this childlike (but not childish) quality which can make magic work, which can control and use the massive animal energies beneath and — literally — between the legs.

All of Dion's sensuality was inward, on magical levels, through the realms of fantasy and imagination; it triumphed over abstract thinking and rationalism, and permitted a greater openness to the intangible, to the Otherworld. At best this let her into new and brighter paths; at worst it took her into dark and primitive realms. Had she carried on without Merl or some suitable priest to balance her out, she would have lost all connection with reality. And she certainly did, though not for some years.

In 1932 she reached what she felt was something of a new direction in her life. *The Mystical Qabalah* was well under way, the Fraternity was on a solid financial footing, and Dion's appeals for money to build a Sanctuary in the Chalice Orchard had raised £113 toward the £150 needed to finish and equip it. She had published *Through the Gates of Death* under the Inner Light's own imprint and must have felt that her own Christianity had been pushed, if not behind her, at least to one side. In many ways she was approaching the peak of her powers then, for she took the unusual step of publishing an excerpt from her Magical Diaries, dating back to Sunday, 1 June 1930, 8.20 to 8.45 a.m.

Seated in Egyptian god attitude facing south-east. Commenced meditation by drawing astral circle. Drew it rapidly and easily and with power. Turning with almost imperceptible quickness to unwind the usual kink of the silver cord in the north-east. Projected astral body to centre of circle, faced it to the east, and invoked God Names of Central Pillar. Clear projection. Consciousness very definitely centered in astral body. Formulated path to a certain astral temple Bright sunshine. Astral body appeared nude. Moved with rapid sweeping dancing motion up path and entered robing room. Refused to robe in usual black robe, so compromised on a white robe with striped head-dress. Astral body swooping and soaring like a bird, very full of vitality.

Outside on path again. Sunshine very bright. Astral body sweeping onwards in strong flight. Bright sunlight on green grass. Grey walls warm with sun. Self in astral body enters temple. Takes seat on stone block, facing east. Did not experience any of the usual difficulty in turning. Consciousness very definitely located in astral body. All sense of physical body lost.

Experienced the sensation of rising in the air while seated on stone block. Went through the roof of building into bright sunlight. Continued to rise rapidly, passing clouds, then saw a sea of clouds below me bathed in sunlight.

Sky began to darken to indigo. Saw crescent moon, very large and bright. Knew I was entering the sphere of Yesod. Determined to push on as the going seemed to be exceptionally good. Saw the Sun of Tiphereth in an area of deep golden sky, like the drop curtain of a theatre, whereas the Moon of Yesod had been real.

Continued to rise on the central Pillar, with no sense of strain but a feeling of breathless rapidity, wondering where I was going next. Borne on as it were, not flying by will power. Made for Kether as the going seemed good, saw Daath below me.

Passed through a sphere in which I saw shadowy angel forms with the traditional harps sitting on clouds all around me. Very misty. Heard snatches of a great choir chanting. Entered a sphere of blinding white light which I believed to be Kether. Could not see or feel anything. Had not even got an astral form. Just a point of consciousness without qualities, bathed in white light. Had some sense of the retention of individualty as a single spark of essential life. No memories, no qualities, thoughts or aims. However, managed to hold to the idea of the experiment. Saw the veils of Negative Existence behind Kether as the darkness of a starless night stretching to infinity.

I was suddenly turned about, facing the opposite way to which I had come. Previously I had looked towards the Tree, as if gazing at a picture of it, so that Geburah was on my left. I found myself backed into it, and expanded to an enormous size, a towering cosmic figure. Nude, Hermaphroditic, powerful, a golden buff colour. The figure was the full size of the Tree. Its feet were planted on the bluish globe of the earth, seen through the clouds. The three Supernal Sephiroth were about the head, but not really in it. Geburah was in the right shoulder and Chesed in the left. The hands gripped Hod and Netzach. Tiphereth was not clearly formulated, but Yesod was distinct as a semi Lune.

Had a tremendous sense of size and power, rising right up through the cosmos, not only the solar system. Felt like a great angelic being. There seemed to be an all-pervading undertone of music and a swinging of spheres in their orbits about me.

Re-absorbed down into Malkuth, entered the temple through the roof and found myself seated on the stone block, robed in black and of normal size.

A disturbance in the street distracted my attention, which so far had not had the vestige of a break. Boys shouting and dogs barking under the window, very loud. Was able to maintain vision nevertheless. The great figure though reduced to more moderate dimension, was overshadowing the temple. I had now got this cosmic figure with my consciousness in it, and also a normal sized astral figure fully robed, with consciousness in it, and they could look at each other. The smaller figure ordered the greater to stop the noise in the street. The greater one stretched out one hand over the disturbing persons, but without effect. Then it projected force in the Sign of . . . The noise ceased.

Consciousness now centred again in the large figure. I did not know quite what to do with it, as I had never expected such a manifestation and did not know its possibilities. Decided to use it to project force on to . . . which it did most effectively, the force was projected in the Sign of . . . and took the form of a downpouring of golden light.

Terrific force pouring like water from a hydrant, full of diamond sparkles of light, out of my hands, from the palms, not the finger tips. Soon force began to come from the solar plexus also, this entered into the base of the altar. Then force began to come from the forehead, this rained upon the altar like a light spray. All the time the force continued to pour from the hands.

The altar appeared as a hollow stone tank which the force was filling. Presently it appeared full to the brim and the force ceased to flow. I had the definite impression that altar and chair ought to be of granite, assumed the dress of an Egyptian priest with Uraeus head-dress and brightly coloured Horus wings . . .

She had a sense that time was up and looked at her watch. Her breathing being very shallow, she waited it for to become normal then used a Sign, followed by a stamp of the foot, to reaffirm her return back to the earth sphere. When she came back to full consciousness she had the sense of a scarlet triangle over the root of her nose, and the feeling as if the skull had been cut away there, exposing her brain.

To Dion, still recovering from the Leadbeater scandals, still aware of her own mannish elements, still very much a married woman trying hard to cater for the needs of her increasingly goat-footed man, it must have been an ecstasy to finally accept her own duality and experience it at the highest level, a sort of *solve et coagula* on the Inner Planes, whereby she found her highest expression in the Light. She became like the woman in the card The Devil who had felt herself chained to the demon she could sense squatting behind her. Only when her eyes had adapted to the gloom, only when she had found her nerve, did she realize that the bond was a 'mind-forged manacle' which could be slipped off at will.

This had been experienced in 1930, but she published the account in March 1932. This must have been when she knew beyond all doubt that she would never keep Merl. It was certainly the year in which she confided to some women pupils that she had married him for the Work, not for love; it was also the year she told people that she would one day lose her contacts as a direct result of publishing her essays on the Qabalah, thus breaking the oaths she had taken in the Golden Dawn. The two statements were not unconnected. She was preparing herself for the day that she felt would surely come, when the Masters and her man would desert her.

This was the time, too, when the rumours started about Merl's sexual activities outside the sacrament of marriage. He was quite taken with Christine Campbell Thompson, who was to become Dion's literary agent, but Dion made quite sure that they never had the chance to work alone. She even thwarted whatever designs he may have had by putting her bright pupil in the charge of Charles Seymour, who was to become an important figure within the lodge. In some ways, from her point of view, it was the worst thing she could have done.

It was said that the chief rumour-monger within 3 QT was William Creasy, whose suspicious mind was aided by an active imagination. This may well have been the reason for his having been reduced to neophyte.

Although there is no evidence to support the idea that Merl was an out-and-out philanderer, it would be surprising if he did not, with all his sensual qualities, have at least one dalliance outside his marriage. Like many others of his ilk, his Christian ethic had been severely battered and probably completely destroyed by his experiences in the trenches. No man who had seen that much death and that much hypocrisy or who had made any nominal Pan-contact, could possibly adhere to the sort of fidelity engendered by the fear of God. Merl certainly strayed at least once, although he ended up marrying the woman in question.

Dion, however, for all her wisdom and power, was capable of a very human jealousy when the circumstances suggested. In her own hard, cool, dutiful, authoritarian and arguesome way, she loved him dearly.

We must look at her then, in the early 1930s, as a Hierophant in the full sense; enthroned, doling out Signs and Wonders, curiously androgynous yet carrying her masculine side within the horns of her lunar persona — her 'Body of Light' — like the old moon being carried in the arms of the new. We can split her still further: there was the fecund and bright aspect of the goddess, The Empress, as she hovered over 3 QT, which was Dion as her followers wanted to see her; while her masculine side, building empires, was hard and armoured, living at a cold and rarified level, secure but alone and often lonely, despite the power.

No one cared about Violet Mary Firth any more, which, apart from the polite conventions of the era, was one of the reasons why no one thought to ask her simple, everyday questions about her background. They never thought about it; they did not care. It was the Mistress of Moon Magic they wanted to see, and what they felt lay behind her. No one saw her as a woman any more, just as a channel for marvels.

This is the power of the Priestess. This is her curse.

9.

SUNKEN LANDS AND THE ISLE OF GLASS

> In Atlantis the Cup or Bowl was the Moon-Bowl (of the *old* Moon and the earliest stages of mankind) in which was a substance in actual contact with the Supernal. These 'substances' are Mysteries . . . and from memories of them have been developed the sacramental rites of various creeds. The finding of the Cup which had been withdrawn from man because of his sins is behind the Grail legend.
>
> Dion Fortune

The Magician stands behind the table which serves as his altar. Before him are the tools of his craft, those which he calls his 'Magical Weapons'; he even thinks of the term in capitals. They are the material symbols of his mastery over the elements. The Sword, which symbolizes Air, and the rational, logical mind; the Cup which equates with Water and the instinctual aspects; the Shield which is the Earth and the physical body; the Wand which proclaims his mastery of Fire and the intuitive, inspirational sides to his psyche. There is a band around his forehead like that which Dion often wore. He holds aloft a crystal rod which signifies attainment in the world of the spirit, at the level of the Adeptus. The sign of infinity is above his head and the slightest of smiles can be discerned on his lips.

This is the condition to which Dion, in her early days, most earnestly aspired. In the course of her Golden Dawn training she would have learnt control of the elements in ascending order: Earth, Water, Air and then Fire, before going on to the more exalted levels.

Although she had troubles with the Air aspects, as already described, which she finally resolved on Glastonbury Tor, her control of the salamanders, or Fire Elementals, was also achieved after a bizarre incident at the foot of that same mound.

Some of her best magic came to be practised at Glastonbury. Some of her more interesting sides emerged here. The Tor and its environs offered a real and earthly solution to the antagonisms within her psyche. The pagan tor and Christian abbey, co-existing quite happily and with remarkable effect, must have offered some hope within her occasionally troubled self.

According to scholarship of the time, the town was the Ynyswytryn of the Ancient Britons, the Avallonia of the Romans, and the Glaestinga-byrig of the Anglo-Saxons. The first and third names were derived from the peculiar position of the place as surrounded with water — literally and poetically 'the isle of the glassy wave' — which it had been before the neighbouring streams were artificially confined within their latter-day limits; a memory too, of the days when the sea had swept to the very foot of the Tor. The second name, Avallonia, was 'the mead of the apple,' the island being then, just as much as in 1923, remarkable for the beauty of its apple orchards.

The famous Benedictine abbey of St Mary to which the town owed its chief celebrity in that era was said to have been founded by Joseph of Arimathea, who had been sent by St Philip, then preaching in France, to evangelize the Druid Isle of Britain. After his arrival Joseph erected on the island of Ynyswytryn a chapel of wattled work, some sixty feet long by twenty feet wide. This was the first Christian oratory in England; it was stated by some to have been the first church above ground anywhere in the world. In the course of centuries, when the abbey necessarily went through many architectural developments, Glastonbury became an unequalled centre of learning; one of the greatest places of pilgrimage in Christian Europe.

And there there was the Tor, less well-understood to the public but even more attractive, the breast of a vast and sleeping goddess, the tower on top being a nipple filled with milk. On good days the energies from the underworld spume into the atmosphere with the sense of a fountain; on other days it radiates an air of near menace.

Around the two, said to be built into the landscape, were discerned huge figures portraying some primaeval zodiac.

And it was at the foot of the Tor, in the Chalice Orchard, that Dion found her most enduring home. For all the attractions of 3 QT, despite the marvels worked there, it is the Chalice Orchard that people most associate with her.

Perhaps it was because here the Christian sense of duality was resolved, for to the Druids of the Glass Isle good and bad, right and wrong, black and white, body and soul were quite unknown. The key to the Celtic philosophy was the merging of dark and light, natural and supernatural, conscious and unconscious. Now, she knew for certain, there was no earthly need to look Eastward. Tibet was a distant dream and would remain so, for within a short trip from London, by courtesy of the Great Western Railways, she could be within the 'holyest earthe in England'. Here, as we have seen, she put down a psychic tendril into the depths and rooted herself for all time.

It is apt, then, that it was here that she made her final rapport with the Fire Elementals and became a magician in full earnest. It was as though the glass town had assumed the property of a lens and brought her own inner light to the point where it could enflame.

She was staying in an old farmhouse in Chilkwell, opposite the Chalice Well where the healing spring of chalybeate waters flowed from the ground. The building, which was owned by a Miss Bath, was very old with low, dark rooms, lit by a big old oil lamp that was hung from a hook screwed into the ceiling. Below this light she worked at the material given her to study by her superiors in the Golden Dawn. One evening, when all of her papers were spread before her, there was a sudden crash and the roar of fire — the hook in the ceiling had given way and the lamp had fallen blazing on to the table. The oil ran in a lake of fire all over the papers and dripped flaming to the floor, setting the carpet alight.

> It was an alarming sight, the flames rose far above my head and were spreading rapidly, and I was alone in the house save for a very old woman. However I managed to keep my self control. I did not possess the Words of Power in connection with the Fire Degree, but I used the words which proclaimed me an initiate, invoked the Order itself, and plunged into the blaze. I felt the soft touch of the flames on my hands, but no heat burning.

She picked up the red-hot metal container of the lamp itself and pitched it out of the window. It landed blazing in the middle of a little lawn and went on burning for some time.

Turning her attention to her precious papers, which were beginning to char at the edges amid the pool of burning oil on the table, she snatched them out of the bonfire and beat out the flames by stamping on them. Finally she trod out the blaze on the floor where the burning oil had soaked into the carpet and then, for reasons she never understood, the burning pool on the table was extinguished, leaving her in total darkness save for a vague light which came from the still-flaming lamp outside the window. She put *that* out with the slop bucket.

> I returned to the pitch-dark room and as I entered the door I felt that I was not alone; there were presences there in the darkness that were not of earth; they were friendly, I felt that, and I received, I do not know how, the impression that they were of a jovial, boisterous temperament, yet under discipline. They stood in a corner of the room which I have since discovered to be the south.

(Within the magical circle, the south was the place of Fire, the west Water, the north Earth, and east Air.)

It made her very thoughtful. No damage was done by a quite considerable fire, except for a slight scar on the table where the red-hot brass container of the lamp had lain till she had pitched it out the window. Yet she had been able to pick it up without any sensation of burning and there were no marks on her fingers. The touch of the flames on her hands had been strange — a velvety soft touch, like butterfly's wings. The papers were no more than scorched at the edges; the carpet was unmarked. The ceiling had a smear of smoke, no more.

Not long after this she took her initiation proper within the element of Fire, and soon began to notice that there was a smell of wood-smoke about the house from time to time. At odd moments, during her meditations, she would smell the aromatic odour that burning pine-wood gives off, see wreaths of soft, grey, sweet-scented smoke curling up from behind her head. Later still as she sat beside a fire that would not burn, trying to coax it into some sort of life, she had the realization that Man was the initiator of Elementals just as the Masters were the initiators of men. At that moment she had one of the surges of rapture that characterize the sudden and unsought-for revelation upon the mystic path. This is quite usual, but what was distinctly unusual was the salamander — the Fire-spirit — which came trailing out of the heart of the fire, now burning fiercely in the hearth.

'It was, I should say, some two and a half feet long from nose to tail, of an elephant-grey colour, the ridges of its neckfolds and back edged with glittering ruby light, exactly like the gay trimmings of a Christmas cracker. Its eyes were glittering jewels of ruby.'

Astonished though she was she was also aware that she was seeing it with her psychic vision, not her physical eyes. The creature's expression was pleasingly and reassuringly mild; its whole bearing was eager and apologetic, in fact, as if it were very anxious to win her approval.

'I went downstairs to my own room, and as I descended the stairs I saw it behind me, flopping along from step to step with its elongated body, exactly like a dachshund. I arrived back in my own room and there it was on the hearth-rug, looking up anxiously into my face. We were both, I think, mutually embarassed.

This was the nearest thing to a pet she would ever have. It had sought her out just as diligently and shyly as she had sought the 'Elder Brethren' on Glastonbury Tor.

Hazel Evans, who had something of her brother's 'sightedness', was aware of it too, seeing it as a trail of smoke on the stairs. Other members of 3 QT came to sniff the aromatic smoke which was its characteristic odour, and a few of them saw it in much the same form as Dion. As the weeks went by he grew much bigger and the ruby edges to his collar and spines became much brighter. Also, he began to assume an upright posture, a distinctly man-like posture. The time came when Dion was drawn to Glastonbury again, and as she 'had no knowledge as to the packing of Elements for transport', she lost sight of her little friend. He never appeared again.[1]

It is easy to mock, but every magician has his own story to tell about the Elementals in his life. Ernest Butler however, made an important point when he recounted a tale about the gnome that he and his wife had seen on the Yorkshire moors. The gnome was visible to them both, dressed as gnomes in his mythology were meant to be — a little man kitted out like a miner. Now Butler, although he had the child-like perception necessary to such magical vision, was also a very wise magus. He knew that he could 'test' the form of the gnome and thus see it in something approaching its true form. He and his wife looked hard at it again with this determination in mind, and the traditional gnome gave way to a pattern of fluctuating light.

Dion knew this too — all magicians do — and her salamander would have reduced itself into a similar abstract arrangement had she wished it to do so. Nevertheless the mind needs such child-like imagery to fasten on to and work through. The romance of such things imbues them with a certain energy over and above that which is intrinsic to them. What is true of the elementals is true of the Masters — which is probably the last explanation that needs to be given as to their true nature: the Masters are what they are; they are not necessarily what they seem.

And as to where the salamander went when he finally disappeared from 3 QT, well that is fairly clear too: he was safe within the confines of Dion's magic Wand, and therefore neatly ordered by the corresponding aspects in her own psyche. From that time on she would carry a portion of Glastonbury's subterranean fire with her wherever she went.

It became quite obvious to Dion that she would need some permanent base within that enchanted town in Somersetshire, as it was then called. She had been staying on occasions with Alice Buckton, a then famous but now forgotten writer who had been instrumental in trying to create the Glastonbury Mystery Plays, on the lines of Oberammagau, and who lived at the Chalice Well. Later in 1924, with Loveday's help, Dion bought a forty-foot hut which had once served as an Officers' Mess and had it put up in the Chalice Orchard, next to the Well, right at the foot of the Tor.

This became in 1928 The Chalice Orchard Club, which was open to the general public from Whitsuntide to Michaelmas as a hostel and pilgrimage centre, the terms being from £2 12s 6d (£2.63) per week. It was originally just something of a *pied-à-terre*, but they had worked hard on the hut's original structure, adding two verandahs and cultivating creepers to grow all over and soften its originally harsh lines. The heavy government timbers stood up to the winter gales of the hut's high perch; the dull red pantiles of its roof sheltered it from the summer heat. Its colours as Dion saw them were full red, deep cream and brown, just as silver and black were the predominant colours of the London centre. On the side towards the east, next to the Tor, was a basking-corner sheltered between two projecting wings. Inside at this end was a long refectory table where the morning sun, coming round the shoulder of the Tor, would melt the butter through the glass. At the western end, on the other verandah which looked toward the sea and the sunset, they could see Dunkery Beacon in Devon, and on a clear night the sea-lights of the Welsh coast.

Dion was quite clear about this arrangement: Fire and Air to the east, where they would glimpse skies 'of an Italian depth of blue' in which disported hawks and bullfinches; and to the west were Earth and Water, and the Celtic depths. And around them both the tops of the apple trees leaned over the verandah rails, in which lanterns were hung for the night, causing Dion to think of herself as a secret priestess in a mystic grove.

Clients were boarded out in a variety of guest-houses down the adjoining street, congregating in the chalet at specific times or else dozing in the hammocks which had been slung from the orchard's trees. Motoring tours were often arranged to the Cheddar Caves and Wells cathedral, and to the sandhills of Bridgewater Bay for an early bathe. Or else guests could sit on the verandahs again and look down to the orchard below where long lines of gay-coloured skeins of wool dried among the apple trees, dyed with lichen scraped from the trees themselves, like multi-coloured versions of the fleece which Jason had once sought.

This was how Dion saw her little retreat in the first year of her marriage, when all things must have seemed possible. It was the one abiding love in her life, and a love which never betrayed her.

It was from this point on, with this point of departure, that she began to explore the Green Ray with the active help of its Lord. In other words she began to work under the aegis of Merlin himself, in this case the actual arch-mage of Britain rather than her husband in his magical identity.

When she was close to the Earth Mysteries, as she was at Glastonbury, Dion's atavistic memories would come through strongly. The glass lens of the town became a telescope: it enabled her to look back along the curvature of light that is evolution, and glimpse her other heartland. To Dion the drowned land of Atlantis lay as close to the surface of her psyche as the fields of Somerset lay below the floods. The tides had only to ebb a little, the waters to drain slightly, and the Old Places could be seen. Sitting in comfort in her Chalice Orchard, looking down the hill toward the old Anchor Inn, she managed to fuse the themes of both Avalon and Atlantis, to create a surprisingly elegant whole.

To her way of seeing, Merlin, Arthur and Morgan le Fay were not single individuals who could be pinned like moths as unique examples of their kind: the names were, rather, initiatic titles which were handed down through the ages. Arthur Pendragon and his cultus (who is paralleled by and often identified with Gwyn ap Nudd) came to be one of the most important of the themes within her life. As she saw it Glastonbury *was* Atlantis, but in a later phase of evolution. 'The Atlantean contacts', she wrote, 'are of great value, since the Age of Aquarius is the Age of Atlantis on a higher arc.' The Tor was nothing more nor less than the sacred mountain which had once risen from the waters and shone.

As we have seen, she had what she felt were her first Atlantean memories at the age of four, when she was presented with the sort of unexceptional hypnogogics that are easily achieved or stimulated. More detailed and enchanting memories came later, which were collected from 1922 onward. To her credit she pointed out that these far memories 'should be treated with reserve varying according to the subject. They are interesting, they may be helpful, but they claim no special authority.' She was never a one for dogma, was Dion.

She gave something of a summary of her visions in her hypnotically intense novel *The Sea Priestess:*

> I could see the scene clearly, as if it were a picture vividly stamped on memory — the sacred city built around the mountain that had been a volcano, just as Pompeii and Herculaneum were built within historical times. I could see the wide alluvial plain that stretched away to a far range of mountains, the land laid bare by the receding sea, and at the very verge of land and water rose the great cone. The cone was flat on top, not pyramidal, because in some previous cataclysm it had blown off its crater, as volcanoes do. And on this level crest were the white buildings of the sacred clan — the great sun-temple with its open court paved with the black and white of alternate marble and basalt, and its two pillars that were the twin gnomons of a time-dial vast as the court, one for the sun, and one for the moon, and calculations were made upon the way the shadows crossed the squares. It was the prototype, Morgan told me, of the Temple of Solomon the King, and all other temples of the Mysteries take after it.
>
> Around the temple were buildings with porticoes and colonnades, beam-spanned, for the Atlanteans, though they knew much wisdom, had not got the secret of the arch any more than the ancient Egyptians had; these were the houses of the priests and scribes that served the temple, and beyond them was the House of the Virgins, built around a court, with no windows looking outwards. It was there that Morgan Le Fay grew to womanhood.
>
> Within were courts leading one into another and surrounded by rooms and colonnades. And there were sunken stone tanks, with steps leading down to them, where the sacred lillies grew; and over them leant trees not unlike mulberry trees, ancient and gnarled, from whose bark oozed the fragrant resins they burnt in the temples. The young priestesses sat under the trees spinning with the spindle and whorl that are more ancient than the wheel. I think that they had not the use of the wheel in Atlantis, any more than they knew the arch.
>
> From the House of the Virgins an underground way led to the

temple, and priests from whom all passion had gone watched over the up-bringing of the young priestesses in the care of the wise women. By this way they were brought into the temple as occasion required, never setting eyes on the outside world nor any undedicated man; and by this way they returned when their work was done, not always virgin.

Beneath the temple a way led by the path of the lava to the very heart of the ancient volcano, and herein was hollowed out a crypt where a rising jet of flame burnt continually, telling those who had eyes to see that the mountain was not dead, but sleeping. This flame, lit by the Earth herself, was to them the symbol of their faith, for all fires are one in nature, though after three kinds — volcanic, solar and terrestrial. It was the leaping of this flame that warned the Priest of the Moon that the catastrophe long foretold was at hand.

Now the Priest of the Moon was other than those who served the flame, though as a young man he had been taken and trained as they had been. He had seen that the worship had fallen on evil days, and had gone back, as men must, to an older and purer faith, tracing the river to the rill till he came to the pure source; and he worshipped the Great Mother under Her forms of moon and sea, and in this he was wise, for with Her are hidden the secrets of human life, though with the All-father are the keys of the spirit.

In his prime he set out to seek a land where life might be lived unsullied by the decay of a dying race, and he travelled with the tin-ships to the Islands of the Sea, where the marts of the sea kings' trade were established — far marts, where men brought strange things, the blue and the purple dyes, and medicinal plants, and silver.

And when the time came that the leaping flame gave warning, the ancient Priest of the Sun, too feeble for that far journey yet knowing what drew near, prepared to die with his temple. And he gave into the hands of the younger man the secret scrolls and sacred symbols. And they went by night by the underground way to the House of the Virgins, and looked at the young girls as they slept in the moonlight, and chose one who had been prepared to serve their purpose, and roused her and led her away wrapped in a dark cloak while the others slept.

And she saw for the first and last time by moonlight the wide spaces of the plain where the spearmen and javelin-throwers learnt their skill, and horsemen rode the two-toed horse; and she went down the winding processional way to the shore, and so to sea. And the land-wind, blowing at dawn, filled their sails and they went swiftly. For a day and a night and a day they went, the rowers toiling till they met the trades. Then, upon the third morning, in the hour between dark and dawn, three great billows heaved their ship as the sea-floor shook, and when the sun rose they saw a dark pillar of smoke and cloud where once was Lost Atlantis.

And the Priest of the Moon, travelling by way of 'thrice-vexed Bermoothes' and the Azores, brought the young girl who was to be his priestess to a place he had prepared in the Holy Isle that is off the Isle of Druids, looking towards the Isle of Saints, which is Ireland. And there he left her in the care of wise women, to be trained in the terrible discipline of the priesthood, he himself coming and going about the wild land, watching its ways, men calling him Merlin.

And when the time came that the summons was sent, they brought the young priestess, now grown and trained, to the priests who had their sacred college on Bell Knowle. And there befell that of which I have already told, so that the sacrifice was in vain, and the sea came in and took the land. And by all the water-ways of the marshes the tide rose, and meadow and field fell back to the sea, and men that had ploughed and sown became fishers and hunters again, living in huts on piles among the reeds who had known stone-built forts and timbered palaces. And Morgan le Fay, priestess of the sea and half-sister of the king, sat in her palace in the island valley of Avalon and watched in the magic well the things to come unfolding.

And she saw her brother the king betrayed by his faithless queen; and the wise Merlin led by the young witch Vivien; and all the evil that comes to lands and men when the sacred hearth-fires die untended.

In what might be called her 'side lectures' she went into more detail still. The Atlantean religion was also described. The important aspect was not so much great knowledge as a very intense training. The priesthood obeyed instructions coming to them from a higher plane. The work of the seers was done in the temple outside the city, the Temple of Naradek, also called the Sea Temple. This was said to be located at the very place where the Atlanteans, who called themselves 'the Sea People,' first landed.

This Naradek Temple was not to be confused with the great Sun Temple in the city itself, which was more for the public, and closely linked with the theocratic aspects of government. It was, rather, the Temple of the 'Sun-behind-the-Son,' and avoided all contact with politics.

The Sun Temple fell upon evil days, as temples tend to do, but the Temple of Naradek never decayed, Dion advised them proudly, remembering her life and lives with Moriarty.

Pure sun-worship was the minor and outer aspect of Atlantean religion. There was also sea-worship, appealing to the illuminati as well as to immediate members of the Royal family. Those who became initiates of the Sea Mysteries were really seers, pure and simple, whereas the adepts of the sun-cult were magicians. It was felt that of the two it was the former who attained the higher spiritual levels, and who had the really potent influence upon Atlantean affairs through the spiritual currents they channelled. Their role was to provide the priestesses to be used as seeresses and pythonesses, not only in the Sea Temple itself but in all those temples where the ritual priests depended upon them.

Very delicate relationships existed between the members of the Sun and Sea Temples. If the priests of the former refused to heed the guidance of the seeress who was loaned to them, the woman would simply wrap herself in her hooded cloak and go back to her mother-temple, brooking no interference. This was considered a terrible thing. If nothing else it broke the Sun Temple's contacts.

Atlantean magic was not infallible. Once, a candidate achieved the role as Priest of the Sun through sheer duplicity, having learnt certain secrets through the unlawful use of a seeress. Armed with the information this woman had given him, he thus achieved highest office. However, when it came to the moment when he had to demonstrate the powers that self-revelation should have given him, he failed miserably. The test required him to materialize an Elemental in the fumes rising from a large bronze tripod which stood below the high altar. Although he knew the theory and the correct invocations as given him by the seeress, his lack of actual attainment was soon revealed for he failed to control the materialization. The rampant Elemental turned on him and made him into a raving lunatic. He died three days later.

Another priest took charge and managed to drive the creature from the temple, although it remained at large upon the astral plane. This priest was then installed as High Priest of the Sun as a matter of necessity, even though he lacked the priestess that all such magi should have. This was because the one who had been chosen to act as both mate and mirror was actually the same woman who had been so used and abused by the late renegade. So, as the High Priest lacked the necessary polarity and was unable to exert the proper magical control, the Elemental continued in its freedom, causing much trouble. Eventually, at the cost of his own life, the High Priest managed to track down and destroy the malign creature.

This, we might be sure, is a memory of Dion's own past life on Atlantis — or one of them — for there are many echoes here of Justin Lucas' caddish use of Veronica in *The Demon Lover.*

The mighty Sun Temple had many aspects. There was the Hall of Mirrors which was a small round temple containing a multitude of mirrors of all different shapes and sizes, being made of highly polished metals. These were fixed on pivots which enabled them to be adjusted at varying angles. Through these the adepts could look into the future. The priestesses who manipulated the mirrors had great responsibilities, for it was possible to manipulate them in such a way as to give inaccurate or misleading results.

Apart from the Hall of Mirrors, there was also a side-chapel to the main temple where stellar magic was performed. This little room was along a passage and down some steps from the Image of the Sun in the main building. The force there was very strange — swift and strong, deadly if it was misused. It was like radium, Dion felt, or at least had strong analogies with radium.

Below the Sun Temple was the Hall of Images, where the spirits of the dead made an almost tangible appearance. This hall comprised four sections: in one of these the powers of Water were controlled by certain processes and it was guarded by a powerful Elemental. Here were held the 'Keys of the Sea' which were eventually misused with such catastrophic effect.

In the Sun Temple, too, was a small rock-hewn image which gave off a very superior and mystic type of magnetism. The image in question consisted of a vast face, the features of which were made of hundreds of smaller faces, and exerted an immense pull upon the awestruck worshipper. For this reason it was always veiled, except to the highest of initiates.

Despite all this exalted magic, the people then did not think as people of Dion's world did. They functioned almost entirely in what we would now call the right brain. The 'concrete mind' that modern man uses as a matter of course was only just being developed then — and only by the priesthood. The higher emotional aspects, too, were being brought into operation, whereas before it was only crude instinct that made any appearance. The ordinary Atlantean citizens, the non-initiates who lived on the lowest tiers, had little more intelligence than dogs.

These higher emotional aspects, which equate with the 'upper astral', were sent from the Inner Planes for the priesthood to work out with the temple-formulae. The Arthurian legend was an example of just such a formula.

There was an aristocracy in Atlantis of course. They were members of the Sacred Clan, being linked by a certain blood-line. They lived on the highest tier, for in a climate where the air was thick and heavy, the sun could penetrate more easily at a higher level. The lesser nobility

— priests and warriors — were also on the topmost level. They were allowed to intermarry but were never prolific breeders.

Everyone led something of a communal life up there, and all wore caste marks on their foreheads. These marks were made by rubbing into a small wound a mixture of blood taken from a high-grade priest, mixed with the juice of a wine-like plant which caused the wound to fester and form a small, round, pitted surface.

In one way Dion felt that it was a primitive civilization, although very highly evolved magically. For example, when a child was born an official came to inspect it; if it was malformed in any way it was smothered. Mothers knew of this, naturally, and so if their own child was even slightly defective they borrowed someone else's and reared their own in secret, or sent it to a lower tier. By this means inherited knowledge and 'powerful occult blood' filtered down to the lower orders . . .

And on and on, evoking a lost world of marvel and cruelty that paralleled the worst and best aspects of the Victorian and Edwardian societies, dragging Atlantis up from the Caribbean depths of the Western ocean, totally unaware that as she did so the unthinkable was happening: slowly, imperceptibly, the British Empire and all its glories were sinking into the waves that Britannia was always said to rule.

That was one thing her vision never foresaw. She would never have believed it anyway.

Avalon and Atlantis then, were two of the pillars which supported the heavens above her own universe. Atlantis was the place of raw and primitive power, Avalon (the mystic realm of which Glastonbury was the outer facade) the place of her heart. She slipped constantly between the two, taking others with her but more often than not going alone.

By the late 1930s there was also a third pillar, one which was more ornate and massive, enscribed with the symbols of the Old Land. These symbols, when deciphered, told the story of the Serpent Power, and how Dion's thwarted sexuality found its best and final expression. This was the period when she gained the knowledge of the time-lost, water-obsessed world which had been regulated by the Nile; and although she never went near Egypt in the flesh, she found a more than adequate substitute within an eldritch former chapel off the Belgrave Square.

But first, before she could get this aspect of her magic properly attuned to the mighty forces of Osiris, Horus and all their minions, there were some other occupants — seen and unseen — who had to be considered and then dealt with.

10.
ISIS IN THE BELFRY

In March 1930 Sir Vincent Henry Penalver Caillard died. He had been an extremely wealthy man who had had an illustrious life by the rather sniffy standards of his class: a diplomat, intelligence officer, director of innumerable companies and president of the Federation of British Industry. Gold medals were flung at him like coinage by grateful governments at home and abroad. He was a financial expert, a prophet of fiscal reform. Aspiring to be a Renaissance Man he also contributed to the *Encyclopaedia Britannica,* wrote lyrics, and once provided a musical setting for Blake's *Songs of Innocence.* He was passionate about all literature and found light relief in motoring, for which he had several fast and very expensive cars. His clubs in the City were Bufonite and Knights, and in his last years he occupied himself as so many in his position did: he became a Justice of the Peace, in the small town of Trowbridge, Wiltshire, spending his country hours in the manor house he owned at nearby Wingfield.

It was not his only property, for he also owned the rather odd but aptly-named Belfry, in West Halkin Street, off Belgrave Square. When he was not doling out justice he was happy relaxing there in the heart of London, with his second wife Zoe, whom he had married in 1927 when he was seventy-one years old. His pet name for her was Bird; she called him Big Fish. It was with Bird's help that he managed to write his book — a book which Zoe felt would help change the world. Despite all his talents, the writing of this book was no easy task. It was not a matter of writer's block, or lack of inspiration; it was simply that when he started writing it he had been dead for years.

The story goes back to a certain George Jobson who had once worked 'as a scientist' for the Graham-Bell telephone company, which might have been expected to know something about communicating across distances. Jobson, when seriously ill, had made a pact with his friend Basil Kirkby that after his death he would attempt to get in touch through a medium, if at all possible. The call-sign they agreed upon was BKK, which happened to be Kirkby's initials. In due course the pre-arranged sign was given, although exactly how we do not know. With this proof came the exhortation 'to give up all thou hast and follow me.' Undeterred by his friend's sudden and uncharacteristic use of the second person singular, the hapless wretch did just that, and devoted the next years of his life to the building, at Jobson's behest, of an instrument that was then called a reflectograph. This wondrous machine required a medium in trance to produce a materialized hand which touched upon various keys — presumably like those on a typewriter. Surprisingly, Kirkby had no trouble in finding just such a medium, a certain Mrs L. Singleton who had the sort of fine features and furs which passed among the upper classes as evidence of a refined spirituality.

However the reflectograph was not quite what Jobson had envisaged, and so he urged Kirkby to build a new variant, now known as the communigraph, this being a combination of pendulum and ouija board set in a high and narrow table. At least it did not need a medium.

It was at this point that Sir Vincent pricked up his astral ears and took note. The next time he 'came through' to Zoe via the usual Spiritualist seance, and with the help of the ever-obliging Red Cloud, he managed to tell Bird to get a communigraph of her own and install it in The Belfry.

She did this. A service of inauguration was held in what she called the 'upper room,' officiated by Archdeacon Wilberforce, no less, who had great sympathy with such pursuits.

To their delight, no sooner had the machine been blessed than Sir Vincent came through with a message. 'Love is mightier than electricity', he said. 'The latter is able to link countries but our love will link two worlds.'

Nice.

Services were held every Wednesday, and followed a prayer to the Blessed Master, Christ. Then, after all lights had been extinguished save for the red glow on the machine which enabled them to see the letters, the task of writing Sir Vincent's magnum opus began, sometimes involving sessions of three hours at a time. The book was to be called *A New Conception of Love*, and was completed with the merry assistance of several on 'the other side' who called themselves, collectively, the Trianon Band. There was the spirit Ethel, who had been Mrs Singleton's guide, and Muriel (also called Star); a Sergeant Murphy who would occasionally entertain them with Irish songs, and Charlie Molesworth, who could never talk in more than a whisper for some reason connected with his mother's presence in the circle around the communigraph. It is not clear how the machine could pick that up.

Zoe and her friends heard how they in The Belfry were making such strides that 'great statesmen, kings, and leaders of many nations' could see the possibilities of giving international messages of counsel and guidance to their respective people. 'We of the Trianon Band are praying to God that our communigraphs may bring universal peace and brotherhood. We can all be Freemasons in the truest sense.'

It was the climax of Zoe's life. She, in the upper room of The Belfry, would become a beacon to the world. She invited anyone to send her questions about the meaning of life to put to Sir Vincent. Many did.

For reasons probably connected with her own illness, Zoe decided to lease The Belfry. She decided to allow a Mrs Evans first refusal for she had heard that the said lady was also a medium, and might be expected to have some sympathy with the important work being done by the Trianon Band.

Mrs Evans was indeed most interested in taking up the lease. She had recently been left a sum of money by Lady Perry, an admirer of hers, and with this she decided to indulge in a piece of personal luxury for once. She fancied that The Belfry would make a good private retreat — a bolt-hole of sorts, and one which she would only allow especial people in for especial purposes, at times convenient to herself alone. The burden of being a semi-public magus was now proving exceedingly heavy.

As Dion stood in the vacant chapel that had been so comfortably converted into living quarters, she was quite aware of all the 'vibrations', as the Spiritualists might say. To her more finely attuned perceptions there was nothing noble about these presences. Big Fish, Ethel, Star, and the lovable Charlie Molesworth were no more than shells, bearers of empty gossip.

And so, by means of an operation known as the Banishing Ritual of the Pentagram, she created a sphere of force around the entire building which whirled the pathetic band into the dread realms of obscurity and endless night.

She was having none of that nonsense. This was to be no mere lodging house for third-rate simulacra. This was to be a *real* beacon, showing the light of the Women's Mysteries. This was to be her very own Temple of Isis.

It is possible that Dion was referring to the Caillards in *Psychic Self Defence* when she described a woman, recently widowed, who elected to idolize her husband after his death and canonized him into the family saint. This woman made a little altar around his photograph and used it as a focus of her meditations after first invoking the Masters, and ignored the reality of the man, who had in truth been an intensely selfish and malignant brute far removed from the dreamy sentimentalist who was to come through to her via the communigraph.

Dion's only concern in those early days was to scour the psychic atmosphere clean of him and anyone (or anything) else. Following this she began the rites and meditations which would slowly attune the whole place towards the active worship of the Goddess.

This was the very height of her life. It was also the beginning of the darkness.

In the tarot sense she had become *The Empress* in more ways than one. There was 3 QT under her rule, Chalice Orchard, and a mysterious connection with St Albans too, perhaps, and now this odd growth in West London. We see Dion at this time enthroned in splendour, bright with achievement, life and energy all around and all keyed-in to the symbol of Venus. The Empress is to the Earth as The Priestess is to the Sea. The latter leads from the Moon toward Venus, while the former leads from Venus toward Jupiter, which in occult parlance is the Sphere of the Masters.

It was during the period of The Belfry that she wrote her novels, that she worked the most appealing magic of her lives and touched upon that energy known as the Serpent Power; it was then that she made new contacts or else renewed those she had once known in the Stella Matutina;

and then that she wore out the last of the real priests ever to work with her on equal terms.

The Belfry itself was more than a mere container for all of this. It was then, and always will be, one of those buildings imbued with a consciousness of its own, a place that is neither fish nor fowl but which is most definitely a creature of some sort. It was originally built in 1830 as a Scottish Presbyterian Church, and attracted, at that time of the Reform Bills, a company of folk 'proverbial for rioting and disorder, for drunkenness and ignorance . . .' Not far removed, Dion might have thought, from the sort of creatures it would attract on the lower astral planes.

She occasionally gave lectures there but on the whole only the select few were allowed entry, and those entirely in tune with the Egyptian nature of the magic. Christ had no place within The Belfry.

Between the years 1935 and 1939 she did a vast amount of writing between her various temples, all of it of an increasingly pagan orientation, and all of it, except for articles in the Society's magazine, fictional. She completed a total of seven novels including three 'lost' novels which are of interest only to the devotee, or else those in whom the purple heart still throbs.[1]

Had Dion devoted her formidable powers and considerable talents to writing, pure and simple, she could have been a great novelist by orthodox standards; or if not a novelist in the first division, at least a promotion challenger from the second. As it was, in her last two novels, *The Sea Priestess* and *Moon Magic*, she achieved greatness within the genre. Quite simply these are the finest novels on magic ever written. Really, looking around at the competition, they are the *only* novels on magic ever written.

In order, her output was as follows: *The Winged Bull* 1935; *The Goat-Foot God* 1936; *The Sea Priestess* 1938; *Moon Magic* 1939/40?. It was reputed that the latter was begun shortly after *The Sea Priestess*, but not completed until a year or so after her death, thanks to the mediumship of a woman who, originally, had started off in 3 QT as a maid.

These were completed by those three novels which she wrote for light relief under the name of V. M. Steele, about which she kept very quiet indeed, and they represented one of her few attempts to do something outside the realm of Magic.

The Winged Bull is in many ways the worst of her books, written almost as though she had forgotten the skills she had evinced in *The Demon Lover* ten years before. She stitched the ideas together in an almost clumsy fashion, going for crude and unexciting action, rather than talking about what she knew. When she describes the ways of the 'chucker out' she is pitiful; but when she gives free rein to her descriptions of the

Otherworld and the inner life of the adept, she becomes (in her other novels at least) superb.

Poor though it is, *The Winged Bull* is nevertheless one of her most important books when it comes to biographical references — or rather, references upon which we can pin biographical suppositions. All her characters are based upon real and recognizable people.

Here we meet the first of her frustrated males — the earthy and worthy Ted Murchison, wandering in the mists which swirled around the British Museum (which Dion thought looked rather like the Royal Palace on Atlantis). He is yearning, as all of her males are yearning, for some sort of answer to life and its problems. As he stands there motionless, 'staring with unseeing eyes into the slowly swirling invisibility', he involuntarily cries aloud 'Evoe, Iacchus! Io Pan, Pan! Io Pan!'

From the fog-bound darkness of the forecourt comes the query: 'Who is this that invokes the Great God Pan?'

Murchison, not long demobbed, is a clear picture of Penry Evans, although in this case he is given an Anglo-Saxon outlook and an Acton background. The voice from the night which answered his call belonged to a Colonel Brangwyn — an equally accurate picture of one Colonel Seymour, who was to become one of Dion's last real priests, one of the last men ever to stand up to her.

Brangwyn is old and wise in the lore and practice of magic. He has seen Pan invoked — effectually — many times, and has known the divine inebriation that Pan's coming can produce. He has a sister too, the lovely Ursula, who has a penchant for Greek dancing in the manner of Isadora Duncan, but who has recently been entangled with the depraved Fouldes, a young occultist who has left a sepsis in her soul, and one which her brother is determined to clear out. Fouldes was once a remarkable personality, 'resembling some such swift creature as a stag, a racehorse, or a greyhound', his mind having the same swift litheness.

Brangwyn's idea was to use Murchison in a pagan rite that would enable Ursula to get clear of Fouldes' fell power. He saw the young and wearied soldier as 'a bulldog type', very staunch and enduring; a creature of earth but with volcanic fire inside him. A winged bull, in fact.

Ursula Brangwyn is, of course, Dion herself. But she is also the heroine of D. H. Lawrence's *Women in Love* and *The Rainbow*, in which the author achieved the sort of self-realization that Dion must have admired. The use of the name could not have been chance, for Dion was a well-read woman, and no literate person with her preoccupations in that era would not have read Lawrence. Either the name is a tribute, of sorts, or else it is an attempt to improve on the Lawrentian vision; an attempt to show how it would operate an esoteric levels.

With Fouldes — the object of Miss Brangwyn's disastrous romance — we find ourselves back in the realm of the demon lovers again, and the possibility of some sub-Crowleyan chappy having once been the perpetrator of an evilly delicious assault upon the psychic and emotional integrity of young Violet. Fouldes is just a more foppish version of Lucas, possibly reassessed through the wiser eyes of age.

This is borne out to some extent by Fouldes' mentor, the ghastly and notorious Hugo Astley, a 'heavily built and pock-marked mulatto', who frequently appeared in the less reputable Sabbath journals: A reference here both to Crowley, and to the delightful English penchant for those Sunday newspapers which specialize in sex and scandal while expressing the utmost outrage and minutest detail.

As Brangwyn explained to Murchison, 'Ursula was a pretty high-grade pythoness till she got messed up; and a pythoness is to an ordinary medium what a medium is to ordinary mortals.' Fouldes, he thought, was an intelligent young man with a nice disposition, and well-blessed with the world's goods, but eventually Astley twisted him. Fouldes' whole strong personality was Astley's work. He burned under a forced draught — and drugs were used too.[2]

Murchison, who took to magic and understood it as though he had been a priest from 'the Oldest Land', knew that his task in this world was to save Ursula from the two black magicians, and eventually win her for himself.

Dion was still, in 1935, trying to work something out of her heart, trying to complete a process begun in 1927 with *The Demon Lover.* She was also trying to come to terms with the fact that Merl was not going to be around much longer — something which needed no power of clairvoyance to know. In this book, and in all her magical novels, she is trying to tell him that, although they are so fundamentally different in character and attitude, so completely unsuited by mortal standards, at least on magical levels they can make a virtue of their differences and meet (and mate) on much higher levels, somewhere closer to the gods.

No shred of Dion's personal correspondence has survived, but in these four occult novels we have something infinitely more important. We have her love letters.

In describing Murchison as he was kitted out in ritual gear in Brangwyn, she is describing Merl as he was in his 'Body of Light': 'He saw at once that his kit was cut on the lines of a tunic of an Egyptian priest, save that it was all gold from head to heel instead of bleached linen. It was absolutely plain save for the rayed sun-disk embroidered on the breast.'[3]

And in the magic they first performed they were 'two forces, not two persons. He was the sun in heaven bringing life to the earth. She was the earth, absorbing it hungrily, drawing it from him to satisfy her crying needs.'

Yet, despite the link that Murchison and Ursula made with such ease, throwing off Astley and Fouldes was another matter. She was sent away to Wales for her safety, although Fouldes tracked her down. There on the Orme he tried to win her back by means of his dark knowledge; the sheepdogs of her landlady saved her; he was driven back to London again, but not before re-awakening the old fascination.

> Love and marriage, if it meant no more than housekeeping and child-bearing, had no attraction for her after she realized the possibilities revealed to her by Fouldes . . . Fouldes was her true mate, and yet she knew that mating with him meant unspeakable degradation and an early death. Murchison . . . was distasteful to her by his roughness. But behind Fouldes loomed Astley, slug-like in his foulness; and to come to Frank meant to come into the hands of this high-priest of evil.

She says a great deal in *The Winged Bull* about Murchison/Merl — or rather how she saw him before he assumed his own formidable power. There are crossed lines of communication within the novel, misunderstandings, and not a few ludicrous scenes, but there is another revealing piece where Ursula suddenly recognizes Murchison's worth as an extraordinarily unselfish man, who was devoted to her in his own way; and yet she had spoiled it all by her snobbery and folly. 'She made up her mind that next time Murchison approached her he should have no cause to complain of her lack of response.'

As Dion recreates Ursula's confusion and heartache upon one of the Ormes in Llandudno, she is telling us as much as she can, or dare, about her own courtship, interspliced with the inevitable should-have-beens that all such reverie brings. And there is the striking exchange:

> 'Tradition has it,' said Brangwyn 'that it was up here on the Orme that Keridwen minded her cauldron.'
>
> 'Who might Keridwen be?' enquired Murchison.
>
> 'She is the Keltic Ceres, and her cauldron is the prototype of the Graal. Ursula, in her better moments, likes to identify herself with Keridwen; but I tell her she is not an Earth-mother.'
>
> 'No, more like a moon-goddess,' said Murchison.

In terms of the novel the inevitable happened and Murchison disposed of both Fouldes and Astley by a combination of honest nature and brute force. He and Ursula went to some unspecified cottage on the coast of

Yorkshire and pondered all that had gone before, both suddenly realizing — and admitting — how much they loved each other. And in the final paragraphs, before they finally consummate their love, Ursula expresses her ideas on marriage:

> 'A real marriage, which has a spiritual side as well as a physical, ought to put one in circuit with the whole universe, for one becomes a channel for the life of the race going on; that is why there is no blessing on a marriage when you close the gates of life permanently against incoming souls.'
>
> 'I cannot imagine anything more wonderful than opening those gates.'
>
> Silence fell between them again, and they watched the fire of driftwood gradually crumble to embers, each deep in the thoughts they shared; and the great bull spread his wings and took off as easily as a bird. Murchison knew instinctively that they had mated, and that nothing now remained to be done but to ratify it outwardly . . .

Poor, poor Dion . . . what is she trying to tell us here, at the age of forty-five, when the menopause had begun, and her husband was more and more likely to leave as the days went by? 'No blessing on a marriage when you close the gates of life permanently against incoming souls.' Untrue of course, and uncharacteristic of Dion herself to say this. Did she, briefly, begin to yearn for a child? Was it actually Merl's fault or mutual choice that they had none? Or was it merely because, marrying at the age of thirty-seven, Chronos was against them?

Whatever the reasons, she allowed us a glimpse of sadness here that is not evident in any of the rest of her work. It was not *Deo, non Fortuna* or her contacts writing with the voice and authority of an Exempt Adept who said this, but a wearied and battered Mrs Evans speaking with the simple voice of a woman.

The protagonist of the next novel, *The Goat-Food God*, is worlds apart from Murchison. Here is a man, Hugh Paston, who is peculiarly negative, peculiarly lacking in any sort of magnetism. He had one very great consolation, however, in the fact that he was also rich — incredibly rich. He had inherited all from his grandfather who had made a fortune in tea. Hugh Paston was also a desperate man, for his wife and a male friend had been killed in circumstances that made it obvious that they were lovers. The scandal made all the papers. It was the sort of news that shocked and appalled people to an extent that we, today, can scarcely comprehend.

Taking refuge in a bookshop during a storm, Paston becomes engrossed in a variety of tomes on magic and related subjects: *The Devil's Mistress* by J. W. Brodie-Innes, *The Corn King and Spring Queen* by Naomi Mitchison, and *The Prisoner in the Opal* by A. E. W. Mason, to name but a few.

The proprietor is one T. J. Jelkes, a man as learned in the occult arts as Brangwyn had been, although far less bold. He recognized Paston from the newspapers and comes to give him a nominal kind of sanctuary. When, in due course, the visitor tells his host that he is suddenly determined to seek Pan by the same methods that others have used to seek Christ, Jelkes blanches (a forgotten reflex in todays shock-proof society), demurs, but eventually gives him full assistance.

There is no need for Paston to go through the long process of *cherchez la femme*, for Jelkes has one tucked away already, Mona Wilton, a talented artist living in reduced circumstances close to the starvation level. She is as far removed from Paston's class as the Firths had been from the Evans.

Identification with actual persons is not so easy here, for although Mona is used to utter the ideas of her creator, she is most definitely not just an arty version of Dion. Physically at least, Mona is a fair description of Christine Campbell Thomson as she was then: 'She had hazel eyes, set wide apart under heavy black brows . . . her hair was rusty brown, like the coat of an ill-kept cat. She wore it *coupé en page* with a straight-cut fringe in front, and a straight-cut bob behind.'

Paston, on the other hand, bears a certain resemblance to Charles Loveday: 'He was tallish, loosely built, and carried himself badly, with awkward jerky, nervous movements . . .'[4] The description continues:

> He had the long-fingered bony hands of a psychic and sensitive . . [Jelkes] judged by the awkward, jerky movements that at the present moment everything was discoordinated, and the fellow had no stamina or staying power. He would go up in brief flares of nervous excitement, and burn out as quickly, like a fire of straw.

Jelkes himself seems to be in some part a mixture of Watkins the bookseller, whom everyone in the occult field in London knew, and also perhaps Arthur Chichester who had the Jesuitical training ascribed to Jelkes.

Every character in Dion's novels has an immediate understanding of occultism in its most sophisticated (though not necessarily most complex) forms. Thus there are no digressions in which basic and tedious ideas are explained to the reader. Her characters are all 'twice-born', all initiates who recover their past lives very quickly and manage to transcend their mean lot. Hence we find that Paston, who hires Mona to find and furnish a temple to Pan, is soon able to discuss the way that Pan is an Elemental force, who comes up from the earth under the feet just as spiritual force sun-force, comes down from the sky overhead.[5]

As we have seen, the locale of this temple was based upon an actual farm, Monks Farm, that they had found languishing on a ley-line connecting Tintagel with St Albans, 'the eastern power-centre'. There was energy along this line, an energy which was preserved in the chalk stratum on which Monks Farm was built, much like the energy that could (and can) be felt in the outcrops of carboniferous limestone on the Ormes, on Brean Down, and Glastonbury Tor.

Now that Paston had bought the farm and ensured that Mona had the finances to renovate it suitably, all he had to do was to link himself with this subterranean power and thus with Pan Himself.

He was helped to an extraordinary degree by the spirit of Ambrosius, a powerful and hawk-like former Abbot who had once been imprisoned for life on that spot for his heretical activities in the sixteenth century. Ambrosius came to possess and obsess Paston. As the tale develops, they begin to merge, to the benefit of the latter and the terror of his interfering relatives. Paston, in brief, takes on some of Ambrosius' power. Mona begins to find him rather attractive.

In Dion's hands this is more than a simple tale of reincarnation, even though Paston does have memories of Miss Wilton during a former life in Ancient Greece. As Ambrosius and Hugh invoke Pan in their separate centuries, Dion brings together their separate tales with no little skill. There is also the telling, and in some ways crucial, comment about who or what Ambrosius really is:

> First of all, he could be the dissociated personality of Hugh himself. Secondly, he might be the spirit of the dead monk manifesting through Hugh, who was negative enough for any sort of mediumship, or thirdly, the explanation might lie in the far-reaching doctrine of reincarnation . . . How could one tell a dissociated personality from a spirit-control, and the spirit-control from a previous incarnation of the same person? Anyway, the practical results were the same, whatever theory might be chosen to explain them.

'Anyway, the practical results were the same . . . ' Within that first word lies a complete revision of her earlier ideas about the nature of those Masters of Wisdom whose will she obeyed. Wearied with her psychologies, and wise beyond the limits of that discipline, she was by now acting *as if*, and taking comfort in its formula of sublime simplicity.

Paston and Miss Wilton come together, as Dion's protagonists invariably do, though never in the tactile sense. The connection that they make is subtle, one that transcends class and all the awkwardness of the 'sex problem' as they used to see it. They eventually come to touch on every level but the physical. Of course they had known each other in previous lives, when Hugh as an Ancient Greek had worn goatskin around his loins and sported a bare torso. And Ambrosius, invoking what the Church in the sixteenth century thought were demons, had regular visions of Mona as she was in the twentieth century, an eldritch creature, a succubus come to tempt him.

An ambitious project, *The Goat-Foot God*; the final judgement being that it is a readable novel which is almost a novel of quality, only hampered by the rather awkward conversations and the shallowness of her characters in places. They are types, no more, but at least they are good types which are mightily redeemed by the scope of the study and her descriptions of the Otherworld. There is also a paragraph half-way through the novel in which we can almost see her muse, the White Goddess, descend and take control of her creative faculties:

> Living in London so long, she had hardly realized what the spring and the morning could mean to her. Some polyanthuses, velvet-brown and wine-purple, had joined the daffodils in the coarse grass at the foot of the old wall, and Mona, made sensitive by her illness, stood and looked at them. Dew sparkled on every grey blade of the dry winter grass, the heavy dew left behind by late frosts, and the little velvety faces of the polyanthuses looked up through it unharmed. The sky was of the pale blue of early spring and early morning; a little mare's tail of clouds to the south showed the way of the wind, which came in soft breaths, blowing away the chill of the dawn. Dark gorse with yellow bloom dotted the unthrifty pasture, silver birches rising among it made a fine lace of twigs against the sky, shot through as the light caught them with a faint haze of new green. The dark firs stood against the skyline as they stood the year through, unchanging. Against the winter grey of the pasture, broad stretches of bracken lay tawny; unfenced, the field stretched away and dropped into a wood with the fall of the ground. The sylvan Pan held his own here, and gave no inch to Ceres.

From this point on she begins to match her vision with skill, something that many writers — and some enormously popular writers — never achieve.

She lets slip more about herself on several occasions as this story of 'love among the moderns' as Jelkes called it, progresses. 'Why had Mona never mated during her thirty-odd years? What was she asking of men that they did not give her? Were there no priest-initiates now to work with her the rites of Eleusis?' Like many people in her circumstances her own standards and taste in the opposite sex were probably too high above the reality of those who were more than willing to try and woo her. If she was a great priestess, then as far as women went she had fussy ideas about potential suitors. Which was why she had married Merl. He was handsome, virile, intelligent, witty, brave . . . the exemplar of the warrior priest. If most people never knew what he saw in her, then somehow, using sight that was not purely physical, they saw each other at a different level, and she touched the Pan within him, aroused some echo within herself. Behind Merl, as with Paston, was the 'All-Father, the First-Begotten Love', while behind her was the Earth-Mother, even if she was past it in terms of gestation. As Merl had become the Priest of Pan, so the priest became the god — '. . . spontaneously, without any volition on his part.'

As she turned her memory back, in this year of 1936 to the days when they had courted and then married, she linked with whatever earth-contacts she had made during her days upon the land in the Great War. 'This was the real invocation of Pan — the surrender to bed-rock natural fact, the return to Nature, the sinking back into the cosmic life after all the struggle to rise above it into an unnatural humanity. Animal is our beginning, and animal our end, and man is a centaur who is related to Pegasus.'

The winged bull, and now the winged horse. Dion, with her Old Gods rampant, was beginning to move very fast.

Whatever real rites those of *The Goat-Foot God* were based upon (and we may be sure they involved her and her husband in the late 1920s and early '30s) Dion began to see that they were not purely selfish. There was more involved, far more, than a kind of sexual catharsis through astral orgasms. She made Paston's problems part of a universal problem: her own awakening part of a much wider awakening. She wondered how far the realization of an idea by one person, even if he spoke no word, might not inject that idea into the group-soul and mind of the race 'and set it working like a ferment.' That which she had worked through with Merl had, she felt, brought something into the world — something that would add to the racial heritage.

She was becoming to her race what a shaman was to his tribe: its mouthpiece, its fount of wisdom; its symbol and its guardian. Whatever the problems she might be facing now in her marriage, whatever the outcome, it was all made worthwhile and eternally valid by the magic they had worked over the years — a magic which had brought great energies down to the earth and also up from those molten depths where lay the earth-soul 'all alive and sentient', from which they drew their vitality.

The themes of *The Winged Bull* and *The Goat-Food God* are Earth and the relationships between man and woman. The problems of human loving as Dion saw them were solved by means of the couple becoming, momentarily, representatives of the God and Goddess, their perfect and divine consummations making themselves felt, gradually, upon the whole race.

What follows next is a natural progression up the elemental ladder, when in her next two novels she resolves their problems not by means of the cthonic powers which lie beneath the Earth, but by means of Water, and the timeless depths of the Bitter Sea.

Written in 1938 nothing very much happens in *The Sea Priestess.* Nothing very much at all. It is no more than a tale about how a rather dreary and asthmatic estate agent, Wilfred Maxwell, falls for an older woman yet ends up marrying his secretary. There is none of the high society background or scandal as provided in *The Goat-Foot God*, none of the crude moments of derring-do as seen in *The Winged Bull*, and none of the portentous atmosphere and melodrama of *The Demon Lover.* Nothing very much happens at all, except that a mentally retarded worker falls into the sea off a locale that is recognizably Brean Down; some friendly girls get quite tipsy; Wilfred makes a crude comment about slop buckets; and the tongues of the locals wag as local tongues do.

Nothing much happens, and yet it is a masterpiece. It is the finest occult novel ever written. No one before or since has come remotely close to matching it.

No matter that her philosophies failed to save her marriage, or that her Masters brought weariness and pain in her final years. No matter that she was never entirely happy in the ceremonial circle when it came to the place of Love. In *The Sea Priestess* Dion gave us something more: she gave us beauty; she gave us the full moon rising.

Wilfred Maxwell lives with his mother and sister in Dickford, for which read Axbridge. During a spell of delirium brought on by a savage asthma attack, he learns to commune with the Moon.

> As I lay there, doped and exhausted and half hypnotized by the moon, I let my mind range beyond time to the beginning. I saw the vast seas of infinite space, indigo-dark in the Night of the Gods; and it seemed to me that in the darkness and silence must be the seed of all being.
>
> With the weakness and the drugs the bars of my soul had been loosened. For there is to every man's mind a part like the dark side of the moon that he never sees, but I was being privileged to see it. It was like inter-stellar space in the Night of the Gods, and in it were the roots of my being.

He has occasion to visit Miss Le Fay Morgan who has been on his firm's books for longer than he has been alive. Expecting a crusty nonagenarian he is not a little surprised to find a woman who is, by any standards, ravishing. She is an adept, of course. Someone rather like Ayesha, in the Rider Haggard novel *She*. Miss Morgan is a woman who has touched the primal fires and been renewed.

As usual, this is tied in with another story of reincarnation. Wilfred sees himself in another age, waiting on the shore as a ship comes from Atlantis carrying the Sea Priestess in question:

> They dropped the sail with a run, and backed water with the oars and just kept her off the sand-bank. And as they drifted past within a stone's throw, I saw, sitting high on the stern poop, a woman in a carven chair. She had a great book in her lap, and at the commotion with the sail she raised her head, and I saw that she had a pale face and scarlet lips, and long dark hair like sea-weed in the tide. Round her hair, binding it, was a gold and jewelled band. For those few moments as the boat wore off the sand-bank I looked into her face and she into mine; and the eyes were strange eyes, as of a sea goddess.

Understandably obsessed by such a woman, Wilfred's persona from this darkest age manages to win his heart's desire: before he becomes a living sacrifice to the sea gods, he spends one blessed night of passion with her. The love he knew that night, the lessons he learned, were carried by his 'seed-atom' down through the millennia.

This priestess from Atlantis had been called to Britain to use her knowledge against the troublesome tides. Miss Morgan had likewise come to Dickford on a parallel mission. She buys the old fort at the tip of Brean Down, and with Wilfred's help converts it into a temple worthy of the sea-gods. She is aided in all this by the discarnate Moon Priest (Charles Seymour) who is her inner mentor, and ultimately Wilfred's too.

Bernard Bromage said that this enchantress was based upon Maiya Tranchell-Hayes, but it is quite clearly an image of Dion herself at this time, though made younger, slimmer, and more sensual in her accoutrements. Miss Morgan is a vamp when the need arises, which Dion could never be. Miss Morgan is alone but never lonely; whereas Dion was rarely alone, often lonely.

The estate agent and the mystic beauty work powerful magic together in lieu of making love. After a mighty rite Wilfred turns up to find that she has disappeared, emtombed within the earth in an act of ritual suicide, the temple he has worked so hard to build wrecked by storms.

Distraught, helpless, he ends up marrying his secretary Molly, a shadow-woman who has nevertheless always been devoted to him. Things fail to gel; they fail to consummate their relationship; Wilfred is still too attached to the Great Soul who has just left him.

Finally, in desperation, Molly herself learns something of the allure of the Sea Priestess, and comes to him one moonset with her arms out towards him in the strange, stiff attitude of the ancient gods, 'like Hathor when she is a hawk,' and Wilfred sees that Molly wears on her neck and wrists the charged sapphires that had once belonged to Morgan.

The outer world disappears; they pass into another dimension through an act of spontaneous magic, and Molly becomes more than just a butcher's daughter, she becomes the silvery figure of Isis — Isis Unveiled. . .

It was the best thing that Dion had ever written and she knew it. She sent a copy to the local paper at Llandudno, introduced herself as a former resident, and asked them to take note of the rhythms in particular: the rhythms of the sea itself.

And even though the manuscript was rejected by several publishers before she decided to publish it herself, at her own expense, and even though it made little enough impact upon the literary scene of the time, who today could deny her the smugness she felt at her achievement?

That time of The Belfry coincided with her most creative period. Paganism was good for her. There is evidence, too, that during this time she was using a different set of contacts, and that Socrates, Carstairs, and even perhaps Lord E were left for the Work still being done at 3 QT and Chalice Orchard.

It was said that Dion went to great expense to install a lift in the building. It was not simply for the purpose of getting her increasing bulk to the top of the stairs with the minimum of effort. She would never have mocked the Goddess like that. It was meant to enable her to rise, quite literally, as Isis, before her priest's magical gaze. Isis Unveiled and Isis Rising . . . she became all things to all men within the inner sanctum of the upper room. It is easy to smile at such apparent folly, but in the right circumstances she could induce in her co-workers the delicious, almost fearful trembling that is sometimes a sign that the gods are near.

In some ways that lift is a symbol of much that was wrong with magic in that era: the belief that it hung upon entirely rational principles, capable of construction and reconstruction, capable of taking Woman in her most exalted and magical expression up into the highest levels. And so it may have done, but one person at least, Charles Seymour, confided to a friend that Dion-as-Isis had trouble with the lift shuddering. It was not easy to rise upon the planes and into the immortal consciousness while the rapidly shaken body clung on for dear life.

Hydraulic vagaries apart, Dion brought the magics of Egypt and Atlantis most fully into her own world during this period. Whatever the state of her Christianity in, say 1930, by 1938 it had been pushed into the rather dainty confines of the Guild of the Master Jesus.

Apart from her own writings, there are two sources which actually describe what she did during this ritual heyday. The first is in Bromage's reflection in the magazine *Light*:

> I was invited, one Saturday evening, to a function which will always remain in my memory as one of the best attempts I have ever witnessed to stimulate the subconscious by means of 'pantomime' drawn from the more ancient records of the hierophant's art.
>
> One was ushered very secretly into the house and then conducted up flights of stairs to the topmost floor where everything was bathed in a deep sepulchral gloom.
>
> One was given a seat with a few carefully handpicked 'others' in a room at one end of which was erected a platform before which hung a curtain.
>
> After a period of meditation and speculation, the space behind the curtain became illuminated and a 'Rite of Isis' began. I am conversant with the celebrated Mysteries which were held in the ancient days at Eleusis in Greece; and happen to know by heart the equally celebrated 'Orphic Poem' which was recited by Initiates of old. Dion Fortune had written round the central episode of Initiation a 'Play', mostly in dumb-show, in which she, her husband, and one or two friends enacted the principal parts.
>
> It was a carefully-studied, conscientiously ritualized performance with excellent regard paid to temple, alterations of currents of energy and correct intonation of the sacred words. But the costumes worn were much more Egyptian than Greek; and I had the feeling that it was *Egypt* which Dion Fortune was seeking to explore and probe; not the more recent occultism of Greece.
>
> I was right. When, later, I discussed the performance with her she admitted that it was the Ancient Egyptian overtones in the Greek symbolism which had always attracted her, and that my own account of a period I had spent investigating the ancient cities of the Nile had thrilled her imagination. For reasons best known to herself, she was convinced that I had some occult affiliation with the great Cat-Goddess who sits enthroned in her 'altar' in the gardens of the Temple of Karnak; and, furthermore, she 'accused' me of casting the image of this dread Being athwart the calculated rhythms of her 'Rite of Isis'.

And the other source is in the Magical Diaries of Charles Seymour, one of the workings being written up as follows:

Thursday October 28th, 1937
11 to 11.30 a.m.
Very Fit.

Tried the Tejas Tatwa — fairly successful. Got into a most desolate mountain place into a big temple very crude: saw a thing like a lion, strangely alive, a great fire, and things that were hardly human. Came back rather tired. Working with Volens in Museum Chambers.

Evening working with CCT and DNF in lecture room 3 QT. Placed the 3 chairs in S altar N. DNF as High Priestess, self middle, CCT left. I put up and cleared Temple at 6.15 p.m. Then did a meditation and got the Cave. At 7 p.m. I went to my room and changed, came back and invoked Isis as the Primordial Mother. Then I deliberately built the Cave and got the P of A, and the idea in very general outlines of the evening working. Got the Black Isis and the Cave very clearly and also a fair head of power. CCT came, I went up to get DNF, CCT went into the Temple and bolted out saying it was full of presences and Things and it scared her. So meditation was effective! We used linked hands.

We 3 went in at 8.10. Invoked Isis. Using the Tatwa method we started from the House of the Virgins, CCT in Black, black litter, black bearers, went to empty Temple where DNF took charge, and to Hall of Sphinxes. Then into an underground passage and suddenly I shot out and found myself standing at the entrance of Cave where I waited for the other two. Then all Three went into cave, and past Anubis the guardian at the curtain. Within was the P of A waiting for us. He took over — and spoke to CCT. He set her certain conditions which she refused at first, and then agreed to them. She then walked to the stone of sacrifice, through the fire burning on the steps and seated herself between the thighs of the Black Isis. I am not clear as to what happened then for the image of the P of A and CCT vanished in a sort of red fog. Later I saw clearly and CCT was leaving her seat, she laid herself on the stone of sacrifice and I saw the P of A bend over her as if sacrificing her(!). Then he vanished and I took CCT back to the Temple of the White Isis. We returned through it to the House of the V where DNF gave the address. Then back to normal. The power was very great, and my eyes were streaming from it. CCT very done at the end, and I think a bit scared. Ended 9.15 p.m. Then while DNF and I were downstairs talking she slept and felt much better.

10 p.m. I found Proctor waiting for me in my rooms and I set to work to get the Osiris contact. Working on my sanctuary I took him through the veil and we found ourselves standing in front of the Ptolemy Gateway and the Temple of Khonsu. We walked through this — and he described what he saw, and then we went to the shrine of Osiris which is to the left (West) of the Temple of Khonsu. We went round this tiny temple and then down into the underground crypt.

Here the whole temple came to life in a blaze of cold soft blue white light. It was so bright that for a moment I thought someone had switched on the light. Then I saw the White Osiris alive — and he turned a ray of power on to us. Next moment Proctor and I were kneeling before him (Proctor right). Isis and Nephythys stood behind him. Thoth was on my left Anubis behind me. Horus was behind Proctor and a little to his right. I was looking into the past and at an initiation. A blaze of light and power came. Suddenly this went and we were back in my room. I was very tired and next moment the people next door began a row.

Proctor was very puzzled because his shoulder was seized by a heavy hand, just before we knelt down, he thought I had done it but opening his eyes he saw my hands on my knees. Anyway I have got that contact, also the curious impression that then I was a woman!

P said he saw the place — not as he knew it now — but as it must have been in the old days. (Very tired but very pleased — both of us.)

Another entry dated 25 March 1938 contains the comment: 'Self fit but very fed up with the Belfry Isis Rite', which suggests that he was finding Dion less than satisfying as Priestess. He actually felt that he was being drained at times, as though she were some black hole which drew in all light and energy and allowed nothing to escape.

But the best and most positive picture of what went on (or what she wanted to go on) during the Belfry period is to be found in her final novel *Moon Magic*.

If *The Sea Priestess* is her best novel then *Moon Magic* is the most accomplished, being a technically superior piece of work in which the limited action of its predecessor is reduced still further, until only two people exist: Rupert Malcom and Miss Le Fay Morgan; not forgetting the odd little temple — formerly a church — that they come to inhabit and revivify down a quiet London street.

It is the same theme, the same endless theme, as repetitive as her constant rows with Merl but honed to sharpness, nothing wasted, and where every nuance is a blatant and final plea to Merl. Malcolm is a brilliant but frustrated surgeon who is married to a neurotic and sexless woman. Miss Morgan, by means of witchery and a magic that had once and will forever grace the temples of the Nile, tries once more to explain to her mage of a husband the true meaning of love and their life on this earth.

Here, finally, is Dion Unveiled, speaking as a real adept, showing an insight into the technicalities of magic which has never been equalled. While beneath it all is the woman upon whom the goddess-form had settled, lonely and weary with the battle.

She also explains very clearly just *how* the rites she worked would go beyond her and Merl and all her Adepti, and influence the very race.

> We hold, we Initiates, that you can bring a thing through from the Inner Planes into manifestation by acting it out symbolically. That is why ritual is used. Now if you and I were to work out together the particular problem I want to solve, it would be solved for the race because we are part of the race, and whatever is realized in our minds becomes part of the group mind and spreads like a ferment.

Again and again she emphasized that sex upon the physical plane was not necessary, that when the Serpent Power was awakened such a crude form of coitus became redundant. In fact this is perfectly true on the rarest of magical levels, and we should beware of dismissing her ideas on sexuality as 'nothing more than' a matter of compensation. She had had these ideas all her lives. They were part of her own gnosis. In *Moon Magic* she brings it superb expression via the Egyptian patterns that she so loved.

> I myself was no longer robed in the dull black of velvet that fits all negative forces, but in soft, shimmering filmy indigo, blue and purple; upon my head was the horned moon, and about my hips was the starry girdle of the constellations, and I knew that I was Isis in her underworld aspect whom the Greeks called Persephone, for all the goddesses are one goddess, personified under different modes.
>
> There was nothing of the human left about me. I was vast as the universe; my head hung among the stars; my feet on the curve of the earth as it swung under me in its orbit. Around me, in translucent space, stood the stars, rank upon rank, and I was of their company. Beneath me, very far beneath me, all Nature spread like a tree-patterned carpet. Alone on the globe that soared through space I stood, with the kneeling man before me, and there were none others in all creation save he and I — I, the ALL-WOMAN, and he, the Archetypal MAN,

and the whole of the manifested universe was summed up in the relationship between us.

It is not clear when the book was written, but it was certainly before 1939. The Second World War was to make such an impact upon her that she would certainly have mentioned it in some way. We do know that the work was only completed some years after her death thanks to the mediumship of Anne Greig. Normally, being a fast and prolific writer, Dion would never have let such a manuscript languish incomplete. But in this case she never finished it in her lifetime because, by this time, Merl had left her. After almost twelve magical, murderous, and sometimes marvellous years, he had gone.

The *Bucks Examiner* dated 4 September 1959, gives us the surprising information that for some time during the 1930s he had been doing research on foodstuffs – particularly the soya bean – from his own little factory. In 1938 the Spanish Republican government invited him out to try and deal with the nutritional problems of children in Spain. He had been in Barcelona only eight weeks when General Franco returned, and he had to flee for his life, leaving behind equipment valued at £2,500. 'Though it was a failure, I am more pleased with that failure than I am with anything else I've ever done.'

Merl began all over again, taking up a post as Tuberculosis Officer at Southwark Borough Council. He might even have come back to Dion except that here, in the urban greyness, he met a woman who seemed to him like a portion of the dawn.

The woman in question was Anne Mower White, who was then an Assistant Medical Officer of Health in Southwark. Merl applied for a divorce and Dion, despite being privately appalled, did not contest the suit. She was appalled because, although she was a representative of mighty Isis in both her dark and bright aspects, she was also, underneath this burden, a mortal woman. She never mentioned him again. She began to conduct herself as though he had never existed. It was the beginning of her darkness.

There is the card Temperance to look at here: it suggests the method of working towards wisdom by deliberate change, pouring one's energy into differing vessels as the need arises. It is the sloughing of old skin, the exchange of masks.

Merl had several masks: he was the Sun Priest, he was a physician; he lived his life through many outlets, none of them really overlapping.

Dion in contrast was the Moon Priestess who had no light of her own and was nothing without the right degree and angle of illumination. People never saw her as anything else; they would not let her be so. She tried to find some outlet from all this by taking on a new identity via the romantic thrillers she wrote under the name of V. M. Steele, but these were dismal pieces which no one knew or cared very much about at all. V. M. Steele was still-born; Dion Fortune almost became mummified.

We can leap ahead in time here as magicians occasionally can, and look at the rest of Merl's life with Anne. According to the testimony of all who knew them they were an extremely happy couple, ideally suited. They lived in a house which Merl designed himself on Weedon Lane, Amersham, looking out on to empty fields. For some reason this mage from the Air sign of Libra was determined to make it draught-free. To the surprise of many of his relatives and former friends back in Wales Merl made a point of renewing contacts, inviting them to join him and Anne in their new home.

His cousin V. W. Williams became close to him at this period and saw a man that was happy with life, very droll and kind, quite passionate about music and possessed of a very definite charisma — a kind and kingly presence.

It seems as though Merl had reached back, via his young wife, via his Welsh relatives, and touched some of the normality he had known before the Great War, and before the Greater War — that between the Darkness and the Light — that his magic had involved him in. And in some ways we can see this reflected in the very appearance and character of Anne. There is a photograph of her: blonde and slim, young and affable, the land around her in full bloom.[7] It is a far cry from the woman he has once posed with in Chalice Orchard, but not very far from the way that Dion would have wanted to look and be herself, underneath the increasing obesity, underneath the burden of the Goddess.

Thomas Penry Evans died in 1959, and with him died a distinctive line of magic. Not that Anne knew anything about this: she was in fact High Church like Violet had once been. She even believed the name of their house to have been derived from the first letter of Penry's Christian name, and the first two letters of her own. She thought it rather clever of her husband to think of that, never dreaming that in the name 'Pan' there was anything more than an expression of their life together. . . The formula of Temperance was not for Dion. It was not possible. She had to take its parallel, that of The Hanged Man, the sacrificed god or goddess who gives up life for the greater good of the race. It is like the journey of Arthur and the three queens in the death-barge to Avalon, except that in her case it was all reversed. The Mysteries of Women often reverse such things: she faced her last years now as the queen, mortally wounded, being ferried to Avalon by three kings: Loveday, Chichester and Creasy. Not exactly what she would have wanted but the only thing that Isis, in those dark aspects that she had deliberately invoked, would allow.

No matter: she would survive, in her own way. More, she could even look back upon it all with some satisfaction and little sense of waste. For she, being an occultist, had been involved in more than an ordinary marriage, more than an ordinary mating; for a dozen years she and Penry had striven together like the two dragons that a previous Merlin had perceived wrestling beneath the earth, and the peculiar magical love-makings that they had perfected in those lustrous years at The Belfry would live on after them both:

> I thought of the complete uselessness and wastefulness, and folly of the sacrifice that had been demanded of him by conventional morality . . . I thought of all the needless, purposeless, long drawn out torture inflicted by the superstitions and conventions of mankind, of which our orthodox morality is one of the worst, and with the power of magic that was upon me at that moment I cursed our modern Moloch to its face and struck at its feet of clay; and what I did then because Malcolm's suffering had moved me, I did magically for all men placed as he, in their varying degrees of frustration and starvation, for thus is magic wrought. That which I did then, in those hours of intense power and emotion up there in the darkness of the moon-temple with the river in flood outside, went into the group mind of the race to work like leaven, as I knew it would when I called Malcolm to the Rite. There is freedom in the world today because of what I did that night, for it opened the first tiny rift in the great barrier and the forces began to move, channelling and eroding as they flowed, till presently the strength of waters came flooding through like the bursting of a dam and all resistance melted away . . .

This, I believe, is where the original manuscript of *Moon Magic* ended, or could have ended. The mighty Isis had found the final missing part of Osiris, and given Man back to himself again. And in doing so they had gone on to create the child Horus, who would be greater than them both. Aleister Crowley, who had prophecied the Aeon of Horus nearly 40 years earlier, would have understood this better than they themselves.

This paragraph expressed the very essence of Dion's philosophy and allowed us a glimpse of a Priestess at the very height of her power and understanding. She was so identified with the sleeping Goddess of the race that she was part of a two-way flow, an occult symbiosis. What she achieved within herself would make an impact within the collective unconsciousness of Womanhood within the West, filtering back through to conscious levels in due course. Likewise, what the slumbering Goddess knew would one day come through to her Priestess, and thence to the world of men. And no one would ever connect it, in any part, to the rites that had been worked within some haunted rooms within the West End of the Moon City.

All this was attained in the fraught peace before the Stukas dived on Poland, and before Merl left. It was a cruel — and typical — magical irony that in setting Man free her own man had left her; and in becoming so perfectly one-in-herself she suddenly found herself a woman alone. She was nearly fifty years old by now. Most of her life had been devoted to Magic, to climbing up the Heaven-tree from the consciousness of Earth, through the Moon, up past the logic of Mercury and the passion of Venus, into the heart of the Sun and upward even further, towards the Abyss that all the magi have to cross some day, stepping boldy but with immense precision across the Sword Bridge.

War was inevitable, really. New Aeons are always heralded by wars. The Abyss which she herself had glimpsed on many levels in many ways was looming before her nation and within the lodge. It needed no magical vision to see that things were going wrong within the world and her own life. And among all her other troubles, she had begun to realise that there were at least two people who worked with her in 3 QT who just *had* to be made to leave . . .

11.

THE MORNING STAR BETWEEN THE MOON'S HORNS

After tea we went to the temple of Atlantis and saw it by moonlight.

FPD

In 1926, still bearing the last shred of the mask known as V. M. Firth, she had gone to the office of Christine Campbell Thomson Ltd with the manuscript of her book *The Problem of Purity*. Like so many others since, but not so many before, she wanted an agent to take on the burden of hawking the manuscript, to promote it for all it was worth. She chose this particular firm not solely because of its reputation, but because Christine Campbell Thomson was one of the very few women making a mark in a cut-throat field.

The Problem of Purity held few attractions for Miss Thomson, even though the actual theme preoccupied her no less than it did most single young women of that era. The book was just not, in her eyes, an especially appealing one, and certainly not likely to enter the best-seller class. Miss Thomson also knew, as only experienced writers and agents know, that very few books ever make much money. Dion surely thought, as all new writers think, that this book was different; that this one would sweep the world. CCT, as she came to be known, had a clearer insight into its very limited commercial appeal; nevertheless, for reasons that she could never later explain, she agreed to try and place the manuscript and did, finally, succeed.

Although this was a woman whom Dion was, briefly, to see as being her heir, there was nothing in that first meeting to indicate what might come: no shocks of recognition from previous lives together in the now-drowned temples of Philae, no visions or dramatic faints. Yet somehow *something* passed between them. A few years later, around the year 1931 or '32, Mrs Evans, as she now was, came back to the offices and asked CCT if she would care to attend a lecture on ceremonial magic that she was giving in the near future. CCT, who had for some time been showing evidence of an increasingly psychic capacity, was more than happy to go.

It was not the first offer of this kind that had come her way. Just after the Great War John William Brodie-Innes had come to her with the manuscript of his last novel, *The Golden Rope*. A dry and wry man, he was also at this time the head of the Alpha and Omega temple in London, in which Dion received her neophyte initiation. A lawyer, a minor novelist known chiefly for his interest in witchcraft, he suggested to Miss Thomson that she might have an aptitude for study along 'certain occult lines'. Perhaps he had seen the marks in her aura from initiations in previous lives. Magicians claim to be able to do this, and some of them really can. The highest adepts, according to Dion, often had the symbol of a great sun disk emblazoned in their auras – symbol of Atlantis. Others have markings discernible as Egyptian cartouches, although not all magicians can see such things. One told me that although she could never see such marks, she felt an almost audible 'ringing' inside when a real adept came near. While someone who knew Dion in the early 1930s had the strongest sensation of a great light shining above her brow. It was shortly after this that Dion started wearing head-bands.

Brodie-Innes it was who eventually did an about-turn and came to support Mathers in the latter's belief in the 'Third Order' behind the Golden Dawn, and thus in the Secret Chiefs. And it is through him that we get close to an intriguing Mystery within a lodge already filled with them.

BI, as they all called him in the manner of the time, believed himself to have been a reincarnation of Michael Scot, the mediaeval wizard. And when CCT made her own contact with Lord E under Charles Seymour's tuition, she was quite sure that the former Chancellor and the Scottish novelist were one and the same. Thus Michael Scot, Lord E and J. W. Brodie-Innes were all the same entity. Yet, as we shall see, the Lord E that they contacted was not the waspish egocentric Thomas Erskine, but instead the slow and reactionary Lord Eldon, also Chancellor, whose real name was John Scott and who claimed something of a family connection with his hierophantic forebear.

This was all beyond Miss Thomson at that time. She was not ready for entry into the mystic group that BI kept alluding to, and not overly enthralled by his talk of past lives. Years later, almost a decade after Brodie-Innes had died, things would change dramatically. When she went through those two columns which formed the porch of 3 QT, she took an almost tangible step into the Otherworld. In many ways she never returned.

To an extent she was a diminutive version of Dion herself in her early days – the Dion who would lock herself in occult combat with her antagonists. One was essentially solar while the other, Dion, was completely lunar; but never at any time did CCT lose herself within the sometimes overwhelming magnetism of her teacher.

She failed the first part of the course: she had marital problems by this time, her husband being a drunken Irishman by the name of Oscar Cook. Also she detested the woman who ran that course, a Claudia Brine, who was to reappear as one of the forces behind the 'Christian Theosophists' who seem to have taken over from the Christian Mystic Lodge when this became completely subsumed by Dion.

Her Magical Motto, or Name, was *Frère Ayme Frère*, taken from her mother's side of the family, but this was rarely used. She was Chris, or she was CCT. Almost no-one called her Mrs Cook, as though they could all see that her marriage was to be brief and doomed.

It was inevitable that, with Dion's increasing output, CCT became her agent. During long lunches at the Strand Palace Hotel or in the Chinese restaurant which had opened in Picadilly, they worked at putting Dion's novels into shape, as Dion had a tendency to 'nod' in the literary sense quite as much as Homer. It was CCT who was used as a sounding board for the regular instalments of *The Mystical Qabalah*, and she who suggested the format of the pot-boiler *Practical Occultism in Daily Life*, which they all referred to — like schoolgirls at prep time — as 'Prac Occ'. When it came to the V. M. Steele novels it was CCT who suggested the name Violet Orchard, although Dion would have none of that. And in the first edition of *The Sea Priestess* that Dion gave to her agent was the inscription: 'To CCT Ltd, from DNF Unlimited'. CCT was also invited to join Mr and Mrs Evans to hear the lecture given by Harry Price on 'The Brocken Spectre Experiment', a piece of foolery based upon a complete ignorance of ritual magic, and which Dion felt was a tale told by an idiot. But when it became clear to Mrs Evans that her husband was not unattracted to the petite young sorceress, Dion made quite certain that in future they would never be in a position to work together alone.

In fact she found the ideal solution: she put CCT in the hands of Colonel Seymour, who was known by the initials of his Motto *Foy Pour Devoir*. CCT agreed to become his personal pupil with some reluctance for she was much attracted to Merl. Seymour, she felt, was a difficult and sometimes prickly customer to deal with. Nevertheless she decided to become his priestess for a short time at least. In fact she had little choice. It was either Seymour, or she could join the rather twee dearies in the Guild of the Master Jesus.

July 1937 marked the start of a relationship that was to last for the rest of their lives and beyond. It also marked the first and only real schism that the lodge would ever know.

Charles Richard Foster Seymour was born on 9 April 1880 in King's County near the border with Galway. He was of a rather higher social class than Moriarty, being one of the landed gentry of Ireland, his family having their seat at Killagally Park.

A career soldier, he began with the Hampshire Regiment and later joined the Indian Army. He fought in the Transvaal and the Orange Free State during the Boer War; during the Great War he served in German East Africa, where he was wounded; he fought with the Rangoon Volunteer Rifles, and also the Burma Rifles. He was in Moscow in 1917 acting as an interpreter, being fluent in Russian; and he later taught at the Staff College in Quetta, where he numbered among his pupils men who would become Britain's Generals during the Second World War.[1]

Seymour was one of the three great magicians in Dion's life, the others being of course Moriarty and Merl. Like them he was a Celt, and exceedingly proud of it. Even those with whom she was not intimately involved expressed some Celtic aspects: Brodie-Innes and Mathers in particular, even if the latter's was a mere assumption. And Seymour's background in occult work was also Masonic, as he was a member of the Grand Lodge of Scotland. It is quite possible that Seymour knew Moriarty during his time in Africa; very likely that he knew Brodie-Innes. Dion certainly knew *him* when he first appeared at 3 QT, but it is not known what or who drew him there.

He was the Colonel Brangwyn of *The Winged Bull:* 'a tall, slight, dark-skinned man; and his black hair, brushed straight back from the forehead, was greying over the ears and receding from the temples.' Burdened with a dismal marriage to a woman who would stand outside 3 QT and scream up at Dion's window demanding that she give back her husband (incidents which disturbed the formidable Mrs Evans not one bit), he became the last man ever to work with Dion on equal terms, the last man never to be afraid of her, nor yet idolize her.

Dion must have seen in him something of the late Moriarty. They were both well-travelled older men, both Irish, both of similar religious background and soaked through with Masonic experience. For a time Seymour replaced Merl as her priest, although as we have noted it was less congenial to him than it was to her.

Before long he took over the editing of the magazine, writing many of the articles himself. Indeed, these articles represented the very best outpouring from the lodge, from a vision that was in no way dependent upon that of its founder.[2] A matriarch, as all connoisseurs of 'inner Celtia' are, he was the real scholar within the group, although he wore his knowledge lightly. Many of the juniors, showing the sort of snobbishness inherent to the middle class backgrounds from which most of them came, felt that Seymour was the man Dion should have married. Merl was too rough, too coarse. Seymour had breeding. Indeed he had; but in the last analysis he was far closer to the spirit of Mr Evans than that of his wife.

The story of Colonel Seymour and Christine Campbell Thomson has been told in detail elsewhere. He is of great interest at this point, however, because it is through him that we encounter one of the more perplexing aspects of the lodge.

Working in the rooms he rented next door, at 2 Queensborough Terrace, FPD spent most of the 1930s training some of the Inner Light's pupils toward making contact with a completely different set of Chiefs to those used by Dion. More, Socrates, and the Master David had no place within the collective psyches of this sub-group. They used Melchisedec of Salem, of course (or rather he used them), but Socrates and Carstairs played no part in their work. They used Lord E, too, who taught them the magic of the Green Ray and showed them Atlantis in its final days, but as we have seen it was not Lord Erskine but Eldon they linked with – the man who had been Chancellor of England immediately before Erskine and immediately after.

Eldon was born plain John Scott in Love Lane, Newcastle-upon-Tyne, on 4 June 1751. His father was a wealthy man who owned several keel boats, a pub, and was involved in coal-mining. Originally intended for the Church and an easy life, John sacrificed it all by eloping with Elizabeth Surtees, who eventually bore him ten children. His maxim was to live like a hermit and work like a horse; he became Lord Chief Justice and was created Baron Eldon of Eldon, in County Durham (Eldon, be it noted, meaning 'from the holy hill'). Politically he was a reactionary, and was nicknamed for a long time 'Bloody Eldon', being as keen to hound Catholics as More had been to harry Protestants. But there is no doubt that as Chancellor under both George III and IV he did much to hold the country together.

Like Erskine, Eldon had enormous quantities of charm. Of middle height, active with regular features and keen sparkling eyes, he was seen at the time as almost the ideal of manly beauty. He was a great drinker, with an inexhaustible fund of witty anecdotes, a good landlord, quietly charitable, a devoted husband – but no church-goer. He died on 13 January 1838 and was buried near his Encombe estate in the graveyard of the weirdly atmospheric Kingston Chapel, set on a high hill in the Isle of Purbeck.

If Erskine once eclipsed him it was a very brief affair. Eldon became a figure of almost Churchillian substance and duration while Erskine became a virtual nonentity.

Had Seymour made a mistake? When Dion talked about Lord E did he get hold of the wrong name yet still make contact with the same entity? Or were Erskine and Eldon (or their Inner Plane presentations) two separate entities?

Neither Seymour nor any of his pupils had any notion of identifying Eldon with More. The Erskine/More connection was common knowledge among the juniors of the post-Merl period, if we may call it that. It seems never to have entered Seymour's head. And although both of the Lords E hearkened their channels back to Atlantean days, the tone and manner of both were very different.

Lord Eldon was not the only anomaly, either. There were Kha'm-uast and Cleomenes III to be considered.

Seymour seems to have made contact with the former via the statue which can still be seen in the British Museum, which he felt was oozing with magnetism. Historically Setne Kha'm-uast was the High Priest of Ptah, a son of Rameses II and overlord of all the magico-religious ceremonies in Egypt. His own centre was in Memphis, and he lived from about 1300 BC to 1246 BC. His mother was the Queen Isit-Nefert. In his youth he had been a soldier; later he became a priest and great scholar. Had he not died some ten years before his father, he would probably have become Pharoah. Seymour identified him as a Merlin figure, potent and ambivalent, neither good nor evil — or beyond both.

Cleomenes III was a Spartan king from the house of Agiad who ruled from 235-222 BC. A vigorous and ultimately maddened character whose ideas on rulership bear odd parallels with the Spartan-inspired *Utopia* of Thomas More, he had defeated the Achaean league at Laodoceia in 227, and then instituted the cancellation of all debts, the redivision of the land, and a return to the old Spartan training. He curtailed the powers of the council and introduced the board of six elders. He was defeated in battle in 222 by the Macedonian king Antigonus Dosun, and fled to the sanctuary offered by Ptolemy Euergetes in Egypt. Imprisoned by the latter's successor, Cleomenes broke out in 219, and, having failed to raise a revolt in Alexandria among his fellow Gnostics, took his own life.

Eldon, Kha'm-uast, and Cleomenes were, one might guess, the contacts used within whatever temple Seymour belonged to before he joined the Inner Light. Given that it is known that he often worked with the Hermes Temple of the Stella Matutina, where Dion found final satisfaction within the Golden Dawn, it is reasonable to assume that Seymour and Fortune worked on parallel lines within the overall aura of 3 QT; and that these were the contacts (or some of them) which held sway within the Belfry, and during Dion's Greek and Egyptian phases generally.

This is obviously one of the points on the caduceus where the three lines of light meet. It is something that will never — ought never — to be completely untangled, lest the whole design collapse.

Whoever or whatever is the truth behind the Eldon/Erskine enigma, Dion certainly made ample use of the Kha'm-uast contact, among others; and very likely the Cleomenes one too. After all, she was an initiate of the Stella Matutina before she ever formed the Inner Light. She had the right to make these contacts if she so wished. And it seems that during a period of the '30s she so wished.

Things did not continue so cosily with Seymour. He began to feel that Dion was, quite deliberately, making him feel unwelcome, unvalued. New initiates were being admitted who seemed far less sympathetic to his own magic. Once, he and she had been intimate on magical levels; once, they had made something of an impact on outer levels too, when he gave his lantern lectures on the Egyptian gods and goddesses, supported by Dion chanting in the background. Now it seemed that she was quite happy to allow the rumours to circulate that the leathery old mage was doing more with his priestesses in his private rooms next door than simply working magic. The only other man of his stature in the lodge had been Merl, who had gone off to Spain, leaving the Colonel to jostle for space with the likes of Creasy and Chichester — both of whom he distrusted, and whom he felt were trying to freeze him out.

Perhaps Dion was basically disturbed by what seemed like a splinter group forming next door. Perhaps she rejected those Stella Matutina contacts on which her paganism rode for the simple reason that her pagan mage of a husband had rejected her.

One of the more curious aspects of this little side-road taken by Seymour and CCT is that their far memories bear more than a passing resemblance to those apparently achieved by Dion Fortune herself: they left Atlantis before the cataclysm, sailing to Britain where CCT was given the initiatic title 'Morgan le Fay'; they had Greek, Roman, and Norse incarnations; they had been burnt at the stake in Avignon, and known each other time and time again in the temples along the Nile.

We can give group reincarnation as one explanation for this: more than one unit of priest and priestess left Atlantis before the end; more than one Cathar had been burnt at the stake in Avignon; while the number of souls involved in Temple Work throughout the vast history of Egypt must be reckoned in hundreds of thousands. Or else we can look upon them as tribal visions, experienced by each person as he or she links, through initiation, with the group mind and memory; not to be taken in the personal sense at all. Or we can deem that these historic selves were not previous incarnations but other parts of a greater self, performing magic in previous epochs which yet exist simultaneously with our own.

It is a matter of choice. It can all be resolved and made to work by acting 'as if'.

In fact, the last far memory or 'simultaneous magic' experienced by FPD and CCT in the Fraternity of the Inner Light was in some respects the most revealing of all. It took place in 2 QT on 13 February 1939 and also in Avebury, the great sun-temple of Britain. It told, more eloquently than invective, exactly how they had come to look upon Dion:

> February 13th, 1939
> Time: 8.30 to 9 p.m.
> CCT and Self.
>
> Room was very quiet and had been carefully sealed beforehand. CCT and Self both fit. Dark of Moon near, weather fine and spring like.
>
> Waited for about five minutes and picked up a place that looked like Avebury as it may have been 3000 to 4000 years ago, except there was a long altar stone in the middle and over it had been built a sort of roof of leaves that looked like beech. It was very early in the morning just after dawn and I think it was about May Day or Beltaine. I noticed the dew on the grass. Then came two priests one carrying a gold hilted bronze sword about 2½ feet long. This was a big man heavily built with a wide face, a big mouth, large teeth with very prominent and pointed eye teeth. The other was a smaller man thin and fanatical looking who carried a large gold cup. Following them were men carrying a rough litter on which lay a young woman about twenty or thirty. Fair hair blue eyes. She was naked with finger nails, toe nails, and nipples painted red. She was not bound.
>
> (Note: I was feeling awful, my back all creepy and I was unable to move in my chair.) Then the woman was placed on the altar stone with her head (face) facing N E looking into a notch in the hills where the sun would appear. This woman was paralysed below the neck – or hypnotized or drugged. But she could move her head a little and her eyes rolled and she was fully conscious. The big priest stood behind her head waiting for the sun to rise to plunge the sword between the painted nipples. The smaller priest with the bowl squatted at her feet to catch the blood from a runnel in the gently sloping stone of sacrifice. The whole temple space was filled with figures. The sun came up after a long wait the priest raised the sword to stab and I recognized him as DNF, the other was Chris, and I was the girl sacrificed on the stone. The big priest had the face of a devil. I ended dead beat both physically and emotionally.

From Seymour's point of view the coming of the war gave him an excuse to leave with dignity. He was invited by the War Office to study intercepted messages, and make sure that there were no international conspiracies between any Germanic or British secret societies. It proved unfruitful; soon he was back with the Home Guard. He never went near Dion, however, and seems to have joined what was left of the Merlin Temple, sister-temple to the Hermes, where he soon took CCT, Paula Trevanion, as well as inviting the Daw family.[3] Here, once more, we find the Kha'm-uast contacts in full flow.

If nothing else Seymour gave the Inner Light, when he was dominant within the lodge, its contact with faëry — although it is ironic that it took a battered old war lord to achieve this. The magic he developed was very like those fragments of Moina's work that have survived, in which the Irish pantheons were invoked, the Sidhe awakened, the Lands of the Ever-Young at least partially explored.

What he gave Dion personally, apart from an increasingly rare ability to look upon her as and treat her as an equal, was contact with Egypt, pure and simple. The Isis rites she had worked with Merl had had Greek overtones, as Bromage had noted, but with the Colonel she got the magic of Egypt in its undiluted form.

The two magics are not inconsistent, for what Seymour and his co-workers did was to leave something in the British psyche very much akin to those faience beads which had once been found under one of the stupendous columns of Stonehenge.

Merl disappeared from Dion's life in Southwark, Seymour in Liverpool. Between them they took the rampant pagan aspects of her magic with them. She never went to Egypt again.

In her last years, as she drew nearer to death and the Sphere of the Masters to which she really belonged, a long-neglected Christ had room to enter once more.

12.

THE COMING OF ARTHUR, AND THE JOURNEY TO THE WEST

> We have been engaged in creating a myth, which by its nature is in harmony with our national tradition. This is readily accepted by the group mind of the race and spreads and multiplies in it like yeast as mind after mind that has the capacity for such ideas picks them up subconsciously and brings them through . . .
>
> Dion Fortune

War came, to the utter astonishment of many — especially the illuminati. Whatever their other virtues, many of the Inner Plane Adepti are as peculiarly inept at predicting war as the British people are at preparing for one. Britons have never, in their long and bloody history, been ready for any war. Dion could have told the world of its imminence if anyone had asked, and a few did. Although it was not through inner sources that she became convinced about Wotan's immenint unleashing, but because she had a great deal of time for Mr Churchill. As she often pointed out, Mr Churchill had been predicting Germany's intentions for some time, and no one listened — well, no one except her. She thought he was a Great Soul.

Reaction among Londoners was two-fold: they girded their loins, stayed, and got themselves ready; or they hurried out into the blitz-free countryside just as quickly as they could.

Dion had no intention of scuttling anywhere. Too old to do a stint on the land again, not well enough to take on any of the civilian tasks such as Air-Raid Precautions, she was determined to stay in London, in the City of the Moon, and work magic for the protection of the nation while the streets around her became as cratered as the Moon itself.

Whatever the emotional truth of her separation from Merl, and whatever the real reasons behind Seymour's defection, the declaration of war on 3 September 1939 gave her something else to look forward to. It had the effect upon her, as it did on so very many others, of concentrating her mind wonderfully upon the situation at hand.

The first months were the so-called 'phoney war', when the bulk of the armed forces were kicking their heels, new divisions were being hastily recruited and trained, and the hopelessly outdated equipment renewed with manic energy. When the bombs finally began to fall, after months of dread anticipation, it was as though the Dweller on the Threshold of everyone's fears had been confronted and controlled. A sense of relief was felt, despite everything.

It affected the Inner Light as it did everything else. Those who were fit and of fighting age hurried to join up. Young men found better things to do than invoke ancient gods. The war came down like a sword and completely severed the development. Those who joined after 1939 knew nothing of what went on before; the only carry-over was with a few women and older men. Creasy, who had by now retired from his job as a bank manager, could still be found within the Sanctuary, as could Loveday (Amor Vincit Omnia), who was of course far too old to do anything very active for the war effort. Under his impulse the Guild of the Master Jesus seems to have evolved into the Church of the Graal.

If the age of forty was a stock-taking time when Dion wrote her *Psychic Self Defence*, then the age of fifty was just as much so. By now, however, she was so much identified with the greater life of the nation that the psychic defence she was now advocating reached out to encompass the whole figure of Britannia.

If she came to associate the international figures of Isis and Osiris with a bitter-sweet time that she would rather now forget, the gods she was to call upon now in this time of national emergency were peculiarly British.

There is a legend, with many variants, of a cave in a mountainside wherein Arthur and his knights lie sleeping. Hanging on the wall of the cave is a great curved horn. In time of dire need, when the fate of the country hangs upon a thread, it needs someone to blow upon that horn to awaken the King who will ride out and do battle.

Dion knew just where this cave was. She had been there many times. Summoning up the last breath in her body, she blew upon that horn mightily indeed. In the glowing cave beneath the Tor, the eyes of Arthur, *Rex Quondam Rex Futurus*, flickered open.

It was not by blowing any actual horn in the sanctuary at 3 QT that she helped awaken him however. She did so by means of a letter. This, she came to feel, produced some of the best magic in her life. This, she was sure, inaugurated a new epoch in her own Otherworldly career.

Not that the letter was in any way comparable to those weighty missives precipitated by Madame Blavatsky and company. This was an open letter to all her pupils. It was so open that it enabled the rawest neophyte to practise magic on equal terms with the most sophisticated adept. The occult world had never known the like. For the first time egalitarianism had raised its head, serpent-like, towards this odd note being sounded.

Paper was in short supply in the autumn of 1939, and so were her magicians. The dais in the East was all but empty. The open letter, properly magnetized, was her only means of maintaining some tenuous link and of pushing on with some sort of group work. There was enough supply of power for this intended letter, or for the monthly *Review*, but not both. She chose the former and in so doing created a new style of working. Really, she had no choice.

The letters would be sent out every Wednesday. This was to ensure that they would arrive at their destinations in good time for the Sunday. The would-be mage was not to open the envelope before then.

The first letter was dated 8 October 1939. On that date each participant would sit or lie in a relaxed attitude, free from strain, feet together and hands clasped, resting on the letter. He would be facing towards London, and the time would be precisely 12.15. The senior Adepti, or what was left of them, would be generating power within the Sanctuary of 3 QT, creating a link between this new group and the group soul of the race itself. This first session, which continued until 12.30, was designed to help them all 'tune-in' to each other and the larger soul of Britain, enabling them to make contact with those spiritual influences at work behind the scenes.

The War, she said, was just one phase of a cosmic plan that was currently being worked out.

The symbol which linked them all was initially that of the Rose upon the Cross. This was seen as surrounded by a golden light of great brilliance, while the Rose itself was limned in that diamond-light which was a sure sign of enormous power.

One of the pupils in the provinces was so shaken by the energies felt behind this that she found herself, in her vision, within the Sanctuary at Glastonbury, shunted there like a train on to another track. Nevertheless it was the right track. In later lessons the Rosy Cross was to be seen as formulated within a wondrous cavern. This cavern was known to initiates as 'the Cavern beneath Mt Abiegnus.' Mt Abiegnus was sometimes referred to as the 'Hill of Vision': its earthly symbol was Glastonbury Tor.

In the light that filled this cavern five figures were initially discerned. Not actual presences but the Shadows of the Masters. In due course, the readers were assured, these shadows would become real. In later weeks the five would become seven, shining with the colours of the spectrum. This meant that the full range of contacts had been made. Then they could get on with the Work proper, which was to bring to the race mind the realization of the support afforded it by cosmic law.

If the ultra-pure Christian Mysticism of her early days was no longer nutrition enough for her spiritual metabolism, and if the exotic diet of her pagan Egyptian workings was no longer palatable, then this new work provided something of an alternative to them both.

In fact the Watchers of Avalon were back in force. Whether they had been pushed aside in some way during the last years before the war, or whether they shared equal billing in another magical programme, no one now can really say. In fact no one now should really care. Magicians can use other systems; the only requirement is the empathy needed to make the contacts. Whatever else the gods and the Secret Chiefs might be, they are not jealous.

Dion was pleased with the results from the start. The Archbishop of York gave a talk on radio that was almost a verbatim reading from the address and meditation given by the Inner Plane Adepti, as printed in the letter. Not that the blessed fellow had read from this, it must be clarified, but he too was giving utterance to those currents that Dion was now actively channelling. A week later the Minister of War, Hore-Belisha, did much the same sort of thing.

By now, in their weekly visits to the Hill of Vision, dark figures could also be seen massing in the background of the cave — figures that were 'touched with light'. This was the rank and file of the nation picking up, telepathically, the messages that were being sent out from the Sanctuary.

In effect it was like the 'silent minute' that so many Christians indulged in at that time, listening to the final stroke of Big Ben on the radio before giving themselves up to silent prayer. Dion was aware of this, and was quick not to make any assertions that hers was the sole magical influence on world affairs. Far from it: witches in the New Forest were performing human (but willing) sacrifice to turn back the German invasion forces; Seymour was reviving the Merlin Temple and tapping the traditional power centres of Britain to help create a shield around the coast; while occultists everywhere were applying their peculiar techniques with great national passion and perhaps some effect. In the parlance of the time, Dion was simply 'doing her bit'.

It is clear throughout her letters that Dion's own politics were somewhat aligned to those of the man she respectfully called 'Mr Churchill'. Unlike on the Continent, it has always been the trend of British magicians to avoid the troubled sea of politics; no one ever knew what party Dion voted for — if any. She had definite ideas about Communism and Fascism, though. Each contained, despite their unfortunate expressions, the seed of a great truth. She even told us what these truths were: the spiritual truth behind Bolshevism was the necessity for increased social organization of life and the abolition of all forms of privilege: this was the Dion speaking who was now allowing neophytes to step behind the veil on equal terms. And the spiritual truth behind Nazism was the need for increased dynamism — the dynamism that would break down old and outworn forms and bring in a return to Nature: this was the jilted woman speaking who was trying to do just that.

Of the two she was probably closer to the latter; and in the working for 15 January 1940, secure within the cave which she had entered via the mystic gate at the side of the Tor, she and her helpers sat before the Masters and invoked the purifying tides of destruction to sweep away all that was selfish in themselves and in their country.

It was a bold thing to do with such an untrained group, she wrote. Great power came down in the symbolic form of a jet of steel-grey water. In the centre of this column was the red-robed Master of the Ray of Geburah. There was a sense of being scoured clean, painfully clean, but at the end of it all these hollow, scrubbed-out people felt a collective sense of the most wondrous peace.

Not long after this, as the war itself took on an active phase leading up to the evacuation from Dunkirk, so too did the magic. They invoked angelic presences, red-robed once more and armed, and saw them patrolling the land from north to south, east to west, keeping watch and ward over the nation's shoreline. Eight weeks later the scope was extended. The line of defence was pushed out to the minefields which lay along the Norwegian coast, down the length of the North Sea, pushing out all that was malign and keeping the darkness at bay.

The cave, too, had seen some additions. On one occasion three rays of light came shooting down like the *awen*, forming themselves into a triangle. One side was coloured red; this was associated with King Arthur. Another side was coloured blue, and linked with Merlin. While the third side, the purple side, was governed by her old friend the Master Jesus. Loveday, although ailing, was not yet finished within the lodge.

This image caused them some problems at first. It just seemed an unbalanced trinity although it obviously worked well enough. Then all became clear when the triangle rotated towards them and they saw that it was really a three-sided pyramid with the Master Jesus at the top, from whom the other three emanated. This trinity now comprised Arthur, Merlin, and to everyone's satisfaction, the Virgin Mary. They felt happier then. This made *much* more sense.

And yet it should have been Morgan. In a previous decade it *would* have been Morgan. Penry, who had come from a part of Wales that was, and is, steeped with the ancient energies of that figure, would have made Morgan's appearance inevitable. As it was, we almost find ourselves back to the pre-Merl days again, when Veronica Mainwaring was still her self-image. Perhaps, also, Dion had identified herself with Morgan le Fay so much during her Atlantean novels that it would have been dangerous to complete this pyramid of light in that way. The Virgin Mary was safer. Far more pure.

Her cloak was the colour of the night sky, covered with silver stars. There was a crescent moon behind her head, horns upward. At her left side was a tall spray of Madonna Lilies.

These were the contacts behind Dion's Second Order. This same Second Order within the Golden Dawn revolved around the same symbol of the Rosy Cross but with Christian Rosencreutz as the dominant figure. Here within the Fraternity of the Inner Light Dion was saving us all the trouble of searching for the mysterious Damcar in the Middle East. She gave us the keys to Avalon instead. No longer would we need to look for CRC, as they called him, sleeping in his vault, deathless and incorruptible; we could have Arthur, our own and true King, dozing lightly in his cave.

To the outsider reading the letters and imagining them all doing no more than looking at symbols moving in their heads, it can all seem quite dreary; a far cry from the spectacles of earlier days. It has to be remembered, however, that these were more than mere pictures. They thrummed with life and presence, very tangible indeed. Here, touching upon those Greater Mysteries where words are useless, inadequate, and where the mind has no comparisons which might help it function in the normal way, these symbols were all that they could cope with. All became a matter of metaphor and simile, parallel and imagery. They struggled along like people in a world of tactile revelation, doing their best to explain it all to the numbed ones who were not yet allowed behind the Veil.

Not that power and majesty were always present. Sometimes the group felt flat, despite expectations. Nothing much would come. At other times, going into the Sanctuary in a personally glum mood, they would come out again astonished by the force that has arisen. It was not always predictable, and not obviously dependent upon any individual whim or mood.

Before long the cave began to develop. A winding stairway appeared which led to a Hall of Learning directly above (but still beneath the mount) which was seen as a great mediaeval library. The stairway continued still further to the Chapel of the Grail above that, and higher yet to the Watch-tower.

This Watch-tower stood upon the mountain-top. Here, if one had grea nerve, one was permitted to join the mysterious cloaked and hoodec

Watcher who was always there. Here, if one could bear the pressure, one was allowed to stare into the change-winds of good and evil, into the heart of the storm, and get prophetic glimpses through the astral turbulence. It was no place for the beginner, Dion warned. Too long there and you opened yourself up to the possibility of psychic attack.

She came to have a great fascination for that tower. In other of its manifestations, she always had.

Its earthly location is clear: it is the tower atop the Tor, dedicated to St Michael. And the identity of the Watcher? She only knew that it was a formidable figure indeed.

Once, they almost saved France. In one of the workings a beam of light shot out and lay like a barrier across France, and into Africa. In all her vast experience of occult work Dion had never seen anything as tangible as that beam; although it had puzzled her as to why it shot across into the Dark Continent. Later, to her chagrin, France fell. No one, least of all the French, expected it. Until then the French Army had been the most up-to-date and highly trained fighting force in Europe. Many of the pre-War strategies had been based upon the assumption — no, the sure knowledge — that this force would not easily be defeated. Yet in April 1940, despite the workings of the Light, France capitulated — with the sole exception of her African colonies.

Dion did not, as so many English people did, put this down to Gallic dislike of serious combat. She who had spent increasing amounts of time upon the Watch-tower had had glimpses of the Other War, and the evil telepathic currents used by the Nazi occultists. She had noted that the Nazi victories were not achieved through force of arms, so much as by the sudden collapse of national will and confidence.

Absurd, but true. As is well known by now there really were strong magical elements within the make-up of the Third Reich. Himmler even had his own tower built as a temple to the Germanic Mysteries. Except that from the Reich's point of view it was Dion Fortune and her like who were the black magicians. The Nazi magi believed that they were working for the Light.

Someone in France wrote to Dion, before the fall of that country, and asked if she would not launch herself in psychic attack upon individual leaders within Germany. Politely, Dion refused. That sort of thing was just not done. Whether we liked it or not, she pointed out, we in England were receiving a new influx of life from the same source that had so disastrously overthrown all human standards in Germany and Russia. 'But' she added, 'if we in this country can maintain the third side of the triangle . . . Christianity, then we shall have a perfect and functional whole instead of the terrible reign of unbalanced force.'

Here she was a Sea Priestess again, in the Summerlands of the West, controlling the gates which managed the tides and stopped them flooding the land.

In October of 1940 there were low-altitude dog-fights in the skies above Queensborough Terrace. An incendiary bomb was dropped next door but one, yet the group held steady in its meditation and had a sense of the most complete peace and rightness. The aerial activity intensified, there was regular bombing on a massive scale. At such moments Dion's pupils became aware that stress had heightened their psychic perceptions and made the Veil as thin as it was ever likely to get. One Saturday night 3 QT was straddled by a stick of four bombs. Its windows were all covered in a diamond-pattern of tape to stop any danger from flying glass, and its very structure was reinforced by powerful magical forces. No damage was done. No damage could be done . . .

Except that on 27 October they were bombed out. Because there were no casualties Dion, who was left standing with more than just egg on her face, claimed at least a partial success in defending the Sanctuary. She commented in the next letter that she and Loveday looked like a couple of sweeps, 'owing to a difference of opinion with the roof which fell in on them but tactfully refrained from hitting them. It has often been alleged that Dion Fortune is a Black occultist, and now she regretfully admits that the allegation can no longer be denied.'

Despite this levity, she also pointed out that everything on the altar in the Sanctuary had been thrown off except the statue of the Risen Christ, which had been shifted to the very edge.

Government officials pronounced the house unsafe. The group moved down the street to 21b Queensborough Terrace while hired men worked hard at making the roof weatherproof again.

Bernard Bromage saw her at this time, when he was working for Military Intelligence. Having close contact with a variety of foreign diplomats, he actually cajoled the Argentine Ambassador to drive him around to 3 QT in some splendour. It had been a few years since he had last had the pleasure, as they said then, and he was surprised by many things.

First, there was his finding that Dion had entered the field of Spiritualism as a lecturer and demonstrator. 'I heard that she was giving "sittings"; that she, like other mediums, had found her "guide". In her case I understood this entity to have been a Scots nobleman of a bygone century.' This was Erskine of course; but I have not yet found any record of her as a Spiritualist medium in the sense understood by Bromage. It is more likely that Dion had become weary of concealing such matters as the nature of her Secret Chiefs, and tired of giving them the usual thin veneer of psychological respectability.

He found her in the basement of 21b QT. 'With typical optimism she informed me that the place was a "fortress" and that we could talk undisturbed by the attentions of the Nazis.'

Then he noticed the other changes, some of which had involved her whole personality.

> As far as I could analyse the transformation, she had surrendered some of her seclusion and had taken a header into the world. She was meeting a more varied assortment of people: she was trying out aspects of herself which had formerly lain dormant. In a word she was trying to move with the times!
>
> Her reception room was now an exotic apartment rich in coloured silks and elaborate hangings. A small girl, of indeterminate nationality, ran in and out with the tea-things. Dion wore, for her, a considerable amount of jewellery; and the 'Sandeman's Port' gown of hieratic cut had yielded to a more mundane (and highly becoming) toilette of black satin.
>
> She had asked me to call because she had a project in mind. It would be an excellent thing, she said, if the leading occultists in London (or, for that matter, in Europe) could be together; that is, pool their knowledge and resources to enrich the common stock . . .
>
> A number of prominent names were mentioned. Alchemists, astrologers, sorcerers, ritualists, writers of learned books and advocates of weird theories . . .
>
> She said she would notify me of the success or otherwise of her enterprise. I parted from her at the door of her basement fortress with the thud of Nazi bombs falling in the distance. (Some time previously she herself had a nasty shock when she had narrowly missed being knocked flat by a boulder when the enemy had scored a direct hit on one of the floors of 3 Queensborough Terrace. But she stood there dauntless and unbowed, like some Brünnhilde or Freya out of remote Northern legend: and I later became convinced that she owed much of her undoubted psychic energy to some Viking strain in her blood!)

It was the last time Bromage saw her.

In some ways this was the nadir of Dion's life, despite her grandiose scheme for a national occult movement — something which she had mooted many years earlier.[1] The great hey-day of rite and ceremony had gone; she did no more writing. On one occasion she telephoned Christine Campbell Thomson for reasons that the latter never understood, and the younger priestess had been appalled at this new version of a Dion determined to move with the times: a large woman grossly overweight, surrounded by adoring women, apparently scoured and bereft of contacts. She in fact believed that Dion had lost her contacts quite early on, as a direct result of writing *The Mystical Qabalah*, and thus provoking the punitive current of the Golden Dawn.

If it was her nadir, yet by nature of the paradox inherent to the Magical path, it was also the very zenith. Dion knew that at a certain stage the priestess acts by virtue of what she is, not by what she does. 'The higher the grade of the initiate the more passive he appears to be upon the physical plane,' she wrote. No one, not even she, could be positive in both planes simultaneously.

It is both apology and truism. It explained her new state to old acquaintances, and expressed old truths to new pupils. People like her, she wrote, were characterized by two things: the power to be still and wait; and the power to be absolutely alone.

She started to go to the Watch-tower a lot. She was drawn to th formidable and utterly lonely Watcher who was always there. It was lik that tower at Sidestrand, now long since toppled into the ocean, whic had once existed in a world that had long since toppled into chaos

Thanks to her vigils there, she could see the future. Before Britain ha aligned with Russia, before America had entered the war, she had foresee the final victory. It would drag along upon the outer planes for a few more years, but the outcome of the war was in no doubt.

More, in the years following, there would be four powers loosed upon the world: the United States of America, the Union of Soviet Socialist Republics, the Chinese Republic, and the British Empire. 'We have not yet realized the part China will play in the new Asia', she noted. No one had; neither had Dion herself realized just how wrong she was in at least one of these respects.

It was just as well that she died before the Empire sank into the waves. It would have broken her heart.

Even so, Dion might have blamed it all on poor leadership. She had had her fill of the weak men who had guided Britain between the wars. Touched by the Lord of the Red Ray, King Arthur, she looked for a man who personified dynamism, and the Nature-contact; awed by the figure of the Blue Ray, Merlin, who had given the Round Table to the land, she looked for a greater sense of social justice and equality. It was her job at that moment to channel a current which would reconcile them both, and ensure that we would never go down the same unbalanced paths as the Germans and Russians.

In part it all came true. Some of her social aspirations were made manifest. If Britain lost India to the independence movement in which Mrs Besant had once been so active, it gained a brief jewel in its battered crown via the Welfare State which Dion had so fondly anticipated.

This figure of the Virgin Mary which had filled the third angle of the basal triangle and reconciled the energies of Arthur and Merlin, was also, in her eyes at least, the purest expression of the three Paths of Womanhood. No matter how deeply involved Dion became with her great strong men and Masters, she never forgot the role of Woman.

The first Path of Womanhood was that of the Mother. This was the Earth-Mother, ever-fecund, home-builder, the Mated Woman. Dion could never be that. She envied such power, but it was never hers.

The second Path of Womanhood was the Path of the Virgin, whose principles were renunciation, dedication, and sacrifice — *and* power, if the renunciation were complete. This was the infinitely potent formula of negation — the Nun's Path. Dion had taken that once. She had almost been happy.

The third Path of Womanhood was peculiarly her own. This was the Path of the Priestess, who is 'neither Mother nor Virgin, but functions mysteriously on the hidden side of things, with powers not understood in the present age. In this aspect she represents a factor, not a person . . . all potent on the inner planes if inert on the physical. She works with neither the physical powers of the Mother, nor the spiritual powers of the Virgin, but with the magnetic powers of her office.' She draws her power from the Earth, and with the cup of the Grail that she carries, she administers the sacrament of Womanhood.

It was beginning again. The group was rebuilding. By 27 April 1941 Dion was announcing to the world that the Society of the Inner Light would soon be resuming its pre-war Outer Court activities. In one sense she had performed the difficult magical trick of getting her pupils to see her as she now saw herself: not as the Priestss of Isis reflected in the lotus pool but as Vivienne, Nimue, and yes, even as Morgan le Fay too, in the latter's more sanitized Christianized version. She was now the woman bearing the Cup of the Grail as seen by the court at Camelot. She knew the secrets of the Fisher King. She knew how to revivify the waste land. Her new group of pupils had no doubt about that at all. The more they began to see in this image, the easier it became to assume the full qualities needed.[2]

As Bromage had noted, she was now dressing very differently indeed, on more than one level. The days of Merl, Seymour and Moriarty were well behind her — for good or ill — and as each of these strong men had departed from her life she did what any woman would do: she bought herself some new clothes, picked up the pieces, and started all over again. It was raiments of Light that she bought, coloured by the Moon within the Western sky. And if she was no longer able to work as one part of a binary, she did her best to sit at the Round Table she was making, on nominally equal terms with everyone else.

Unfortunately she was not a well woman. Although the leukaemia would come on quickly in her last weeks, her general health in her final few years was not good. Like the Fisher King she had come to serve, and like the British Empire she worked for, her energies were leaking away as insidiously as in the days when she had leaked prana.

She even issued a disclaimer in her usual light-hearted style saying that she was not, despite many rumours, either dead or dying. She had had a heavy cold, that was all.

But she had more than that.

In the darkness, in her lonely bed, she kept very still and became aware of all the currents in the Otherworld, she grew convinced that one of the disgusting black magicians who stood behind the Führer was making a personal onslaught upon her. This foul creature had an Eastern inspiration. To her dismay, to her horror, Lord E seemed unable or unwilling to help. Nor did she have anyone left within 3 QT who had the sort of stature or knowledge to help. Loveday was an old man by now and very ill himself; Creasy was too gentle and no youngster either; there was 'Uncle Robbie', as they all called him, but his nickname spoke for itself; while the only vigorous young man of any standing, Arthur Chichester, whom she called her 'young Sun Priest', was away fighting his own sort of war.

So she did what she had done so many times in the past: she kept the occult vigil while the sun was below the horizon, and hung on desperately, matching her limited staying-power against the attack until the moon-tides changed, and the force of the onslaught blew itself out.

The people around her thought she was going 'a bit funny', although none of them would ever specify exactly how. Fiercely protective towards these people, she had become, against all her inclinations and wishes, something of a mother-figure to them. They in their turn, in the years since, have repaid her with fitting loyalty.

Yet it was not the mother-figure of 'hearth and garth' she exemplified but the dark, sterile Mother of Saturn, the sphere of Binah on her beloved Tree of Life.

> The Mother aspect of Binah finds expression in the title of Marah, the Sea, which is given her. It is a curious fact that Venus-Aphrodite is represented as being born of the sea-foam, and the Virgin Mary is called by the Catholics Stella Maris, Star of the Sea. The word Marah, which is the root of Mary, also means bitter, and the spiritual experience attributed to Binah is the Vision of Sorrow. A vision which calls to mind the picture of the Virgin weeping at the foot of the Cross, her heart pierced by seven swords . . . of the descent of life to the planes of form.

In a previous life, before *Deo, non Fortuna* was ever conceived, Mary had been her middle name.

Not all was glumness though; that is not the true nature of the dark goddesses she served. She even found the whimsy to take upon herself a nickname. In her last days they called her 'The Fluff', and she liked that. It was derived from her habit of running her finger along the backs of the furniture and crying out in mock ire 'Fluff!' whenever she found that the rest had been less than perfect in their dusting. It was also a name which took her back to her younger days, before the obesity, before the gods, when she had seen herself as a dancer, light and floating across the world. The last person to give her such a pet name had been Penry, who for reasons that will never now be recalled used to call her Furry Evans. She liked being called The Fluff. It made her feel human again.

She was taken back in other, more subtle ways: if the Master Jesus was back within the lodge at the head of that pyramid of light, Rakoczi, the Hungarian Master, had also returned. Some of her pupils, Chichester in particular, had very strong contacts with him, but she was not too interested. Those days were gone.

The war progressed. A very different war this time: Alamein and Anzio, the Normandy beaches and the great struggle for Caen; the heroic debacle of Arnhem and the manic race for Berlin . . . No need for archangels guarding our coastline now. The Wild Hunt had been unleashed. It would not rest until two towns at the eastermost point of the globe knew beyond all doubt that a new and terrible Aeon had begun.

Dion, who had fought against the East in a very different war all her lives, must have felt a grim sense of revenge.

Not much is known of her at this time, except that she was a deeply unhappy and world-weary woman, profoundly dissatisfied with her Magic, feeling herself in something of an impasse but knowing in her ancient heart that she would never win through this stage towards some new gold dawn. Linked as she was with the egregore of the nation, the end of the conflicts in Europe and Japan found her as someone old before her time, battered inside and out, and half-dreading the battles of the peace that stretched ahead. As the months went by she wanted nothing more than that the Horseman should come and bring her to some dignified end.

The story goes that Uncle Robbie, who was then living in one of the bed-sits at 3 QT, was approached by Dion complaining of toothache. As a qualified dentist he consented to examine her jaw. The next thing the rest of the group knew was Uncle Robbie bursting back into the room by himself with the words: 'Christ! She's had it!' It is not clear how he came to that conclusion, but he was right. She had only a short time to live.

The war in Europe had been over almost nine months: a whole gestation. The Nuremberg Trials were under way and Mr Churchill was about to bring down an Iron Curtain between Russia and the West. Epstein had produced his sculpture 'Lucifer', and Picasso had shown the world his cubist painting 'The Charnel House'. Mutiny was incipient within the Indian Navy at Bombay, and Britain was to recognize the independence of Trans-Jordan. While in realms beyond the purely earthly, the astronomer Bay received radar echoes from the moon.

For the Sea Priestess, who saw the world being swept by new and strange tides, it was time to go home.

In January 1946, the woman who had wrestled with the androgyny of the human spirit was admitted to the Middlesex Hospital, in the heart of London, the City of the Moon. It was a fitting month to go, for Janus was the deity who kept the gates of heaven, his two faces looking into

Time Past and Time Future. Those who visited her then, in the large ward, thought that they had never seen her look so lovely. She had the sort of glow that comes to the surface of the earth at dusk, as if the setting sun draws all the energies of the rock and soil to the open, in one final blush. What they saw was the life force leaving her — the inner light.

And it was beautiful.

There is no record of her last moments or of her last words. Only the memory that she was glad to go — that and the will she had made which left all her money to Chichester and Creasy, for the furtherance of the Work; plus a small regular sum to her cousin, Enid Mary Chambers, whom she had known as a girl in Llandudno, all those lives ago.

She had come to us from the depths of the interstellar space which had so fascinated her, moulded and magnetized by the Moon she had passed on her way down, falling from the heavens into dense matter. As a mortal woman she had quibbled about Blavatsky, scorned Mrs Besant, taken up the torch of Anna Kingsford and fought with Mrs Mathers on the Inner Planes, and all so that she could take herself and a portion of her race through the Pylon Gates towards the Otherworld, leading us all a little closer to a knowledge of the Earth, the Waters, and the

Mysteries of Women. Her task had been, as she wrote in a story after her death, 'to stress the ancient Moon powers for healing of present day social ills in order that the profounder spiritual work could thus proceed unimpeded in the next age.' At the end of her life she could say that she had achieved what few women of her era or class had ever done: like some old wise woman from a Chaucerian fable she had sovereignty in her grasp: over Earth and Water, Fire and Air, and their aspects within her psyche; over the inner and the outer worlds, past and future, and the darkness and the light that strives between the sexes.

Whatever the reality behind her Masters, however ephemeral her philosophies, we cannot but respect her for the way she gave herself completely, unremittingly — even bloodily — to this task of bringing wisdom to the world. And in her emotionally fraught, magically demanding relationship with Merl she had striven with all her might to bring to the race new insight into the nature and potential of Woman, banishing the last earth-bound spirit of the Victorian age as she did so. As she fought for her own happiness and understanding, so did she fight for all women. She taught us too, that the land is a living being, our nations real entities; and that if we can only learn to sit still and listen, with all the wonder of a little child, the veiled goddess within the Earth and below the Moon will talk to us. Slowly, secretly, the 'door which has no key' will open.

Which leaves nothing more to do but to say the ancient words that we have said to this great priestess, this Daughter of Heaven and Earth a thousand times, in a thousand temples, throughout the aeons:

Dion, Dion, Dion . . . we'll always know you.

Afterword

Dion Fortune continued to rule the lodge via her mediums for some years after her death. Eventually a complete and formal banishing ceremony was performed because it was felt that her continued presence was becoming unproductive and even unhealthy. As the history of the Society of the Inner Light after her death on 8 January 1946 is not really in my province or sphere of interest, I would refer those interested to *The Story of Dion Fortune* by Carr Collins and Charles Fielding, as well as Francis King's *Ritual Magic in England* and Ithell Colquhoun's *The Sword of Wisdom*, for less sympathetic comments.

I will be criticized for being less than objective in my study of Dion and magicians generally. However, in an ailing world filled with small men who measure things, it is not something that will cause me to lose much sleep.

I will also be criticized for revealing the identities of her Secret Chiefs, as it is often felt in occult circles that this in some way destroys their validity. In my defence I can offer two comments. First, this has all been an open secret for many years. I was first told about Thomas More and Socrates in the library of the Theological Seminary in Lexington, Kentucky, where I used to go to read books on Magick. Second, the Christian Mysteries have not been diminished one whit by a public knowledge of the rites and Contact behind them.

I have no personal connection with the Society of the Inner Light. In our brief and necessary correspondence they have always been cordial, straight, and as helpful as they could be within the limits of their oaths, obligations, and desires. I have never at any point sought their approval for this work, while they in their turn have maintained a consistently neutral stance. Really, all they want to do is get on with their Work. I have no idea what goes on behind their doors today. I do not know if they use the same contacts or indeed any at all. I am not being secretive: had I known I would probably have used the information as a counterpoint and worried about the morality later. All I can offer is the rumour that after many debatable and probably necessary changes, the Society of the Inner Light is once more a potent group with high standards.

If they or anyone else feel that my revelations will in any way hurt them, then perhaps I should offer up details as to my own Secret Chiefs in what might be an act of magical self-destruction. I offer this information as Dion would have done: for what it is worth . . .

Although I achieved a very strong and radiant contact at the age of fourteen with what I then supposed to have been 'the Master Jesus', that entity means nothing to me now. I was lying on the couch at the time, pretending to be ill and skiving school. I had been reading a book on Raja Yoga and a novel by Lloyd C. Douglas.

The longest contact in my life lasted for some ten years, from 1974 onwards. He was priggish, insistent, often very tedious, but he taught me many things. The link between us was through the boy Mithras, somehow. I called this contact, simply, Bert, and through the years got quite blasé when a wide variety of seers told me about the D. H. Lawrence figure overshadowing me. Finally in 1984 I wrote an as yet unpublished and probably unpublishable novel entitled *Shimmying Hips* on the unlikely themes of sex, football, and magic, set in the 1930s and intended as a quite deliberate parody of Bert's style and concerns. I have never seen him since. Sometimes, I rather miss him.

In 1976 I wrote a massive tome that was then entitled *Western Magic*. I was quite certain it would save the world, suggesting as it did a complete replacement of the Judaeo-Christian images of the Qabalah with those of a genuinely Western vitality. During the writing of this and other works which still languish in my cupboard I used the pen-name Michael Scot, who seemed to dog me at that time, and who was moreover a fellow Northumbrian — according to some legends. He faded after a while but reappeared in the early '80s when I became intimate with Christine Hartley. *Western Magic* was later re-written — and badly — as *Gate of Moon*.

Dancers to the Gods was a ritual; a test. I believe that the act of typing up the Magical Diaries from the Seymour and Hartley originals put me in touch, in some sense, with the contacts behind them both. The house we lived in then, already haunted by an earth-bound spirit that Dolores Ashcroft-Nowicki eventually dealt with, was often filled with the presence of Kha'm-uast, the Priest of Anubis, and Penry Evans. Especially Penry Evans. On two occasions I had strong contacts with Lord Eldon, one of them at his burial place when, in high summer and at noon, the sky turned completely black and hailstones swept the hillside; and the other was a very brief one in my car as I left Hawkwood College, Gloucestershire, in May 1983. On the other hand I have never felt any contact with Cheiron, who was so important to Seymour and Hartley, nor yet Cleomenes III; and this not for the lack of trying.

Likewise Thomas More and Socrates leave me largely unmoved — especially the latter. Oddly enough, despite the fact that I know he did not exist, David Carstairs has caused a few twinges in my psyche.*

Throughout all of this I have experienced a Guirdham-esque saga which has encompassed Lindisfarne and Brittany as they were in the Dark Ages, so-called, and which centred around an obscure entity named Ywi, or Yvius, to give him the Latin variant. This has still not resolved itself.

The obvious question is, have I ever felt any contact with Dion herself?

The answer is yes. During the writing of *Dancers* I had intense and lucid dreams about her on many occasions, in which she provided me with the information that I had been manically searching for. The details she gave me in this wise were comprehensive, cogent, convincing — and always wrong. When one is faced with the choice of *Kelly's Directory*, or revelations of the Third Eye, then I have long since learnt to grab the former and run. On the other hand, against all logic, I believe that she was present in other ways more reliable than that of dream. It was the sense of her presence during the daylight hours that was most important: she seemed to put things in my path.

All of which, incidentally, I had to pay for in some way — and not always willingly. My wife got the brunt of this during one period, being wakened regularly by someone whispering in her ear. I am quite certain that this was not me. In fact, from her description, it could only have been Dion. Finally one night I awoke and became most clearly aware of that woman's presence. Gathering up my nerve I had the presumption to use some simple banishing techniques against her. She came around to my side of the bed and, not without affection, slapped me quite tangibly across the face. I had to laugh.

The last time I felt her presence was in early 1985 when she seemed to help me with an essay entitled *The Microcosmic Doctrine* which Dolores published somewhere. The essay tried to encapsulate some ideas on the tribal nature of modern magic that had been niggling at my consciousness for some years. It was — and is — my assertion that each magician belongs to a tribe, or clan, which exists as much on the Inner Planes as in the world. The tribe had different leaders, or Chiefs, from

*As if to prove the magical law that Mystery shall always prevail, information has just come in which leads me to accept that Carstairs may well have existed after all: that his parents remarried, and that Dion did correspond with one of them. My source is 'Charles Fielding', whose knowledge is first hand, and whose experience in magical matters is vast.

time to time, and can offer each member access to its collective wisdom.

After writing that she disappeared.

I have never made a cult of these Chiefs, never indulged in worshipping them. I am not worried as to their exact nature and have long since given up entreating them for lots and lots of money and awesome powers. They come and go, like the postman. Sometimes they bring nice things. Every now and again I lambast them something awful. They are part of me as I am part of their tribe. And I have come to believe that rather than accept the strings of reincarnational identities as given in *Dancers to the Gods*, we would be better employed using this tribal model, and the concept of overshadowing. There is more to life and lives than reincarnation alone.

During the writing of *Dancers* the pressure was enormous. As is always the case when I write, we had domestic disasters involving water, one after the other with endless variety and ingenuity. These have pursued us wherever we go, only stopping when the writing stops. The pressure was maintained, but to a lesser extent, with the writing of *Priestess*, although the various presences seem to have taken their leave mid-way through. Perhaps they will come back and perhaps not. I can't say that I will be too bothered either way.

The only real development is that while I did not particularly like Dion during the writing of *Dancers* and was keen to push my own bias towards Seymour and Hartley, now I really do like her. Very, very much.

These are the only secrets I have that are worth telling. Time will tell whether such revelations are injurious or not.

Aficionados of my occult plagiarism will recognize that I have stolen from my own books and used images, *bon mots*, and often whole paragraphs from writers who are far better and wiser than myself: Ursula le Guin, Jean Overton Fuller, Des Kavanagh, Elizabeth Sutherland, R. J. Stewart, William Gray, John Symonds, Martin Ebon, David Annwn, Frank Harris, Michael Herr and Edward Whitmont, to mention only those whom I can remember. It is obvious that I have made little attempt at a critical analysis of Dion Fortune's work, as this will come from someone else in due course. And as more material assuredly becomes available, so will there be more biographies that will look at Dion in a totally different and perhaps more comprehensive way.

Good luck to them all.

End Notes

Chapter 1

1. Or perhaps something did. The story was told to me by Keyworth's granddaughter, Dolores Ashcroft-Nowicki.
2. *Applied Magic*, pp. 56-7, Aquarian Press.
3. See *Women's Mysteries*, by M. Esther Harding for a discussion of the paradox whereby the Cosmic Whore and the Eternal Virgin are one and the same.
4. *Psychic Self Defence*, p. 79, Aquarian Press.

Chapter 2

1. There is also the cave on the western side of the Great Orme known as Ogo Arth, or 'cave of the bear'. The Orme itself was sometimes called Pen Gogarth, derived from the name of the tribe which at one time inhabited the headland.
2. *More Violets*, 1905, London.
3. Having just found a reference to his in-laws, the Crowe family, as running the Royal Pier Hotel in Weston-super-Mare, it is more than likely that he had come back to the West Country to be near his sister. As to the final fate of the Craigside Hydro, it was demolished during the years of Flower Power by a man called Ian Smith acting on behalf of a company from Sheffield. The birthplace of the Sea Priestess was reduced to a rubble that formed the car park for the Asda superstore.
4. Maiya Tranchell-Hayes described Violet's mother as a keen Christian Scientist. In terms of Violet's own development the teachings of Mrs Eddy concerning the spiritual equality of men and women would have left their mark. In that movement women have always enjoyed significant roles as church officers.
5. See *Dancers to the Gods* for more details of this.
6. See *Hero with a Thousand Faces* by Joseph Campbell, for a more

detailed discussion of the journey through madness.

7. *Light*, Spring 1960; courtesy of the College of Psychic Studies.
8. *Psychic Self Defence*, pp. 18-19.
9. *Psychic Self Defence*, p. 19.

Chapter 3

1. The now out-of-print *In the Astral Light* by John Symonds provides an excellent introduction to Blavatsky's life, and is in many ways more sympathetic than his later book on Crowley.
2. The *O.E. Library Critic*, April 1937.
3. Quoted from *Theosophical History*, a stimulating and independent journal which tackles a wide variety of intriguing topics. Published by Leslie Price, 46 Evelyn Gardens, London.
4. *In the Astral Light*, p. 74.

Chapter 4

1. It would seem that one of her near neighbours was Maiya Tranchell-Hayes, who assumed great importance as a magical teacher.
2. Or by the hallucinogenic effects of ergot in rye.
3. According to *The Story of Dion Fortune* by Charles Fielding and Carr Collins, another member of his group, Amy Campbell, had also been a member of the Theosophical Society in East London, South Africa. Presumably their connection began then.
4. Quoted from an as yet unpublished manuscript of his on Mystical Christianity.

Chapter 5

1. Quoted from the article 'Dion Fortune', published in the magazine *Light* in 1960.
2. 'Ceremonial Magic Unveiled', *Occult Review*.
3. See *The Elder Brother*, by Gregory Tillett, Routledge Kegan Paul.
4. Quoted in *O. E. Library Critic*.
5. Perhaps her father as a solicitor had some knowledge or admiration for the man. Perhaps she had learned of him from her historian uncle. Someone has even suggested to me that she got it wrong, that it was an earlier entity she got who also bore the soubriquet True Thomas, namely Thomas of Ercildoune, rather than Thomas Erskine.
6 See Jasper Ridley's *The Statesman and the Fanatic*, a dual biography of Wolsey and More.

Chapter 7

1. This system of tarot attribution is taken from William Gray's *Magical Ritual Methods*, Helios Books.

2. I am indebted to my dear friend E. Marion Griffiths for these myths and more. Born in the same year as Penry and probably going to the same school, she has been a constant source of information on things Celtic. Readers ought also to be aware of the debt I owe to the book *The Underworld Initiation*, by R. J. Stewart, Aquarian Press which in its field is one of the most important this century.
3. *Psychic Self Defence*, p. 73.

Chapter 8

1. The early services were run not only by Loveday but also by Ernest Butler and Charles Seymour. I have met three people who, while not particularly Christian themselves, attended these mornings and found them very effective. Contrasting the calibre of these men with the vapidness of the average English career-vicar, this is not surprising.
2. Quoted in *The Return of the Goddess*, by Edward C. Whitmont.

Chapter 9

1. *The Journal of the Society of the Inner Light*, July 1932.

Chapter 10

1. These were *The Scarred Wrists*, 1935; *Hunters of Humans, 1936, and Beloved of Ishmael*, 1937.
2. Although Dion undoubtedly experimented with one of the hallucinogens available at that time — especially to someone whose husband could prescribe them — her final assessment was that of every magician of stature: keep away.
3. We have a picture of Dion in her own Body of Light as described by Christine Campbell Thomson in her Magical Diary: 'I saw the High Priestess clearly . . . she wore brownish-yellow linen robes with straight line pattern of dull red bordering and a linen veil. She had a big jewel on her breast.'
4. Loveday was to contract Parkinson's Disease.
5. She had obviously been reading and was influenced by *The Rainbow*, by D. H. Lawrence.
6. Dickford, Dickmouth, and Starber would equate nicely with Axbridge, Weston-super-Mare and Brean. On the other hand so would Highbridge, Burnham and Brean fit the bill. Yet I have been unable to find any trace of the Smiths, Firths, or Crowes having lived in Highbridge as stated by Messrs Collins and Fielding in their *Story of Dion Fortune*. They seem to have derived this information from someone who had simply made a cursory analysis of the Sea Priestess and drawn some hasty conclusions.

7. She was thirteen years younger than Penry.
8. I would point out here that *Sun Magic* does not exist. This was referred to in a piece 'received' from Dion after her death. Rather cleverly written in the first person, people have since taken it literally. If the tale were true then it meant Dion would have received her initiation in the Rue Mozart, Paris, when she was five years old. *The Death of Vivien Le Fay Morgan* was a short story, no more.

Chapter 11

1. See *Dancers to the Gods* for more complete details about the lives and magic of Seymour and Christine Campbell Thomson.
2. See *The Forgotten Mage*, a collection of FDP's essays edited and introduced by Dolores Ashcroft-Nowicki.
3. These were Anthony Daw, Susan Daw, and their mother. Anthony Daw was the young priest that Seymour found for CCT to work with when he himself became too old to do her magic justice.

Chapter 12

1; If she had not met Crowley before this she must have done now, through her laudable but doomed scheme. It is highly unlikely that they ever worked together, even though Crowley tried to imply that she was in some way beholden to him. When his *Book of Thoth* came out, he sent her a copy inscribed to the Priestess of Selene.
2. See *Gate of Moon* for an analysis of the Three Queens/Morgan/Binah/Saturn symbolism.
3. *The Mystical Qabalah*, p. 148.
4. Bill Gray, who should know, thought him one of the most psychic men he had ever met. At first meeting Uncle Robbie correctly diagnosed and accurately predicted the outcome of an ailment that had been troubling him for some time.

Index

The publishers wish to thank the following for their kind permission to reproduce photographs in the plate section of this book:

C. W. Daniel & Co.; Her Majesty the Queen; Hulton Picture Library; The National Portrait Gallery.